# EU Energy Relations with Russia

This book provides a detailed analysis of the legal framework in which the energy trade between the European Union and the Russian Federation has been conducted. Using case studies of eight member states, it critically examines the EU's ability and the duty of its Member States to conduct their external energy trade in accordance with the principle of solidarity. Providing a comprehensive analysis of the principle of solidarity as provided in the *acquis communautaire* of the EU, the book critically analyses the legal framework pertaining to EU-Russia energy trade to ascertain whether, and to what extent, it satisfies the requirements of the rule of law.

**Umut Turksen** is a Professor in law at Coventry University, UK and an executive of the Commonwealth Legal Education Association.

# Routledge Research in EU Law

For a full list of titles in this series, please visit https://www.routledge.com/Routledge-Research-in-EU-Law/book-series/ROUTEULAW

# EU Energy Relations with Russia

## Solidarity and the Rule of Law

Umut Turksen

Routledge
Taylor & Francis Group

LONDON AND NEW YORK

First published 2018
by Routledge
2 Park Square, Milton Park, Abingdon, Oxon OX14 4RN

and by Routledge
711 Third Avenue, New York, NY 10017

*Routledge is an imprint of the Taylor & Francis Group, an informa business*

*British Library Cataloguing in Publication Data*
A catalogue record for this book is available from the British Library

*Library of Congress Cataloging in Publication Data*
Names: Turksen, Umut, author.
Title: EU energy relations with Russia : solidarity and the rule of law /
Umut Turksen.
Other titles: European Union energy relations with Russia
Description: New York : Routledge, 2018. | Series: Routledge research in
eu law | Includes bibliographical references and index.
Identifiers: LCCN 2017041452 | ISBN 9781138041752 (hbk)
Subjects: LCSH: European Union--Russia (Federation). | Energy policy--
International cooperation. | Energy industries--Law and legislation--European
Union countries. | Energy industries--Law and legislation--Russia (Federation) |
Trade regulation--European Union countries. | Russia (Federation)--
Commercial treaties | European Union countries--Commercial policy | Russia
(Federation)--Commercial policy | Rule of law--European Union countries. |
Rule of law--Russia (Federation)
Classification: LCC KJE5112.R87 T87 2018 | DDC 346.2404/679--dc23
LC record available at https://lccn.loc.gov/2017041452

ISBN: 978-1-138-04175-2 (hbk)
ISBN: 978-1-315-17417-4 (ebk)

Typeset in Galliard
by Taylor & Francis Books

# Contents

# Acknowledgements

Writing this book would not have been possible without the generous support from Kingston Law School and Coventry Law School. I would like to thank Jacek Wojcek for his hard work, which gave the initial impetus for this book. My thanks also go to Adam Abukari. I would like to dedicate this book to my late father, Onur Türksen (1949–2013), who always stood up for fairness and equality.

> "Laws and principles are not for the times when there is no temptation: they are for such moments as this, when body and soul rise in mutiny against their rigour ... If at my convenience I might break them, what would be their worth?"
>
> – Charlotte Brontë, *Jane Eyre* (1847)

coming years.[16] Given this recent digression of EU-Russia energy relations it is necessary to consider the adequacy of the current EU legal mechanisms of energy security management.

This book critically evaluates whether the existing legal framework of the EU-Russia energy relations operates in light of the 'solidarity' principle and explores if and to what extent it ensures trading practices that result in a reliable energy supply from Russia to the EU. The legal analysis, based on socio-legal methodology, focuses only on the external aspects of the energy trade framework and does not cover any of the internal measures found in Member States. Accordingly, the institutional and legal tools conferred to the EU by the Member States in the Treaties are examined so as to establish the EU's competence in monitoring and enforcing this principle. Moreover, the contribution of the Court of Justice of the European Union (CJEU) in clarifying the division of competences between the EU and the Member States as well as the effectiveness of the Common Foreign and Security Policy in energy dealings with Russia are considered. Discussion is geared towards finding whether the EU has sufficient legal tools to speak with one voice in line with the 'solidarity principle'[17] when it comes to external energy relations with Russia. There is no single definition of solidarity in the EU however; it is seen as both a principle that distinguishes the EU and its Members from other international organisations[18] and a fundamental value on which the EU (especially the Single Market) is based. Given the actual and potential vulnerabilities the EU faces both economically and politically,[19] it is argued that the principle of solidarity (embedded in the *acquis*) shall be a guiding principle in energy relations of the EU[20] as it does in many other economic spheres. Indeed, the EU Commission

16 Granholm N, Malminen J and Persson G (eds), *A Rude Awakening – Ramification of Russian Aggression towards Ukraine* (FOI June 2014) 75.
17 For example, Article 3(3) Treaty of the Functioning of the EU (TFEU) requires the EU to establish an internal market, which shall promote solidarity among Member States. Article 4(3) Treaty on the EU (TEU) (as amended by the Lisbon Treaty) provides that the Member States are required to sincerely cooperate with the EU and with each other. Articles 2 and 21 of the TEU stipulate 'solidarity' in international relations. Article 24 TEU states 'mutual political solidarity' among MS and Article 31 TEU underlines the 'spirit of mutual solidarity' in EU's external action. Chapter IV (Articles 27–38) of the Charter of Fundamental Rights of the European Union is entitled 'Solidarity.' In C-159/91 and C-160/91 [1993] *Poucet v Assurances générales de France (AGF) et Caisse mutuelle régionale du Languedoc-Roussillon (Camulrac), Pistre v Caisse autonome nationale de compensation de l'assurance vieillesse des artisans (Cancava)* ECR 637, the Court of Justice for the EU has also recognised 'solidarity' as a fundamental principle; Ross has even suggested solidarity to be conceived as a potential 'new constitutional paradigm for the EU'; see Ross M, 'A New Constitutional Paradigm for the EU' in Ross and Borgmann-Prebil (eds.) *Promoting Solidarity in the European Union* (Oxford University Press, 2010).
18 Hartwig I and Nicolaides P, 'Elusive Solidarity in an Enlarged European Union' (2003) 3 *Eipascope* 19.
19 For a detailed analysis of energy vulnerability in the context of EU–Russia energy relations, see *supra* note 7, Christie.
20 A Common Energy Policy has been of limited effect because the security framing contributed to the further legitimisation of EU member states' reluctance to cede

states that efficient and fully integrated energy networks are the backbone of the single market[21] and 'energy security dimension is [recognised as] one of the cornerstones of the Energy Union strategy, a key political priority of the Juncker Commission'.[22]

While the EU institutions in general,[23] the EU Commission in particular, have been keen to assert the centrality of market liberalisation to its future energy policy and energy diplomacy and create a unified policy towards energy relations, this stance has been countered by the Member States' bilateral energy agreements with Russia. These practices are discussed with reference to a number of examples so as to illustrate different EU Member States' approaches to energy trade with Russia. Part 4 of this monograph is devoted to the critical analysis of the current legal framework for EU – Russia energy trade – which could provide sincere cooperation – yet lack a number of elements to ensure legal certainty and security. Part 5 provides a commentary on future prospects of the EU–Russia energy relations (including short-, mid-, and long-term strategies for energy security) in light of the current affairs.

sovereignty in the energy domain. The European Parliament and the Commission in particular spoke in favour of a 'Common foreign energy policy strategy' owing to the recognition of the fact that energy supply could not be dealt with only within the market sphere, but also needed a strategic, foreign policy approach, enabling the EU to maintain a unitary position in international energy relations. The necessity of setting new instruments to govern energy at the EU level was also supported by the academic community. Natorski M and Surrallés A, 'Securitizing Moves to Nowhere? The Framing of the European Union's Energy Policy' (2008) 4(2) *Journal of Contemporary European Research* 71.

21 European Commission, 'Single Market Act II-Together for New Growth' COM 2012/573 final.
22 European Commission, 'Towards Energy Union: Sustainable energy security package' (*Press Release Database*, 16 February 2016) <http://europa.eu/rapid/press-release_ IP-16-307_en.htm> accessed 12 May 2017.
23 European Council, '4 February 2011 Conclusions on Energy' [8 March 2011] EUCO 2/1/11 Rev 1.

# 1 Russia as an important supplier of energy for the EU

In order to put forward the argument that solidarity is a legal obligation and necessary in the EU's external energy trade, it is important to provide the reasons and the logic behind it. The Russian Federation (Russia) is the primary energy supplier for the EU.[1] Russia is known to have the largest natural gas reserves (about 18%) and seventh largest crude oil reserves in the world. It is also the biggest exporter of oil and gas to the EU, with its supplies accounting for 25% of oil and 33% of gas.[2] In 2016, Russia's share in the EU imports of natural gas was 38.2% (37.5% in 2015) and its share in EU imports of petroleum oil was 29.2% (32.5% in 2015).[3] (See Table 1.1.)

The EU as a whole is the world's largest energy importer; importing approximately 55% of its energy supply – nearly 84% of its oil and 64% of its natural gas.[4] The EU's overall dependency on gas imports is expected to rise significantly by 2030[5] with its energy consumption rising by 15% in comparison to the demand in 2000. This is particularly true with respect to EU's imports of

1 *Supra* Introduction, note 7, Haghighi. Also, see, Piebalgs A, 'EU-Russia Energy Relations: Common Goals and Concerns' (2009) 2 *Oil Gas & Energy Law*; European Commission, 'A European strategy for sustainable, competitive and secure energy' (Green Paper) COM (2006)105 Final.
2 Europe's Energy Portal, 'Energy Prices Report' (*Energy Prices from past to present*) <www.energy.eu/#dependence> accessed 12 December 2016; Eurogas, 'Statistical Report' (*The European Union of the Natural Gas Industry*, 2012) <www.eurogas.org/uploads/media/statistics_2012_21.11.12.pdf> accessed 29 November 2016; Russia provides 100% of gas imports of at least seven Member States of the EU; European Commission, 'EU Energy Policy Data' (Commission staff working document) SEC (2007) 12.
3 EUROSTAT, EU imports of energy products – recent developments, April 2017, <http://ec.europa.eu/eurostat/statistics-explained/index.php/EU_imports_of_energy_products_-_recent_developments> accessed 14 August 2017.
4 In 2011, oil made up about 37%, coal nearly 18%, and nuclear energy 12% of the EU primary energy supply; European Commission, 'Market Observatory for Energy' (*Key Figures*, June 2011) <http://ec.europa.eu/energy/observatory/eu_27_info/doc/key_figures.pdf> accessed 12 December 2016. For the most recent data see, <http://ec.europa.eu/energy/en/data-analysis/market-analysis>.
5 European Commission, 'Towards a European Strategy for the Security of Energy Supply' (Green Paper) COM (2000) 769 Final.

*Table 1.1* Eurostat – Extra-EU imports of natural gas, shares (%) of main trading partners, 2016[6]

| Partner | Value (Share%) | Net mass (Share%) |
| --- | --- | --- |
| Russia | 39.7 | 38.2 |
| Norway | 34.1 | 35.8 |
| Algeria | 15.2 | 14.3 |
| Qatar | 5.1 | 5.8 |
| Nigeria | 2.1 | 2.1 |
| Libya | 1.4 | 1.5 |
| Others | 2.4 | 2.3 |

the natural gas. The future projections show that European gas production is expected to decline[7] and the reliance on imported natural gas will grow considerably,[8] a fact recognised already in the EU Council Directive 2004/67/EC.[9] A growing reliance on natural gas is mainly due to its increasing popularity as a substitute to less eco-friendly fuels and its relatively low price in comparison with other energy resources such as coal and oil.[10]

On average, the EU's dependence on Russian energy is 26%[11] however; the level of dependency strongly varies (see Table 1.2) between the Member States (MS).[12] Out of 28 EU Member States only Denmark and the United Kingdom are independent on oil imports, and the same countries with the addition of the Netherlands have no dependency on gas imports.[13] Andris Piebalgs, former Energy Commissioner for the European Commission stated that 'the relationship [with Russia] is one of interdependence not dependence which means that Russia needs us much as we need Russia … sales of Russian raw materials to the EU

---

6  *Ibid.*
7  Energy Information Administration OIAF, 'International Energy Outlook 2004' (*doe/eia-0484*, April 2004) <www.energieverbraucher.de/files_db/dl_mg_1084170436.pdf> accessed 25 November 2016.
8  Energy Information Administration OIAF, 'International Energy Outlook 2005' (*doe/eia-0482*, July 2005) <www.eia.doe.gov/oiaf/ieo/pdf/0484(2005).pdf> accessed 29 November 2016.
9  European Council Directive 2004/67/EC of 26 April 2004 concerning measures to safeguard security of natural gas supply [2004] OJ L127/92, Preamble para 13.
10  E.g. coal and oil; see, Nies S, 'Oil and gas delivery to Europe: An Overview of Existing and Planned Infrastructure' (2008) 3 *Oil, Gas & Energy Law* <www.ogel.org/article.asp?key=2761> accessed 26 November 2016.
11  Woeehrel S, 'Russian Energy Policy Toward Neighbouring Countries' (*Congressional Research Service*, 2 September 2009) <www.fas.org/sgp/crs/row/RL34261.pdf> accessed 12 December 2016.
12  For the list of the most dependent MS on Natural Gas Supplies see Table 1 in Cohen A, 'Europe's Strategic Dependence on Russian Energy' (*Backgrounder 2083 on Europe, Russia and Eurasia*, 5 November 2007) <www.heritage.org/Research/Europe/bg2083.cfm> accessed 12 December 2016.
13  *Supra* Introduction, note 7, Haghighi.

*Table 1.2* EUROSTAT – Share (%) of Russia in national extra-EU imports of each Member State, 2016, trade in value.[14]

| Country | Share (%) of Russia in national extra-EU28 imports | |
| --- | --- | --- |
| | Petroleum oils | Natural gas |
| Belgium | 25–50 | 0–25 |
| Bulgaria | 75–100 | 75–100 |
| Czech Republic | 50–75 | 75–100 |
| Denmark | 0–25 | 0–25 |
| Germany | 25–50 | 50–75 |
| Estonia | 75–100 | 75–100 |
| Ireland | 0–25 | 0–25 |
| Greece | 0–25 | 50–75 |
| Spain | 0–25 | 0–25 |
| France | 0–25 | 0–25 |
| Croatia | 0–25 | 0–25 |
| Italy | 0–25 | 25–50 |
| Cyprus | 0–25 | 0–25 |
| Latvia | 0–25 | 75–100 |
| Lithuania | 75–100 | 25–50 |
| Luxembourg | 0–25 | 0–25 |
| Hungary | 75–100 | 50–75 |
| Malta | 0–25 | 0–25 |
| Netherlands | 25–50 | 25–50 |
| Austria | 0–25 | 75–100 |
| Poland | 75–100 | 75–100 |
| Portugal | 0–25 | 0–25 |
| Romania | 25–50 | 75–100 |
| Slovenia | 0–25 | 75–100 |
| Slovakia | 75–100 | 75–100 |
| Finland | 75–100 | 75–100 |
| Sweden | 25–50 | 0–25 |
| United Kingdom | 0–25 | 0–25 |

contribute to over 40% of its federal budget and the EU represents almost 80% of cumulative foreign investments in Russia. This clearly shows interdependence …'.[15] The EU Commission's Green Paper (2006) emphasises the

14 EUROSTAT, EU imports of energy products – recent developments, April 2017, <http://ec.europa.eu/eurostat/statistics-explained/index.php/EU_imports_of_ener gy_products_-_recent_developments> accessed 14 August 2017.
15 *Supra* note 1, Piebalgs.

EU's interdependency with its 'energy partners' and confirms that '... the EU, as Russia's largest energy buyer is an essential and equal partner in this relationship.'[16] Others indicate that 50% of Russia's budget is generated through the sale of oil and gas with the EU being the dominant buyer of this commodity.[17]

It is clear that Russia is and will continue to be, an important supplier of energy to the EU in the foreseeable future and it is engaged in promoting its Nord Stream and South Stream pipelines[18] which are designed to feed Europe. Kratochvil and Tichy opine that 'the energy interdependence between Russia and the EU is to some extent asymmetrical in favor of the EU as Russia is more dependent on the EU energy market than the EU is on the Russian energy supplies'.[19] This asymmetry is created by two factors: a) the EU can replace its energy suppliers easily; b) Russia's current energy policy and infrastructure rely heavily on the EU energy market both in terms of geography and finances.[20] Despite these factors, both parties see mutual benefit emanating from cooperation and strategic partnership in energy trade.

This interdependence is formally recognised by the *Roadmap of the EU – Russia Energy Cooperation to 2050*.[21] However, this relationship is also described as one of 'asymmetric interdependence' whereby Russia has been able to exploit divisions within the EU and pursue bilateral energy trade agreements with a number of Member States and uses its energy as leverage in diplomatic, trade, economic and political disputes.[22] Furthermore, if we were to confirm Christie's argument that 'it is rational for Europeans to understand Russia as an ambitious geopolitical player whose ruling elites are motivated by a combination of nationalism, domestic political survival and national economic gain'[23] then it becomes even more necessary to place this relationship on a legal, predictable mandate rather than

16  *Supra* note 1, EC Green Paper (2006); Similarly, field experts seem to also confidently embrace the notion of interdependency, stating that 'It is a common understanding that Russia and the EU are extremely interdependent in terms of energy'; Seliverstov S, 'Energy Security of Russia and the EU: Current Legal Problems' (2009) 2 *Oil Gas & Energy Law* <www.ifri.org/sites/default/files/atoms/files/noteseliverstovenergysecurity.pdf> accessed 26 November 2016.

17  Assenova M, 'Russian Energy Review in 2012: Consolidating State Control in an Uncertain Market' (2013) 10(10) *Eurasia Daily Monitor*, <www.jamestown.org/single/?no_cache=1&tx_ttnews[tt_news]=40333> accessed 12 December 2016.

18  At the time of writing this monograph, the South Stream Pipeline (SSP) project has been put on hold; Bierman S, Arkhipov I and Mazneva E, 'Putin scraps South Stream Pipeline after EU pressure' (*Bloomberg*, 1 December 2014) <www.bloomberg.com/news/2014-12-01/putin-halts-south-stream-gas-pipeline-after-pressure-from-eu.html> accessed 12 December 2016.

19  Kratochvil P and Tichy L, 'EU and Russian discourse on energy relations' (2013) 56 *Energy Policy*, 391–406.

20  *Ibid.*

21  European Commission, 'Energy Roadmap 2050' (*European Union*, 2012) <https://ec.europa.eu/energy/sites/ener/files/documents/2012_energy_roadmap_2050_en_0.pdf> accessed 25 November 2016.

22  *Supra* Introduction note 9, Judah B et al., p. 49.

23  *Supra* Introduction note 7, Christie, p. 276.

leave it to less certain power politics. In the current global economic crisis, secure energy relations and supply are imperative for the functioning and growth of the EU and its common market effectively. Accordingly, solidarity among the EU Member States is essential and hence it is expressed explicitly in the provisions of EU law.

## 1.1. What is the security of energy supply?

Consideration of energy as a security issue is not a recent phenomenon. During the oil crisis in 1973 when the OPEC cut the supply of oil and oil prices increased by 400 percent, the vulnerability of oil dependent economies was exposed.[24] Subsequently, energy has become not only a key economic issue but also a threat or a risk for the functioning and development of economies and markets.[25] It is worth noting that the concept of energy security is understood differently in different contexts:[26] the use of fossil fuels and its effect on global warming and other environmental considerations; suppliers' concerns over terrorist or pirate attacks on pipelines and refineries; and state intervention and nationalisation of foreign investments, are some of the prominent examples which raise security issues.[27]

The concept of 'security of energy supply'[28] is used interchangeably with a term having the same meaning as 'energy security'.[29] Energy security is vital for everyday activities of a functioning society[30] thus the need for reliable sources of adequate

24 Issawi C, 'The 1973 Oil Crisis and After', (Winter, 1978–1979), 1(2) *Journal of Post Keynesian Economics*, pp. 3–26.
25 Dyer H and Trombetta J M, *International Handbook on Energy Security* (Edward Elgar, 2013), p. 3.
26 Chester L, 'Conceptualising energy security and making explicit its polysemic nature', (2010) 3 (4) *Energy Policy*, 202–212.
27 For various discourses and construction of energy as a security issue see, *supra* note 25, Dyer and Trombetta.
28 The definition of 'security of energy supply' has been a subject to an extensive discussion; see Saga B, 'Introduction of Competition in Gas Markets: Effects on Contract Structures and Security of Supply' in Hancher L (eds), *The European Energy Market: Reconciling Competition and Security of Supply*, Vol. 13 (Bundesanzeiger, 1995) 93; see Barton B and others, 'Introduction' in Barton B and others (eds), *Energy Security: Managing Risk in a Dynamic Legal and Regulatory Environment* (Oxford University Press 2004); Cameron D P, *Competition in Energy Markets: Law and Regulation in the European Union* (2nd edn, Oxford University Press 2007); Alhajji F A, 'What is Energy Security? (5/5)' (2008) LI (2) *Middle East Economic Survey* <http://archives. mees.com/issues/204/articles/7861> accessed 14 December 2016.
29 Maican O-H, 'Some Legal Aspects of Energy Security in the Relations Between EU and Russia' (2009) (9)4 *Romanian Journal of European Affairs* 29, <http://beta.ier. ro/documente/rjea_vol9_no4/RJEA_2009_vol._9_no_4_Some_Legal_Aspects_of_ Energy_Security_in_the_Relations_between_EU_and_Russia__.pdf> accessed 14 December 2016.
30 Most of the industries, such as agriculture, mining, construction and manufacturing rely heavily on the energy supplies. The level of demand for energy varies from country to country and from industry to industry depending on a number of factors; see *supra* note 7, Energy Information Administration, International Energy Outlook 2004.

supplies of energy is '… central to states' security, economic development and stability'.[31] In the *Campus Oil* Case, the Court of Justice for the EU held that energy in the modern economy, is 'of fundamental importance for a country's existence since not only its economy but above all its institutions, its essential public services and even the survival of its inhabitants depend upon them'.[32]

Security of energy supply is currently at the top of the agendas of most EU states[33] and the EU,[34] which makes it an international security issue. Security of supply is also 'a cornerstone of European energy policy'[35] being one of its three main objectives.[36] From Russia's perspective, energy security is defined as the '… state of protection of the country, its citizens, society, state, economy from the threats to the secure fuel and energy supply' and 'the full and secure provision of energy resources to the population and the economy on affordable prices that at the same time stimulate energy saving, the minimization of risks and the elimination of threats to the energy supplies of the country'.[37] Russia has repeatedly used energy both as a foreign policy tool in the form of a threat or punishment for states that have conducted policies that Russia dislikes.[38] Russia has used its energy exports not only as a coercion tool but also as a commodity, which empowers its government 'to act independently of criticism from recipient countries that otherwise could be inclined to publicly condemn Russian foreign policy actions'.[39]

31  Flynn C, 'Russian roulette: the ECT, transit and Western European energy security' (2006) 4 *Oil, Gas & Energy Law*.

32  Case 72/83 *Campus Oil Limited and others v Minister for Industry and Energy and others* [1984] ECR 2727.

33  *Supra* note 31, Flynn.

34  The EU's official view on Energy Security: 'Energy supply security must be geared to ensuring, the proper functioning of the economy, the uninterrupted physical availability at a price which is affordable while respecting environmental concerns. Security of supply does not seek to maximise energy self-sufficiency or to minimise dependence, but aims to reduce the risks linked to such dependence'; *supra* note 6, EC Green Paper (2000). More recently, see Commission, 'Energy Union and Climate: Making energy more secure, affordable and sustainable' (*European Commission Priorities*) <http://ec.europa.eu/priorities/energy-union/index_en.htm> accessed 14 December 2016.

35  *Supra* note 16, Seliverstov.

36  Amongst 'sustainability' and 'competitiveness' – *Supra* note 1, EC Green Paper (2006).

37  Ministry of Energy of the Russian Federation, 'The Summary of the Energy Strategy of Russia for the Period of up to 2020' (2003) approved by the Decree No 1234-p of August 28, 2003, and 'Energy Strategy of Russia for the Period up to 2030', issued by the Government of Russian Federation, <http://www.energystrategy.ru/projects/docs/ES-2030_(Eng).pdf> accessed 05 July 2017.

38  Nygren B, *The Rebuilding of Greater Russia: Putin's Foreign Policy Towards the Baltic CIS Countries* (Routledge 2008) and Lucas E, *The New Cold War: Putin's Russia and the Threat to the West* (Palgrave Macmillan 2008). For example, Russia cut off gas to the Czech Republic when it supported the US missile defence plan in 2008; see Elder M, 'Russia exerts its power' *Financial Times' News* (31 October 2008) <www.ft.com/content/07d25ee2-a6e1-11dd-95be-000077b07658> accessed 14 December 2016.

39  Harsem O and Claes D H, 'The interdependence of European–Russian energy relations' (2013) 59 *Energy Policy* 784–791 <http://ac.els-cdn.com/S0301421513002851/1-s2.0-S0301421513002851-main.pdf?_tid=382aa63e-baf2-11e6-b250-00000aab0f02&a

It is argued that this 'gas-for- silence' strategy has influenced an ex-German Chancellor not to criticise Russian actions in the context of conflict in Chechnya[40] and Russia uses bilateral trade negotiations as a way to silence European leaders on contested political issues.[41]

Thus, as in any other defence and international relations policy conducted at the EU level, energy policy of the EU also requires a unified and cooperative approach among its Members. This would allow the EU to have a strong standing and gravity of bargaining power when dealing with its business partners in the energy field. The EU's small number of energy suppliers, Russia, Iran, Iraq and Saudi Arabia and in the Caspian, ex-Soviet countries such as Kazakhstan, Azerbaijan, Turkmenistan, and Chechnya, have not developed liberal open markets nor do they have democratic governance based on the rule of law; and in almost all these jurisdictions power politics determine energy policy. Furthermore, energy is the only efficient and credible Russian export sector and arguably the most important commodity for its economic stability. Energy as the bloodline of the Russian economy is somehow a weakness for Russia and therefore makes Russia a fierce trade partner.

It has been argued 'that the sustainability, efficiency, and security of European energy supply will best be achieved not by hastily deciding to reduce dependence on Russian gas, but through the creation of a carefully and cooperatively managed "interdependence" between Europe and Russia'.[42] If this strategy was to be adopted, then it is essential that such cooperation needs to be based on legal obligations and certainty. Given the lack of such reassurances within the current EU–Russia energy trade relations, there is an even greater incentive for the EU to establish solidarity in its external energy relations with Russia.

cdnat=1480946196_5d5250b8308cfafd55c39f2c3bded786> accessed 14 December 2016.
40 Aalto P, *The EU–Russian Energy Dialogue: Europe's Future Energy Security* (Ashgate, 2008).
41 Hughes J, 'EU Relations with Russia: Partnership or Asymmetric Interdependency?' [2006] LSE Research online <http://eprints.lse.ac.uk/651/1/Hughes.EU-Russia. 2006.pdf> accessed 15 December 2014.
42 *Supra* note 39, Harsem and Claes.

# 2 Legal framework for the EU external energy policy

'The EU has been characterised as a normative power in international relations based on an acceptance of market liberal values, rules and norms and the dissemination of these rules abroad.'[1] While the EU set off to create a fully integrated regulatory regime for its internal energy market via a number of legal instruments[2] whilst continuing its efforts to materialise a multilateral energy trade regime,[3] the concept of the EU's competence in the area of energy policy could be viewed in a broader context of the EU's external energy policy and international affairs.[4] It has been suggested that the EU's external energy policy has three distinct dimensions.[5] In one of the dimensions the EU is acting[6] as two distinct entities:

1  Kuzemko C, 'Ideas, power and change: explaining EU-Russian energy relations' (2014) 21(1) *Journal of European Public Policy* 58–75, 58; Also, see Wagnsson C, 'Divided power Europe: normative agencies among the EU "big three"' (2010) 17(8) *Journal of European Public Policy* 1089–1105; Youngs R, *The EU's Role in World Politics: A Retreat from Liberal Internationalism* (Routledge 2010).

2  The EU internal energy market is regulated under the Third Energy Package which consists of two Directives and three Regulations: Directive 2009/72/EC concerning common rules for the internal market in electricity and repealing Directive 2003/54/EC; Directive 2009/73/EC concerning common rules for the internal market in natural gas and repealing Directive 2003/55/EC; and Regulation (EC) No 714/2009 on conditions for access to the network for cross-border exchanges in electricity and repealing Regulation (EC) No 1228/2003; Regulation (EC) No 715/2009 on conditions for access to the natural gas transmission networks and repealing Regulation (EC) No 1775/2005; Regulation (EC) No 713/2009 of the European Parliament and of the Council of 13 July 2009 establishing an Agency for the Cooperation of Energy Regulators.

3  International Energy Charter 2015, http://www.energycharter.org/process/international-energy-charter-2015/overview/.

4  The notion of policy could be defined as a 'set of coherent norms and values, forming a political regime'; Belyi V A, 'The EU's External Energy Policy' in Roggenkamp M and others (eds), *Energy Law in Europe: National, EU an International Regulation* (Oxford University Press 2007); the general definition of a regime provides that regime is a formation of 'implicit or explicit principles, norms, rules, and decision-making procedures around which actor's expectations converge'; see Krasner D S, 'Structural causes and regime consequences: regimes as intervening variables' (1982) 36 (2) *International Organisation*, pp. 1–21.

5  *Supra* note 4, Belyi.

6  Bretherton C and Vogler J, *The European Union as a Global Actor* (Routledge 2006).

i  as a single economic block with its internal (regional) law making powers and external law making powers within the international/supranational organisations;[7] and

ii  as an intergovernmental organisation expressing the geopolitical security preferences of individual Member States.[8]

The analysis in this book adopts the former perspective as it aims to focus on the legal framework, instead of issues of diplomacy and international politics, which fall under the latter.

## 2.1. European Union as a single economic block

The EU treaties provide specific competences and powers to the EU institutions in well-defined areas (e.g. free movement of goods, competition policy, etc.) and it is in these areas that the Member States have given up their sovereignty to a great extent. This is also acknowledged and reiterated on a number of occasions by the Court of Justice for the EU (CJEU). For example, the CJEU spoke of the new legal order constituted by the EU for whose benefit the Member States had limited their sovereign rights[9] and that not only the law stemming from the treaties cannot be overridden by rules of national law but also national courts have a duty to give full effect to provisions of EU law.[10] It is also established that where there is a conflict between EU and national law, the national law rule must set aside that rule.[11]

The crucial issue in analysing competences of the EU regarding the external energy policy is the marking of the division of the competences between the EU and the Member States. As a general rule, the more the issue is related to the basic community principles, the more likely it is that it will fall within the competences of the EU. Expansion of these basic 'common' principles results in the gradual extension of the EU's competences. Treaty on the Functioning of the European Union (TFEU) 2009 provides that the EU has the authority to negotiate and conclude international agreements in areas regarded as the common commercial policy.[12] Furthermore, where the Union promulgates common rules in order to

---

7  On this level the EU is acting under the European Union competence and is externally represented by the Commission.

8  On this level the EU's actions fall under Common Foreign Security Policy (CFSP) with its international representation by the High Representative for the CFSP.

9  Case 26/62 *NV Algemene Transport en Expeditie Onderneming van Gend & Loos v Netherlands Inland Revenue Administration* [1963] ECR 1 and Case 6/64 *Flaminio Costa v ENEL* [1964] ECR 585.

10  Case 106/77 *Amministrazione delle Finanze dello Stato v Simmenthal SpA* [1978] ECR 629 and Case 11/70 *Internationale Handelsgesellschaft mbH v Einfuhr- und Vorratsstelle für Getreide und Futtermittel* [1970] ECR 1125.

11  Case C-213/89 *The Queen v Secretary of State for Transport, ex parte: Factortame Ltd and others* [1990] ECR I- 2433.

12  Consolidated version of the Treaty on the Functioning of the European Union (TFEU) [2012] OJ C 326/47, Article 207.

implement such a common policy, the Member States of EU have no longer been authorised to individually or collectively conclude other obligations with third parties affecting those rules.[13] The issue of the division of competences between the EU and the Member States analysed here is closely tied to the question of whether the EU can and shall speak in solidarity with one voice in the area of energy policy and security.[14]

### 2.1.1. *From the European Coal and Steel Community to the Treaty of Nice*

The first European Treaty, establishing the European Coal and Steel Community (ECSC) in 1952[15] was primarily concerned with the distribution of domestic energy resources amongst its original six Member States (MS).[16] In the 1940s and 1950s the primary energy resource was coal. Internal coal and gas resources were sufficient and the reliance on oil imports was minimal. In the following years oil began to slowly substitute coal as an energy resource due to its competitive price. Subsequently, the European Community's (EC) focus began to shift from internal regulation of coal to external supplies of other energy resources. This shift has not been legally reflected in the treaties and the MS were free to determine their relations with non-EC countries.[17] This lack of legal mandate on the EC's 'external security of supply' was only partially justifiable, because while the energy reserves were sufficient at that time, the future dependence on external energy resources was foreseeable. On the other hand, Article 95 of the ECSC established a legal avenue which provided that the necessary (additional) powers might be granted to the Community upon the unanimous approval from the Council of Ministers.

Subsequent treaties – the European Atomic Energy Community (EURATOM) Treaty, 1957 and European Economic Community (EEC) Treaty, 1957 which were later amalgamated (together with ECSC, 1952) by the Merger Treaty 1967,[18] covered all the main energy activities, including the rational use of natural resources and the funding of common infrastructure projects.[19] One of the important additions was Article 103 EEC that offered the Council a possibility

---

13  Case 22/70 *Commission of the European Communities v Council of the European Communities* [1971] ECR 263, 274.

14  *Supra* Introduction, note 7, Haghighi, p. 67.

15  The Treaty itself expired in 2002, but some of its provisions were incorporated into subsequent treaties; for details see Treaty establishing the European Coal and Steel Community, ECSC Treaty [1951] <http://europa.eu/legislation_summaries/institu tional_affairs/treaties/treaties_ecsc_en.htm> accessed 12 December 2016.

16  Article 3 of the ECSC states "…to promote a policy of natural resources rationally and avoiding their unconsidered exhaustion". For a historical overview see, *supra* Introduction, note 7, Haghighi.

17  *Supra* note 4, Belyi.

18  For details, see Treaty establishing a Single Council and a Single Commission of the European Communities (with protocol concerning the privileges and immunities of the European Communities and final act) (concluded at Brussels on 8 April 1965, entered into force on 1 July 1967) 1348 UNTS 80 (Merger Treaty).

19  *Supra* note 4, Belyi.

(upon the proposal from the Commission) to adopt measures in a case of difficulties that may arise in supply of certain products, including energy supply. The EURATOM Treaty on the other hand, did not stipulate any measures that would contribute to the security of the energy supplies and indeed 'favoured' the use of nuclear energy over the use of imported fossil fuels.[20]

All subsequent treaties[21] with the exceptions of the EC Treaty[22] and the Maastricht Treaty, 1992 did not provide any other provisions helping to secure the energy supply to the EU.[23] Thus, there was very little legal imperative or duty for the EU and its Member States to act jointly when it came to energy policy and contracts with non-EU countries.

## 2.1.2. From the European Community[24] Treaty to the Treaty of Lisbon – The EU

The reason why both Treaties (the European Community Treaty and the subsequent Lisbon Treaty) should be analysed together is that their combination most accurately portrays the current position of EU law in the area of the external energy relations. With the Treaty of Lisbon 2007[25] (ToL) in force since 1 December 2009, the EC Treaty has been amended and number of other changes have been implemented,[26] but the majority of these provisions have not yet been tested. The provisions under the EC Treaty were put to practice for a number of years and arguably provided a solid basis for the reforms under the ToL.

Article 5 of the EC Treaty 1957, stated that 'the community shall act within the limits of the powers conferred upon it by this treaty and of the objectives assigned

---

20 Oil, gas or coal; EURATOM [2012] OJ C 327/1, Articles 64 and 66. While the provisions (Arts 64 and 66) of this legal instrument have not changed, the reference to the legal instrument is now cited under the consolidated version (CONSOLIDATED VERSION OF THE TREATY ESTABLISHING THE EUROPEAN ATOMIC ENERGY COMMUNITY) See http://www.wenra.org/media/filer_public/2015/01/06/wenra_handbook_part_1_-_european_legal_framework_in_nuclear_safety.pdf.
21 Single European Act [1986] OJ L 169/1, Treaty of Amsterdam Amending the Treaty on European Union – the Treaties Establishing the European Communities and Certain Related Acts (*European Communities*, 1997), Treaty of Nice Amending the Treaty on European Union – the Treaties Establishing the European Communities and Certain Related Acts [2001] OJ C 80/1.
22 Analysed below.
23 The Maastricht Treaty included a reference to measures in the sphere of energy in Article 3 EC, in the context of sustainable development. However, the article did not determine the ways through which the activities under this article should be put in place, rendering it unusable by the Community. Subsequent treaties (Nice and Amsterdam) also contained Article 3, but similarly without detailed rules on its implementation.
24 'EC', 'EU' and the "Community" will be used interchangeably in this text notwithstanding the changes brought by the Treaty of Lisbon in 2009.
25 For details, see Lisbon Treaty [2007] OJ C306/1.
26 For the general analysis, see Fairhurst J, *Law of the European Union* (9th edn, Pearson Education Limited 2012); Kaczorowska A, *European Union Law* (Routledge-Cavendish 2013).

to it therein'. Thus, once the powers had been assigned to the Community, the MS were prevented from taking unilateral action.[27]

The powers conferred to the Community[28] by the EC Treaty fell into two categories: explicit and implicit.[29] Explicit powers were listed in Articles 3 and 4 of the EC Treaty in the form of 'objectives'. None of these expressly stated whether the EU has competence[30] in relation to the energy or energy security. However, the Community developed the internal powers that were not expressly derived from the treaty, but from global and/or general objectives. In the area of energy security, the EC's powers were extended through the use of the 'flexibility clause' pursuant to Article 308. This provision enabled the Community to expand the legislation into the areas where no separate legal basis was provided. In other words, Article 308 allowed the EC to adopt measures only if no other provision in the Treaty did.[31] This article was extensively used in the area of energy, for a wide-range of purposes such as concluding various international trade agreements including the Energy Charter Treaty.[32]

The EC Treaty also provided two other provisions allowing the EU to grant internal measures in the field of energy: Article 95 provided a solution to the difficulties that may arise in the harmonisation of the internal market, whereas Article 100 was drafted to be used if and when 'severe difficulties arise in the supply of certain products'.[33]

Similar to the EC Treaty, Article 13(2) TEU (as amended by the Treaty of Lisbon) has reinstated the obligation on the EU to act pursuant to the principle of conferral. Article 2(6) TFEU stipulates that the scope of the EU's competences should be determined by the treaties. It introduces three categories of Union's Power: exclusive competence;[34] shared competence;[35] and actions to support, coordinate or supplement the actions of the Member States.[36] According to Article 4(2)(i) TFEU, 'energy' falls in the area of shared competence between the EU

27 Case 6/64 *Flaminio Costa v ENEL* [1964] ECR 585, 593 & 584.
28 Now the 'Union'.
29 For further analysis, see *supra* note 26, Kaczorowska.
30 Treaty establishing the European Community [Consolidated version 2002] OJ C325/33, Article 133 on Commercial Policy; TEC [Consolidated version 2002] OJ C325/33, Article 111(3) concerning the exchange rate system for the ECU in relation to non-Community currencies; TEC [Consolidated version 2002] OJ C325/33, Article 174(4) on the protection of environment; TEC [Consolidated version 2002] OJ C325/33, Article 181 on development co-operation; TEC [Consolidated version 2002] OJ C325/33, Article 310 on association agreements.
31 *Supra* Introduction, note 7, Haghighi, p. 72.
32 Analysed below.
33 Additionally, there were two other areas of the EC Treaty where energy was mentioned for purposes different than the security of supply: Article 154 EC related to the establishment of trans-European networks in the area of energy and Article 175 EC on MS' choices of the different energy sources in the context of environmental protection.
34 TFEU [2012] OJ C326/47, Article 3.
35 TFEU [2012] OJ C326/47, Article 4.
36 TFEU [2012] OJ C326/47, Article 6.

and MS. It means that MS can only legislate and adopt legally binding acts if this right has not yet been exercised by the EU.[37]

### 2.1.3. The principle of solidarity – 'More than a token with a lustrous aura'?[38]

In recent years, the EU Member States have increasingly been called upon to act in solidarity both in legal,[39] political[40] and economic[41] terms and contexts. For example, the global economic crisis and its impact on the EU as well as the on-going refugee crisis, international terrorism, and Ukraine conflict[42] have required collective action.[43] More recently, Brexit negotiations have given rise to both legal and political unified stance and response among the 27 Member States of the EU.[44] As Borgmann-Prebil and Ross aptly observe and demonstrate, calls for adherence to and exercise of solidarity have coincided with various crises across the EU. In tandem with these events, the literature also reveals that there has been a growing interest in the principle of solidarity from scholars in academic discourse.[45] This monograph illustrates that there is clear evidence from the CJEU jurisprudence and the EU Commission which indicate that solidarity is no longer a mere political concept for internal issues and it is becoming a dominant feature of external trade (i.e. energy trade and investment) and external security issues. In this context one can observe the tensions between national and supra-national competences whereby Member States' desire to exercise their sovereign powers has to be checked against their loyalty and obligation to adhere to the principle of solidarity and act in the interest of the EU. Perhaps, as a direct result of such

37 Case 6/64 *Flaminio Costa v ENEL* [1964] ECR 585, 593 & 584.
38 Cited by Ross M, 'Solidarity – A New Constitutional Paradigm for the EU?' in Ross and Borgmann-Prebil, *Promoting Solidarity in the European Union*, (Oxford University Press 2010), p. 24.
39 Turksen U, 'Current Problems and Future Prospects for EU Solidarity in Energy Trade', (2014) Vol. 12 (4) *Oil, Gas and Energy Law*.
40 Bockenforde E W, *What holds Europe together?* (Central European Press 2006) p. 32.
41 Buntenbach A and others, 'Solidarity in the Economic Crisis, Challenges and Expectations for European Trade Unions' (*Friedrich Ebert Stiftung International Policy Analysis*, May 2011) <http://library.fes.de/pdf-files/id/ipa/08073.pdf> accessed 12 December 2016; Fernandes S and Rubio E, 'Solidarity within the Eurozone: how much, what for, for how long?' (2012) 51 Notre Europe, Policy Paper, <www.insti tutdelors.eu/media/solidarityemu_s.fernandese.rubio_ne_feb2012.pdf?pdf=ok > accessed 12 December 2016.
42 EU Commission, European Civil Protection and Humanitarian Aid Operations, Ukraine, <http://ec.europa.eu/echo/where/europe-and-central-asia/ukraine_en> accessed on 17 August 2017.
43 Juncker J C, 'State of the Union 2015: Time for Honesty, Unity and Solidarity' (*European Commission Press Release Database*, 9 September 2015) <http://europa. eu/rapid/press-release_SPEECH-15-5614_en.htm> accessed 12 December 2016.
44 European Commission, Brexit Negotiations, <https://ec.europa.eu/commission/ brexit-negotiations_en> accessed 07 August 2017.
45 Borgmann-Prebil and Ross, 'Promoting European Solidarity: Between Rhetoric and Reality' in Ross and Borgmann-Prebil, *Promoting Solidarity in the European Union*, (Oxford University Press 2010), ch. 1.

tensions, it has been difficult to provide a single and all-compassing definition of solidarity. Rather, various definitions have been provided in different contexts. For example, the principle of solidarity has been defined by Advocate General Fennelly as an 'inherently uncommercial act of involuntary subsidization of one social group by another'.[46] This monograph does not challenge this definition yet it presents the view that energy security requires a holistic, teleological and single market oriented approach to the definition and exercise of solidarity. Accordingly, its puts forward a notion that both commercial and uncommercial interests require the EU Member States to act in solidarity when it comes to energy security and trade in general and in the context of energy trade with the Russian Federation in particular.

The recent surge in interest pertaining to solidarity in the academic literature,[47] politics[48] and religion[49] is somehow surprising given the fact that the spirit and/or the principle of solidarity has been recognised for a long time as one of the founding and guiding principles of the European Communities.[50] Solidarity, as a moral and legal force, has not only found expression in the realisation of fundamental freedoms (e.g. free movement of goods and services, citizenship), fundamental rights (e.g. equality and non-discrimination, environmental protection) but also provided policy direction for social justice, fairness and security and contributed to the effective functioning of the EU.

Since the very start of the European Project, solidarity has been articulated both in legal and political contexts. For instance, the Preamble to the Treaty Establishing the European Coal and Steel Community Treaty (1951) stipulated that 'Europe can be built only through real practical achievements which will first of all create real *solidarity*, and through the establishment of common bases for economic development'.[51] Later in the Single European Act (1986) and in the Maastricht

---

46  Case C-70/95 *Sodemarev Rgione Lombardia* [1997] ECR I-3395, para 29.
47  Ross provides a review of the recent academic literature written on solidarity from philosophy, social theory and sociology perspectives. See, Ross M, 'Solidarity – A New Constitutional Paradigm for the EU?' in Ross and Borgmann-Prebil, *Promoting Solidarity in the European Union* (Oxford University Press 2010) ch. 2. Also see, Desierto D, 'Namur Declaration of 05 December 2016: An EU-Values Driven Path to Negotiating and Concluding Economic and Trade Agreements', 7 December 2016, http s://www.ejiltalk.org/namur-declaration-of-5-december-2016-an-eu-values-driven-pa th-to-negotiating-and-concluding-economic-and-trade-agreements/   accessed   07 August 2017; and Azaria D, 'Community Interest in International Energy Law: A European Perspective', Lauterpacht Centre for International Law – University of Cambridge, 14 March 2016, <https://sms.cam.ac.uk/media/2201583> accessed on 7 July 2017.
48  Grimmel A and My Giang S, *Solidarity in the European Union* (Springer, 2017) and Sangiovanni A, 'Solidarity in the European Union' (2013) 33 (2) *Oxford Journal of Legal Studies*, pp. 213–241.
49  Caroll J, (quoting from Pope Francis), 'Pope Francis Proposes a Cure for Populism', *The New Yorker*, 28 March 2017, <http://www.newyorker.com/news/news-desk/p ope-francis-proposes-a-cure-for-populism> accessed on 07 August 2017.
50  Giddens A., *Europe in the Global Age* (Cambridge Polity Press, 2007), p. 112.
51  Emphasis added.

Treaty (1992) 'solidarity' appeared alongside 'cohesion'.[52] The Preamble to the Lisbon Treaty (2007) not only commits its signatories 'to deepen the solidarity between their peoples while respecting their history, their culture and their traditions' but also expands it in numerous policy areas and activities of the EU and its Member States. One of the important changes brought by the ToL in relation to energy is indeed the *principle of solidarity*.[53] This principle has been promoted by the Commission since the 1990s and appears in various parts and contexts[54] of the ToL including the security of the energy supplies. Lisbon Treaty provisions indicate that solidarity is not some distant possibility but an expectation in the transnational and supranational governance structure of the EU. With explicit identification and requirement of solidarity in several areas of EU competence, the potency and distinctiveness of this principle have also been strengthened by the jurisprudence of the Court of Justice of the European Union (as identified below). Subsequently, within the different contexts and notion of solidarities, solidarity in energy trade and security necessitates a degree of normative and legal gravity. Solidarity within the EU context thus represents Stjerno's view that solidarity is 'readiness for collective action and a will to institutionalise it through the establishment of rights and citizenship'.[55]

For example, Article 194(1) TFEU provides that in the context of establishment of energy market and protection of environment,

> Union policy on energy shall aim, in a spirit of *solidarity* between Member States, to:
>
> i    ensure the functioning of the energy market;
> ii   ensure security of energy supply in the Union.

However, Article 194(2) states that the measures taken under Article 194 shall not affect the MS's right to choose energy resources and suppliers.[56] Thus, Maltby argues that 'solidarity' in this context is vague[57] and Konstadinides opines that the

---

52 *Supra* note 48, Sangiovanni.
53 TFEU [2012] OJ C326/47, Article 4(3).
54 TEU [2008] OJ C115/13, Article 21 states that: 'The Union's action on the international scene shall be guided by the principles which have inspired its own creation, development and enlargement, and which it seeks to advance in the wider world: democracy, the rule of law, the universality and indivisibility of human rights and fundamental freedoms, respect for human dignity, the principles of equality and *solidarity*, and respect for the principles of the United Nations Charter and international law'.
55 Stjerno S, *Solidarity in Europe: The History of an Idea* (Cambridge University Press, 2009) p. 325.
56 Nevertheless 'measures significantly affecting a Member State's choice between different energy sources and the general structure of its energy supply' (TFEU [2012] OJ C326/47, Article 192(2)(c)) may be passed through the special procedure specified in Article 192(2) of TFEU [2012] OJ C326/47.
57 Maltby T, 'European Union energy policy integration: A case of European Commission policy entrepreneurship and increasing supranationalism' (2013) 55 *Energy Policy*,

solidarity clause (under Article 222 TFEU) renders solidarity as an 'interpretative, rather than legally binding commitment'.[58] This is not completely accurate because Article 222 TFEU[59] stipulates solidarity in situations arising from atrocities and in crisis management, including modern threats from non-state agents such as terrorist organisations and manmade disasters, etc., areas which do not necessarily fall into the economic realm and policy. Whereas the other legal provisions outlined here are linked to the Single Market and intra-community trade activities thus are directly linked to explicit aims and objectives of the Treaties for which the EU has competence.

It is important to note that rules on Single Market have consistently been held to have direct effects and supremacy.[60] It seems that the requirements of solidarity in the economic field and energy policy are clearly articulated and there has been 'prior consultation' between Member States and political institutions of the EU. Therefore, it could be argued that the principle of solidarity has a degree of gravity as a constitutional benchmark and may be invoked as a duty on Member States in the context of common internal and external energy policy. The Treaty objectives are intrinsically far too valuable to be held hostage to the norm of state sovereignty and discretion provided by Article 194(2) and, therefore, ought to override that norm.

Indeed, in the context of bilateral investment treaties (BITs) signed with countries outside of the EU, both the treaty provisions (e.g. Articles 63–66 and 218 TFEU) and Court of Justice of the European Union jurisprudence[61]

435–444 <http://ac.els-cdn.com/S0301421512010798/1-s2.0-S0301421512010798-main.pdf?_tid=496055c0-bbd3-11e6-8ae1-00000aacb361&acdnat=1481042862_6ba 74f0fc84c48a4126a2722cf17cd54> accessed 28 November 2016.

58  Konstadinides T, 'Civil protection in Europe and the Lisbon "solidarity clause": A genuine legal concept or an article exercise' (2011) Uppsala Faculty of Law Working Article 3, <www2.statsvet.uu.se/LinkClick.aspx?fileticket=ywEQQ722UuI%3D&ta bid=3159&language=sv-SE> accessed 12 December 2016.

59  TFEU [2012] OJ C326/47, Article 222 states: 'The Union and its Member States shall act jointly in a spirit of solidarity if a Member State is the object of a terrorist attack or the victim of a natural or man-made disaster. The Union shall mobilize all the instruments at its disposal, including the military resources made available by the Member States, to … assist a Member State in its territory, at the request of its political authorities, in the event of a natural or man-made disaster'.

60  The doctrine of 'direct effect' applies in principle to all binding EU Law including the Treaties, secondary legislation and international agreements. See Case 26/62 *Van Gend en Loos* [1963] ECR 1; Case 6/64 *Costa v ENEL* [1964] ECR 585 and Case 11/70 *Internationale Handelsgesellschaft* [1970] ECR 1125. Also, note that Article 4 (3) TEU stipulates that 'Pursuant to the principle of sincere cooperation … the Member States shall take any appropriate measure … to ensure fulfilment of the obligations arising out of the Treaties … [and] shall facilitate the achievement of the Union's tasks and refrain from any measure which could jeopardise the attainment of the Union's objectives.' Declaration 17 under TFEU states that '… in accordance with well settled case law of the Court of Justice of the European Union, the Treaties and the law adopted by the Union on the basis of the Treaties have primacy over the law of Member States, under the conditions laid down by the said case law.'

61  Case C-522/04 *Commission of the European Communities v Kingdom of Belgium* [2007] ECR I-5701; Case C-205/06 *Commission of the European Communities v*

confirm that member state interests *cannot* override the EU common interests.[62]

According to the Court, the treaty provisions empower the Council to take restrictive measures against third states, which may include also states with which EU Member States have concluded BITs. The Commission is also in the opinion that in the case of 'hypothetical incompatibilities' between the BITs and the EU *acquis*, the BITs must be either brought into line with EU law or, if that is not possible, the BIT in question shall be declared void.[63] Indeed, in its judgment on 16 May 2017, the CJEU held that entering into bilateral Open Skies agreements as an individual EU Member State was a breach of the community's single market policy which was traditionally governed by bilateral agreements.[64] In this opinion, the Court of Justice of the European Union referred to its judgment of 31 March 1971, *Commission v Council* (22/70, EU:C:1971:32), whereby the Court stated that, 'when the European Union adopts provisions laying down common rules, whatever form these may take, the Member States no longer have the right, acting individually or even collectively, to undertake obligations with third States which affect those rules' (see also, *inter alia*, judgment of 5 November 2002, *Commission v Denmark*, C-467/98, EU:C:2002:625, paragraphs 77 to 80). Citing this jurisprudence, the CJEU expressed that in particular when 'the Community, with a view to implementing a common policy envisaged by the Treaty, adopts provisions laying down common rules, whatever form these may take, the Member States no longer have the right, acting individually or even collectively, to undertake obligations with third countries which affect those rules'. It seems clear therefore that when Single Market considerations and interests of the EU are concerned, unified action (solidarity) is a requirement. In parallel with this argument, it can be asserted that external energy trade is not an exception although the judgments by the Court of Justice of the European Union have not expressly used the term solidarity in this context, yet.

   *Republic of Austria* [2009] ECR I-1301; Case C-249/06 *Commission of the European Communities v Kingdom of Sweden* [2009] ECR I-1335; Case C-118/07 *Commission of the European Communities v Republic of Finland* [2009] ECRI-10889 and Case C-384/09 *Prunus and Polonium* [2011] ECRI-3319.

62 By the Lisbon Treaty, foreign direct investment (FDI) has been added to the exclusive external trade competence of the EU; TFEU [2012] OJ C326/47, Article 207.

63 UNCITRAL ad hoc investment arbitration case (*Eastern Sugar BV (Netherlands) v The Czech Republic*) [2007] Partial Award, SCC Case No 088/2004. For further analysis and critique, see Nappert S, 'EU-Russia Relations in the Energy Field: The Continuing Role of International Law in EU–Russia relations in the energy field' in Talus K and Fratini P (eds), *EU-Russia Energy Relations* (Rixensart, Euroconfidentiel SA 2010) 103–118 and Strik P, *Shaping the Single European Market in the Field of Foreign Direct Investment* (Bloomsbury Publishing 2014).

64 The CJEU Opinion 2/15, Opinion pursuant to Article 218(11) TFEU – Free Trade Agreement between the European Union and the Republic of Singapore, 16 May 2017, <http://curia.europa.eu/juris/document/document.jsf;jsessionid=9ea7d0f130 d60c4e643954774a1eb178a8d0ac0d1a74.e34KaxiLc3eQc40LaxqMbN4Pax4Se0? text=&docid=190727&pageIndex=0&doclang=EN&mode=req&dir=&occ=first&pa rt=1&cid=402364> accessed 07 August 2017.

Even in response to events strictly within the scope of Article 222 TFEU, Member State discretion is confined to criteria. The lack of clear interpretation and invocation of the principle of solidarity has been addressed by the Council Decision (2014/415/EU).[65] Accordingly, in the implementation of the Solidarity Clause, the political authorities of the affected Member States may invoke the Clause if they conclude that the crisis overwhelms their response capabilities. This clause has been instilled as a major pillar in strategies dealing with new threats such as cybercrime and cyber-security and defense.[66]

In addition, Article 122(1) TFEU provides that in a case of severe difficulties in the supply of 'certain products notably in the area of energy', the Council, on a proposal from the Commission, may decide upon the measures appropriate to the economic situation. That decision shall again be reached in a *spirit of solidarity* between MS.

The Treaty of Lisbon also foresees a possibility of difficulties in cases of energy crisis when Member States have an obligation to consult each other and take necessary steps to resolve these problems, placing the issue of energy security in a broader context. These instances are laid out in Article 347 TFEU and are 'clearly defined and do not lend themselves to any wide interpretation'[67] which does cover 'measures taken for reasons of public safety and security'.[68]

'Energy', unlike other areas covered by the Treaty, does not contain an express encouragement for the MS to foster co-operation with third countries and international organisations. It has been suggested that such 'categorisation of the Union's policy in the field of energy is designed to allow the Union to embark on activities at the external level because nothing in the provision limits the competence of the Union in this respect'.[69]

Article 308 EC which was extensively used in the area of energy has been modified in the Treaty of Lisbon under Article 352 TFEU. Article 352(1) TFEU provides the Union with a general legislative power: 'If action by the Union should prove necessary ... to attain one of the objectives set out in the Treaties, and the Treaties have not provided the necessary powers, the Council ... shall adopt the appropriate measures'. On the one hand the scope of Article 352(1) TFEU is wider than of Article 308 EC as it refers to the objectives of the EU and is not confined to the internal market, which was the case under Article 308 EC. On the other hand, its application is limited, as it requires unanimity in the Council and the consent of the European Parliament.[70] Furthermore, over-reliance

65 Council Decision of 24 June 2014 on the arrangements for the implementation by the Union of the solidarity clause (2014/415/EU) [2014] OJ L192/53.
66 Pawlak P, 'Cybersecurity and Cyberdefense: EU Solidarity and Mutual Defense Clauses' (June 2015) European Parliament Briefing <www.europarl.europa.eu/RegData/etudes/BRIE/2015/559488/EPRS_BRI(2015)559488_EN.pdf > accessed 12 December 2016.
67 Case C-13/68 *SPA Salgoil v Italian Ministry of Foreign Trade* [1968] ECR 453, 463.
68 Case C-222/84 *Marguerite Johnston v Chief Constable of the Royal Ulster Constabulary* [1986] ECR 1651, para 26.
69 *Supra* Introduction, note 7, Haghighi, p. 81.
70 *Supra* note 26, Fairhurst J.

on this article would no longer be necessary as the EU has gained express legal basis in the area of energy,[71] which is likely to expand as the secondary legislation becomes denser.[72]

While Article 95 EC which made reference to energy in the context of environmental protection has been 'transferred' to the Treaty of Lisbon under Article 114 TFEU, it adds no further competences to the EU regarding energy security. Nevertheless, the EU institutions which are endowed with the responsibility to devise both an internal and external common energy policy and strategy have indeed given heed to the principle of solidarity in EU secondary legislation. For example, the EU Commission highlighted the importance of completing the internal market in natural gas and indicated that the existing rules and measures were not adequate[73] and titled its Second Strategic Energy Review as 'An EU Energy Security and Solidarity Action Plan'.[74] While Regulation (EC) No. 663/2009 requires MS to implement the aforementioned Action Plan in light of solidarity among MS,[75] EU Directive 2009/73 provides that the MS '*shall* cooperate in order to promote regional and bilateral *solidarity*' (emphasis added).[76] It is important to note that the use of the term 'shall' indicates that there is an explicit obligation on the Member States to cooperate. The EU Directive 2009/119/EC[77] also calls upon the MS to cooperate with the Commission so that Community-wide solidarity and cohesion in regards to energy (oil) policy can be ensured and the objective of this Directive[78] can be achieved.[79] Similarly, the European Parliament (EP) has consistently made reference to solidarity in its recent reports and legal

---

71 TFEU [2012] OJ C326/47, Article 4(2)(i).
72 *Supra* Introduction, note 7, Haghighi, p. 83. Also, see the CJEU jurisprudence explained below.
73 Directive 2009/73/EC of the European Parliament and of the Council of 13 July 2009 concerning common rules for the internal market in natural gas and repealing Directive 2003/55/EC [2009] OJ L211/94.
74 European Commission, 'Second Strategic Energy Review: An EU Energy Security and Solidarity Action Plan' (Communication from the Commission to the European Parliament, the Council, the European Economic and Social Committee and the Committee of the Regions) COM (2008)781 final, SEC (2008) 2870–2872.
75 Regulation (EC) No 663/2009 of the European Parliament and of the Council of 13 July 2009 establishing a programme to aid economic recovery by granting Community financial assistance to projects in the field of energy [2009] OJ L200/31.
76 Directive 2009/73/EC [2009] OJ L211/94, Article 6.
77 Council Directive 2009/119/EC of 14 September 2009 imposing an obligation on Member States to maintain minimum stocks of crude oil and/or petroleum products [2009] OJ L265/9, recital 13.
78 Article 1 of Council Directive 2009/119/EC of 14 September 2009 imposing an obligation on Member States to maintain minimum stocks of crude oil and/or petroleum products [2009] L 265/9 provides the objective as ensuring 'a high level of security of oil supply in the Community through reliable and transparent mechanisms based on solidarity amongst Member States'.
79 *Ibid*. Recitals 28 and 33; similar provisions are present: in regards to electricity in Directive 2009/72/EC [2009] OJ L211/55, Recital 24; in regards to oil and petroleum products in Directive 2006/67/EC [2006] OJ L217/8, Recital 18; in regards to natural gas supply in Directive 2004/67/EC [2004] L127/92, Recital 13.

proposals.[80] The European Council which is endowed with the duty to 'provide the Union with the necessary impetus for its development and shall define the general political directions and priorities thereof',[81] has instructed the EU Commission to prepare a communication on energy supply security and cooperation and coherence of the EU's external action in its energy trade and relations.[82] As the primary EU institution in formulating its foreign policy, the Council opined that the EU ought to take appropriate action so as to develop 'mutually beneficial energy partnerships with key players and around strategic corridors, covering a wide range of issues, including regulatory approaches, on all subjects of common interest, such as energy security, safe and sustainable low carbon technologies, energy efficiency, the investment environment and maintaining and promoting the highest standards for nuclear safety' and asserted that action ought to be taken as soon as possible 'to develop a reliable, transparent and rules- based partnership with Russia in areas of common interest in the field of energy and as part of the negotiations on the post-Partnership and Cooperation Agreement process and in the light of on-going work on the Partnership for Modernization and the Energy Dialogue'.[83] Subsequently, the EU Commission produced a *communiqué* titled, 'The EU Energy Policy: Engaging with Partners beyond Our Borders' in September 2011.[84] The *communiqué* recognised that the EU 'energy cooperation requires a new and strong legal base. Therefore, the negotiations on the New EU-Russia Agreement need to address crucial topics like access to energy resources, networks and export markets, investment protection, reciprocity, crisis prevention and cooperation, level playing field, and pricing of energy resources'. The proposal also urged Member States to inform the Commission in advance of any bilateral negotiations with third countries in the energy field so that a structured approach can be adopted.[85] This approach also included a proposal to vest in the Commission the power to review draft intergovernmental agreements and at EU level, negotiate agreements with third countries in order to materialise the core EU objectives. Indeed, such approach has been evidenced in the context of the multilateral treaty between the EU and Azerbaijan and Turkmenistan in which the Commission on behalf of 27 EU Member States agreed to the establishment of the Trans-Caspian Pipeline System.[86] This has been

---

80 See, for example, Wagner S F, 'Energy Infrastructure Priorities for 2020 and Beyond (2011/2034 (INI))' (*Committee on Industry, Research and Energy*, 14 June 2011), which makes reference to solidarity seven times.
81 Lisbon Treaty [2007] OJ C306/01, Article 9.
82 Council 4 February 2011 Conclusions [8 March 2011] EUCO 2/1/11 Rev 1 < http://register.consilium.europa.eu/doc/srv?l=EN&f=ST%202%202011%20REV% 201> accessed 12 December 2016.
83 *Ibid.*
84 European Commission, Communication on security of energy supply and international cooperation – 'The EU Energy Policy: Engaging with Partners beyond Our Borders' [2011] COM (2011) 539 final, SEC (2011) 1022–1023 final.
85 *Ibid.* p. 18.
86 European Commission, 'EU starts negotiations on Caspian pipeline to bring gas to Europe' (*Press Release Database, IP/11/1023*, 12 September 2011) <http://europa. eu/rapid/press-release_IP-11-1023_en.htm?locale=en> accessed 15 December 2014.

yet another sign of the development of the principle of solidarity within the EU's external energy trade relations.

In addition, jurisprudence of the CJEU indicates that the principle of solidarity must inform Member States' action and implementation of secondary legislation.[87] As Ross opines, solidarity in the EU is a real and viable 'constitutional principle'[88] and it could be argued that it is becoming one of the general principles of EU law. Furthermore, on the back of such legal and political rationale, the EU Commission has been trying very hard to establish itself as the leading institution in creating a common external energy and security policy for the EU,[89] without explicitly invoking the principle of solidarity as a benchmark for enforcement against non-abiding EU Member States.

In conclusion, it can be argued that EU solidarity is expressed in primary and secondary legal provisions of the EU, therefore, it cannot and should not be confined to specific policy area and/or distinct sectors of social life such as economy, arts, health and safety, consumer rights, sports, etc. Rather, it should be seen as a founding constitutional principle that:

i    embraces co-existence in its generic sense;[90]
ii   underpins the European sense of belonging and informs all activities of the EU (in which the EU has been given the competence) including its external energy trade.

The EU legal instruments refer to solidarity as a requirement but do not define it. In order for the principle of solidarity to have a unified understanding and application, there seems to be a need for a specific judicial opinion on the subject matter. Perhaps the line of thinking behind the following judgment of the CJEU can be incorporated in the interpretation and solidification of the principle of solidarity:

It follows from the need for uniform application of Community law and from the principle of equality that the terms of a provision of Community law which makes no express reference to the law of the Member States for the

87  In Joined Cases C-411/10 and C-493/10[2011] ECR I-0000, the CJEU held that treaty aims and obligations (e.g. common asylum policy) are to be governed by the principle of solidarity and fair sharing of responsibility (para. 93); also see Judgment of the Court (Sixth Chamber) of 29 September in Joined cases 351/85 and 360/85 *Fabrique de fer de Charleroi SA and Dillinger Hüttenwerke AG v Commission of the European Communities* [1987] ECR 3639; and C-56/99 *Gascogne Limousin viandes SA v Office national interprofessionnel des viandes de l'élevage et de l'aviculture (Ofival)* [2000] ECR I-3079 where the CJEU held that in the context of the pursuit of an objective recognised by EU law, all Community producers, regardless of the Member State in which they are based, must together, act in a spirit of solidarity and equality.
88  Ross M and Borgmann-Prebil Y, *Promoting Solidarity in the European Union* (Oxford University Press 2010) 4.
89  Talus K, *EU Energy Law and Policy: A Critical Account* (Oxford University Press 2013) 248.
90  *Supra* note 40, Bockenforde, pp. 32–33.

purpose of determining its meaning and scope must normally be given an autonomous and uniform interpretation throughout the Union.[91]

### 2.1.4. Developments by the Court of Justice of the European Union (CJEU) in the area of energy security

The CJEU's institutional role conferred by the Treaties represents a significant transfer of jurisdictional authority, previously embedded within national courts, and underpins the supremacy of EU law. For many years, the CJEU has been involved in clarifying the division of powers between the EU and Member States. Most of the EU's powers and competences in the area of energy security and supply were implied prior to the ToL,[92] consequently it was even more important to draw a clear demarcation line separating these competences. It can be asserted that the CJEU is 'both willing and able to assert itself as the highest court in a constitutional order adjudicating on competences'[93] and its 'opinion may be sought on the questions concerning the division of competences between the Community and the Member States'.[94] It is however up to the EU institutions to initiate such inquiry for the CJEU's perusal. So far, the Commission, as the main EU institution endowed with the duty of monitoring the Member States' compliance and ensuring the aims and objectives of the Treaties are achieved,[95] has not challenged either any unilateral Member State activity in the energy sector or dominance of any energy supplier such as Gazprom. This is somehow surprising from a purely legal perspective because the *acquis communautaire* clearly enables the Commission to uphold and enforce the principle of solidarity in general and in the context of external energy trade in particular.

#### 2.1.4.1. Article 30 EC Treaty – Public policy grounds and 'necessity'

Initially, the CJEU opined that the Member States were the best authorities to make decisions on the security of their energy supplies thus it has given deference to executive decisions within Member States. However, this view began to change giving a way to the expansion of the external competences in energy relations to the Community.[96]

In the *Campus Oil* case,[97] the CJEU held that even if the Community rules on the matter of energy supply exist, the complementary measures of MS on a

---

91  Case C-66/08 *Seyman Kozlowski* [2008] ECR I-6041 para. 42.
92  Primarily through the use of Article 308 (see above) and up until the ToL.
93  Bast A and Bogdandy A, 'The European Union's Vertical Order of Competences: The Current Law and Proposals for its Reform' (2002) 39 *Common Market Law Review* 227, 238.
94  Opinion 1/94 *the Competence of the Community to Conclude International Agreements concerning Services and the Protection of Intellectual Property* [1994] ECR I-5267, para. 9.
95  TFEU [2012] OJ C326/47, Article 17.
96  *Supra* Introduction, note 7, Haghighi, p. 84.
97  Case 72/83 *Campus Oil Limited and others v Minister for Industry and Energy and others* [1984] ECR 2727.

national level should not be excluded. Therefore, the MS were permitted to derogate from the basic Treaty principles under Article 30 EC (now Article 36 TFEU) on 'public security' grounds, *inter alia* due to the 'necessity' of securing the energy supplies. The CJEU's rationale for this decision was the fact that petrol was very important to each country's existence and economic security.[98]

In the case of *Commission v Hellenic Republic*,[99] the issue of 'necessity' of securing the energy supply was reconsidered. Although the facts of this case were similar to the *Campus Oil*,[100] the CJEU interpreted the notion of 'necessity' more strictly and held that it should be interpreted beyond 'purely economic reasoning' and expressed the need for 'less restrictive' measures than straightforward derogations. This decision changed the threshold for the MS' ability to restrict trade in energy.

Members States' freedom to derogate from the Treaty provisions due to the 'necessity' of securing energy supplies was further limited in the Opinion of the Advocate General in the *Preussen Elektra case*.[101] It remained doubtful[102] whether it was still possible to rely on the 'public security' exceptions under Article 36 TFEU if these particular issues have been addressed by the EU in the form of a secondary legislation.

### 2.1.4.2. *Implied EU external powers and the doctrines of 'necessity' and 'effect'*

The EU can acquire legal personality (i.e. a capacity to be represented internationally and to enter into international treaties with third parties) only through transfer of that power from Member States to the EU. This could be done in two ways: through explicit reference to the provisions of the Treaty[103] or through the progressive development of the CJEU's case law that originates from the case of *ERTA*.[104] In *ERTA* it was held that if there is any common rule that deals with externalities,[105] the EU has an implied external power in the field covered by this common rule.[106]

---

98 Another reason for this stance may be the fact that in the 1980s there were no real attempts to create an internal energy market for oil and gas.
99 Case C-347/88 *Commission v Hellenic Republic* [1990] ECR I-4747.
100 Case 72/83 *Campus Oil Limited and others v Minister for Industry and Energy and others* [1984] ECR 2727.
101 Opinion in C-379/98 *Preussen Elektra AG v Schleswag AG* [2001] ECR I-2099.
102 The doubt remained as the Court's decision was made on the environmental protection grounds; See paras 68–81.
103 E.g. Ex Article 281 EC and Article 47 TFEU granting the EU a 'legal personality', i.e. 'capacity to enter into contractual and other relations with third States, and bear full responsibility for one's actions'; Leal-Arcas R, 'EU Legal Personality in Foreign Policy?' (2006) 24 *Boston University International Law Journal* 165, 167.
104 Case 22/70 *Commission v Council* (ERTA) [1971] ECR 263.
105 In ERTA, the 'common rule' was provided under Regulation No 543/69.
106 It is important to limit the external competences of the Member States to prevent the existing internal community rules from being affected by their individual actions. The more measures adopted in a certain field, the more likely it is that the Community will acquire an exclusive competence; see Opinion 2/91 Opinion delivered pursuant to the

Furthermore, the EU has the power to enter into international agreements in policy areas for which it has competence and may add to the agreement without the need for an additional legal basis.[107] This principle was later developed by the CJEU and has been referred to as the 'necessity doctrine'. The 'necessity doctrine' grants the EU an authority to enter into international agreements if it is necessary for attaining objectives of the EU,[108] but only when the 'attainment of the objectives' of the Treaty is inextricably linked to the externality.[109]

Another important doctrine developed by the CJEU extending the external competence of the Community, is the 'effect doctrine' stating that if the international commitment falls within the area covered by the external measure, then the 'effect' is established.[110]

The operation of the two principles – 'necessity' and 'effect' – has two major consequences for energy security. Firstly, the more energy related measures come to existence the more the EU competence in this area will be. Secondly, the gradual expansion of the internal and external competence of the EU might lead to its exclusive competence in some aspects of energy security policy.[111]

While there is, a linguistic certainty pertaining to the principle of solidarity therefore an implicit and explicit duty to observe this principle is placed on Member States, political questions and the intent of the Member States have continuously hindered the realisation of solidarity in the energy relations between the EU and Russia. In other words, the provisions pertaining to the principle of solidarity have been considered as precatory.[112] 'Precatory treaty provisions are deemed judicially unenforceable not because of the parties' (or anyone's) intent, but because what the parties agreed to do is considered in our system of separated powers, a "political" task not for the courts to perform.'[113] This trend can clearly

second subparagraph of Article 228 (1) of the EEC Treaty; Convention N° 170 of the International Labour Organization concerning safety in the use of chemicals at work [1993] ECR I-1061.

107 Case C-268/94 *Portugal v Council* [1996] ECR I-06177.

108 Opinion 1/76 Draft Agreement Establishing a European Union Laying up Fund for Inland Water [1977] ECR 741.

109 Opinion 1/94 the Competence of the Community to Conclude International Agreements concerning Services and the Protection of Intellectual Property. Article 228 (6) of the EC Treaty [1994] ECR I-5267.

110 Open Skies cases of 5 November 2002: Cases C-466/98 *Commission v United Kingdom* [2002] ECR I-9427, C-467/98 *Commission v Denmark* [2002] ECR I-9519, C-468/98 *Commission v Sweden* [2002] ECR I-09575, C-469/98 *Commission v Finland* [2002] ECR I-9627, C-471/98 *Commission v Belgium* [2002] ECR I-9681, C-472/98 *Commission v Luxemburg* [2002] ECR I-9741, C-475/98 *Commission v Austria* [2002] ECR I-09797, C-476/98 *Commission v Germany* [2002] ECR I-9855.

111 Cremona M, 'External Relations and External Competence: The Emergence of an Integrated Policy' in Craig P and Búrca G (eds), *The Evolution of EU Law* (Oxford University Press 1999).

112 As opposed to 'obligatory'.

113 Vazquez M C, 'The Four Doctrines of Self-Executing Treaties' (1995) 89 *American Journal of International Law* 695, 712.

be seen in the context of external energy policy and deference afforded to Member States by the CJEU in external affairs.

However, the objectives of the EU are worded in *mandatory* terms. For example, Article 3 (3) TEU states that:

> The Union *shall* establish an internal market. It *shall* work for the sustainable development of Europe based on balanced economic growth and price stability, a highly competitive social market economy, aiming at full employment and social progress, and a high level of protection and improvement of the quality of the environment. It *shall* promote scientific and technological advance. It *shall* combat social exclusion and discrimination, and shall promote social justice and protection, equality between women and men; solidarity between generations and protection of the rights of the child. It *shall* promote economic, social and territorial cohesion, and solidarity among Member States. It *shall* respect its rich cultural and linguistic diversity and shall ensure that Europe's cultural heritage is safeguarded and enhanced.

This provision, created by the Member States, is clearly intended to establish legal effects. In relation to questions of intent, the CJEU does not concern itself with the intentions of the Member States in assessing the legal effects of the Union provisions it is called on to interpret and apply. Instead the CJEU assesses the language of a provision in light of the overall purposes of the Treaties (teleological approach). In this regard, a 'general' interpretive assumption is that all individual Union measures are intended by the Member States collectively to fit within the overall scheme of the Union legal order, which is based on the achievement of the Treaty objectives. Yet, in the context of state practice and solidarity in the energy relations with Russia, such intentions are hard to come by (explained by examples in Chapter 3).

The above analysis portrays that the EU has placed a great emphasis on strict open and competitive market principles in the field of energy trade (at least within its Single Market). Elsewhere in the world, in Russia in particular, state monopolies, or at least state-intervention seems to be the rule. As it is demonstrated below, this creates challenges and poses real risks for the EU and its Member States.

# 3 Member States' practices

Finding evidence of solidarity in external energy trade – namely between the EU Member States and a third state – is like a quest for the Holy Grail.[1] Such evidence is particularly hard to come by in the context of EU–Russia energy trade.

Historically, each EU Member State has had a different relation with Russia. The scope of this book does not allow for a detailed analysis of each Member State, yet these differences can be explained in light of historical, geo-political,[2] social, economic factors and national interests. The European Council on Foreign Relations (ECFR) study[3] found five distinct trends among EU Member States when it comes to their foreign policy towards Russia:

- 'Trojan Horses' (Cyprus and Greece) who often defend Russian interests in the EU system, and are willing to veto common EU positions;
- 'Strategic Partners' (France, Germany, Italy and Spain) who enjoy a 'special relationship' with Russia which occasionally under-mines common EU policies;
- 'Friendly Pragmatists' (Austria, Belgium, Bulgaria, Finland, Hungary, Luxembourg, Malta, Portugal, Slovakia and Slovenia) who maintain a close relationship with Russia and tend to put their business interests above political goals;
- 'Frosty Pragmatists' (Czech Republic, Denmark, Estonia, Ireland, Latvia, the Netherlands, Romania, Sweden and the United Kingdom) who also focus on business interests but are less afraid than others to speak out against Russian behaviour on human rights or other issues; and

1 Britannia, King Arthur in Legend, The Holy Grail, http://www.britannia.com/history/arthur/grail.html accessed 08 August 2017.
2 Interestingly, statistical data indicates a direct correlation between a state's geographical proximity to Russia and that state's dependence on Russian energy; Eurogas, 'Statistical Report' (*The European Union of the Natural Gas Industry*, 2012) <www.eurogas.org/uploads/media/Statistics_2011_09.12.11.pdf> accessed 25 November 2016.
3 Leonard M and Popescu N, 'A Power Audit of EU-Russia Relation' (*Policy Paper, European Council on Foreign Relations 2007*) <http://fride.org/uploads/file/A_power_audit_of_relations_eu-russia.pdf> accessed 29 November 2016.

- 'New Cold Warriors' (Lithuania and Poland) who have an overtly hostile relationship with Moscow and are willing to use the veto to block EU negotiations with Russia.[4]

It can be argued that this wide spectrum of factors has shaped the energy relations with Russia whereby Member States negotiate gas imports with Gazprom bilaterally. Consequently, some of the EU Member States have got much better deals than others and Gazprom has insisted that the gas pricing agreements should be kept confidential.

**Bulgaria** as an ex-communist bloc country under the Soviet Union found herself vulnerable during the January 2009 gas crisis and still finds herself pushed into a corner by Russia.[5] For instance, Gazprom had linked gas prices to the South Stream Pipeline participation and inserted clauses to its contracts, which required Bulgaria to finance this project,[6] exclude competition and impose penalty payments if new contracts are not expedited.[7] EU law stipulates that such agreements ought to work in line with the aims and objectives of the EU and its single market (including competition and the Third Energy Package)[8] and requires that stakeholders such as civil society groups, local residents, environmental organisations, be consulted on such large construction projects. At the time of the South Stream Pipeline agreement between Russia and Bulgaria, the EU Commission had not been informed about the environmental impact assessment of this project nor was

4  Harsem Ø and Claes D H, 'The interdependence of European–Russian energy relations' (2013) 59 *Energy Policy* 784–791, 787.
5  Judah B, Kobzova J and Popescu N, 'Dealing with a Post-Bric Russia' (*European Council on Foreign Relations*, 2011) 53 <www.ecfr.eu/page/-/ECFR44_RUSSIA_REPORT_AW.pdf> accessed 25 November 2016 and Assenova M, 'Protests against Rising Energy Prices in Bulgaria: Will Sofia Follow Warsaw and Kyiv's Lead on Shale Gas?' (2013) 10(29) *Eurasia Daily Monitor*.
6  Euractiv, 'Russian-Bulgarian energy relations near melting point' (*EU news and policy debates across languages*, 13 November 2012) <www.euractiv.com/energy/russia n-bulgarian-energy-relatio-news-515999> accessed 15 December 2016.
7  EurActiv, 'Gazprom links gas price to South Stream participation' (*EU news and policy debates across languages*, 12 August 2012) <www.euractiv.com/energy/gazprom -links-gas-price-south-st-news-514481> accessed 15 December 2016.
8  Russian President Putin branded the EU's efforts to liberalise the energy market as 'no better than terrorism'; Feifer G, 'Too special a friendship: Is Germany questioning Russia's embrace?' (*The Big Read*, 24 January 2013) <www.rferl.org/content/germa ny_and_russia_too_special_a_relationship/24262486.html> accessed 15 December 2016; also note that the Third Energy Package directive is designed to promote competition and prevent the monopolisation of energy industries in EU countries; this has a direct impact on Russia. That is because in several EU countries, and particularly the Baltic states, Russia is responsible for both the production and the transportation of natural gas. Subsequently, its interests would directly be threatened by this directive. There have already been several countries that have actively tried to enforce this directive on Russia, such as Lithuania, while other countries have started to implement the process legally, like Slovakia; EurActiv, 'Russia-EU energy politics' (*EU news and policy debates across languages*, 16 November 2011) <www.euractiv.com/energy/ russia-eu-energy-politics-analysis-508992> accessed 15 December 2016.

there any transparency in regards to the other provisions of the agreement. Subsequently, the Commission referred Bulgaria along with Romania to the CJEU (under Article 258 TFEU) for failing to fulfil their obligations under EU law.[9] Following the Commission's enforcement action, a further letter was sent to Bulgarian authorities requiring them to suspend work on the project.[10] Subsequently, it was reported that the Bulgarian Prime Minister Plamen Oresharski ordered all work on the pipeline to be stopped.[11] Eventually the project was terminated unilaterally by President Putin.[12]

**Poland,** as a country previously under the control of Soviet Union, has a history of strained relations with Russia. It is therefore not surprising that the fact that 45% of Poland's energy imports come from Russia is perceived as a threat to Poland's energy security.[13] Russia's dominance is enhanced by its large share in Polish oil and gas imports and a lack of Polish share in Russia's imports. Poland's position is complicated by the fact that the country hosts a number of energy routes from Russia to West Europe. Thus, as a consumer and a transit country, Poland is important not only for Russia but also for the region. In some instances, Poland has been able to utilise its EU member status and its logistical transit position in taking contrasting stances against Russian initiatives. For instance, Poland delayed the new EU–Russia Partnership and Cooperation Agreement by several months following its meat export dispute with Russia.[14] In addition,

9 European Commission, 'Internal energy market: Commission refers Bulgaria, Estonia and the United Kingdom to Court for failing to fully transpose EU rules' (*Press Release Database*, 24 January 2013) <http://europa.eu/rapid/press-release_IP-13-42_en.htm> accessed 15 December 2016; Regulation (EC) No 715/2009 of the European Parliament and of the Council of 13 July 2009 on conditions for access to the natural gas transmission networks and repealing Regulation (EC) No 1775/2005 [2009] OJ L211/36; and Regulation (EC) No 1775/2005 of the European Parliament and of the Council of 28 September 2005 on conditions for access to the natural gas transmission networks [2005] OJ L289/1; European Commission, 'EU gas market: Commission refers Bulgaria and Romania to court to ensure European law is properly implemented' (*Press Release Database*, 24 November 2011) <http://europa.eu/rapid/press-release_IP-11-1437_en.htm> accessed on 15 December 2016; also note that Antoine Colombani, spokesperson to Competition Commissioner Joaquín Almunia, said the Commission had opened an antitrust case against Gazprom in September 2012.
10 BBC, 'Bulgaria halts work on gas pipeline after US talks' *BBC News* (8 June 2014) <www.bbc.co.uk/news/business-27755032>accessed 15 December 2014.
11 RT, 'Bulgaria halts Russia's South Stream gas pipeline project' *RT Business* (8 June 2014) <http://rt.com/business/164588-brussels-bulgaria-halts-south-stream/> accessed 15 December 2016.
12 Vihma A and Turksen U, 'The Geoeconomics of the South Stream Pipeline Project' (2015, Fall/Winter Issue) 69(1) *Journal of International Affairs.*
13 Honorata N, 'Poland's energy security strategy' [2011] March 2011 Issue, *The IAGS Journal of Energy Security*, <www.ensec.org/index.php?option=com_content&view=article&id=279:assessing-polands-energy-security-strategy&catid=114:content0211&Itemid=374> accessed 15 December 2016.
14 Sharples J, 'Russo-Polish energy security relations: a case of threatening dependency, supply guarantee, or regional energy security dynamics?' (2012) 6(1) *Political*

Poland has lobbied hard for 'energy solidarity' and Europeanisation of energy security since the 2006 Russia-Ukraine energy crisis[15] and sought to diversify its energy supplies.[16] For instance, in 2006, Poland presented a joint position on the diversification of energy supplies to Central and East European countries, prepared together with the Czech Republic, Hungary and the Austrian EU Presidency, and also promoted a joint action plan (worked out with the Czech Republic, Slovakia, Austria, Hungary, Slovenia, Croatia and Romania) to reduce dependence on Russian natural gas. This was a clear indication that Poland wanted a joint action in energy relations with Russia.

The efforts by Poland have, to a certain extent, been hampered by the German engagement with Russia, which resulted in Germany being branded as a Russian 'Trojan horse' within the EU.[17] As an influential member of the EU, **Germany** relies heavily on Russian energy supplies and is Gazprom's largest customer and Russia's biggest trading partner in general. Germany's successful export-driven economic success depends partly on Russian energy supplies. For many years Germany and Russia enjoyed smooth energy trade relations and as a result Germany has been able to concede special deals from Russia to the point that the previous German chancellor, Gerhard Schroeder, is one of the board directors for the North European Gas Pipeline (NEGP) who complimented President Putin as a 'flawless democrat'.[18] It is argued that promise of a steady flow of cheap Russian energy has encouraged German politicians to surrender a degree of sovereignty by reducing their enthusiasm for EU unity and collective action, on international policy in general[19] and on the energy front in particular.[20] For instance, Merkel

*Perspectives* 35 <www.politicalperspectives.org.uk/wp-content/uploads/PP_6-1_Rus so-Polish-energy-security-relations-2.pdf> accessed 15 December 2016.

15 Roth M, 'Poland as a policy entrepreneur in European external energy policy: towards greater energy solidarity vis-à-vis Russia?' (2011) 16 (3) *Geopolitics* 600–625 <http:// dx.doi.org/10.1080/14650045.2011.520865> accessed 16 December 2016; Maltby T, 'The development of EU foreign policy: Enlargement and the case of external energy security policy towards Russia, 2000–2010' [2010] *Political Studies Association* <www.psa.ac.uk/journals/pdf/5/2010/1630_1484.pdf> accessed 16 December 2016.

16 *Supra* note 14, Sharples.

17 Rettman A, 'Polish FM in Wikileaks: Germany is Russia's Trojan horse' (*EU Observer*, 16 September 2011) as cited in Judah B, Kobzova J and Popescu N, 'Dealing with a Post-Bric Russia' (*European Council on Foreign Relations*, November 2011) <www. ecfr.eu/page/-/ECFR44_RUSSIA_REPORT_AW.pdf> accessed 25 November 2016.

18 *Der Spiegel*, 'SPIEGEL Interview with Ex-Chancellor Gerhard Schröder' 23 October 2006, http://www.spiegel.de/international/spiegel/spiegel-interview-with-ex-cha ncellor-gerhard-schroeder-i-m-anything-but-an-opponent-of-america-a-444069.html> accessed on 07 August 2017.

19 Note that when the Bush administration campaigned to put Ukraine and Georgia on a path to NATO membership, which provoked anger in Russia, Merkel led the opposi- tion to the plan and blocked progress. Williamson H., 'Germany blocks ex-Soviets' NATO entry', *Financial Times*, 1 April 2008, <https://www.ft.com/content/a b8eb6a6-ff44-11dc-b556-000077b07658> accessed 8 August 2017.

20 *Supra* note 8, Feifer 107.

led the effort to block proposed EU regulations that would have restricted foreign companies from buying European energy utilities.[21] These measures were aimed at slowing Gazprom's monopoly in the energy market.

Russia sees its relationship with Germany as a valuable asset for asserting greater influence in European Union affairs[22] thus provides certain privileges in return. For instance, Gazprom has signed deals containing flexible and favourable terms that have proved very profitable for its German partners, such as its main Nord Stream collaborators: energy giant E.ON and chemical giant BASF. These companies each control almost one-quarter of the Yuzhno-Russkoye gas fields that will provide most of the supplies for Nord Stream. Germany, the Netherlands and France have a 49% stake in the Nord Stream project, which is another indication that there is a cultivation of bilateral agreements rather than a unified approach among EU Member States when it comes to energy security and relations with Russia.

Gazprom negotiates bilaterally between itself and its corporate partners in the EU, which results in an asymmetric bargaining power in favour of Gazprom. Whilst Gazprom benefits from a centralised data analysis, individual European energy companies end up competing against each other with incomplete information about one another and about supply prospects. As analysed by Westphal in detail, Germany's bilateral relationship with Russia has been beneficial to Germany, yet this markedly state-centric approach to energy has somewhat undermined international/regional governance and regulation, namely the common EU approach.[23] However, more recently, with Germany's initiative, the EU Joint Political and Security Committee with Russia was established and a Polish-German joint letter called for a coordinated EU approach to Russia 'based on shared interests and objectives'.[24] These developments could be seen as the start of a convergence amongst two Member States who traditionally differed in their relations with Russia. However, it does not amount to an EU level solidarity as required by the legal instruments outlined in Chapter 2 above.

21 Feifer G, 'Too Special a Friendship: Is Germany Questioning Russia's Embrace?' *European Dialogue*, 25 July 2011, <http://www.eurodialogue.eu/too-special-friend ship-germany-questioning-russias-embrace> accessed 08 August 2017.
22 Stelzenmuller C, 'Germany's Russia Question: A new Ostpolitik for Europe' (April/ March 2009) 89 *Foreign Affairs* <www.foreignaffairs.com/articles/russia-fsu/ 2009-03-01/germanys-russia-question> accessed 16 December 2016; the Russian approach has been twofold: to build up its relationship with Germany as the pipeline and contracting hub; and to squeeze the alternative supplies from the Caspian, by trying to continue the Soviet strategy of routing its exports via Russia, whilst frustrating alternative (non-Russian) outlets via (for example) Georgia. For further analysis, see, Helm D, 'Russia, Germany and the European Energy Policy' (*Open Democracy*, 14 December 2006) <www.opendemocracy.net/globalization-institutions_governm ent/energy_policy_4186.jsp > accessed 16 December 2016.
23 Westphal K, 'Germany and the EU-Russia Energy Dialogue' in Aalto P (ed.), *The EU-Russian Energy Dialogue: Europe's Future Energy Security* (Ashgate 2008) ch. 5.
24 Sikorski R and Westerwelle G, 'A New Vision of Europe', *The New York Times*, 17 September 2012, <http://www.nytimes.com/2012/09/18/opinion/a-new-vision-of-europe.html> accessed 21 June 2017.

Haukkala states that Germany is a good example of the 'schizophrenic attitude' the EU Member States have portrayed in the field of energy trade with Russia. Germany's lead in developing common multilateral and liberal approaches to energy by pushing for the ECT in the 1990s and support for the liberalisation of energy markets at the domestic level in the 2000s are in stark contrast with its strong bilateral energy relationship with Russia which in turn has undermined common EU energy policies. It is argued that the building of the Nord Stream gas pipeline between Germany and Russia coupled with the close partnerships between German and Russian energy companies weaken the EU Commission's attempts to extend the EU energy order beyond its own borders.[25] While Germany has not been alone with these actions (Italy, France and the Netherlands have displayed similar inconsistent behaviour), as one of the strongest drivers of the EU economy and dominant member within the EU decision making mechanisms, arguably the gravity and damage of Germany's actions outweigh others.

**Italy** is the Russian Federation's third largest trade partner and purchases approximately 15% of its oil and 30% of its gas from Russia.[26] Similar to Germany, Italy has benefited from certain preferential treatment conferred by Russia: for example, South Stream AG, was a joint company comprised of Gazprom and ENI, Italy's main oil company. The South Stream project (now derailed) had rivalled the Nabucco project which was supposed to diversify the EU's energy supplies thus reducing reliance on Russian energy. It is argued that Italy was keen to endorse the South Stream project with the prospect of profits by politically connected companies.[27] However, there is also another factor behind Italy's stance; it is expected that gas production in Italy[28] (along with Germany and the United Kingdom) will decline substantially over the next two decades.[29] Therefore, there is a need to find alternative supply.

One of the other leading energy consumers in the EU, **France** has also forged strong links with Russia. The leading French electricity group, Électricité de France (EDF), has acquired a minority stake in this venture in tandem with Gazprom's advances to enable the French GDF SUEZ to participate in the Nord Stream pipeline.[30] In addition, France's Total energy company is closely linked to

25 See Haukkala H, 'Towards a Pan-European energy order? Energy as an object of contention in EU-Russia relations' (2014) 12 (4) *Oil, Gas & Energy Law*, 1–26.
26 Farnesina, Italian Ministry of Foreign Affairs, New Italian/Russian Relations (*Macro Areas*) www.esteri.it/MAE/EN/Politica_Estera/Aree_Geografiche/Europa/I_nuovi_rapporti.htm accessed 16 December 2016.
27 Smith C K, 'Russia-Europe Energy Relations – Implications for U.S. Policy, Center for Strategic & International Studies' (*CSIS*, February 2010) < https://csis-prod.s3.amazonaws.com/s3fs-public/legacy_files/files/publication/100218_Smith_Russia EuropeEnergy_Web.pdf> accessed 16 December 2016.
28 Index Mundi, Italy Natural Gas Production, <http://www.indexmundi.com/italy/na tural_gas_production.html> accessed on 14 August 2017.
29 Kjarstand J and Johnson F, 'Prospects of the European Gas Market' (2007) 35 *Energy Policy* 874.
30 Smeenk T., 'Russian Gas for Europe: Creating Access and Choice', Clingendael International Energy Programme, 2010, <http://www.rug.nl/research/portal/files/13025746/16_thesis.pdf> accessed 14 August 2017.

various Russian companies. France is the third biggest EU exporter to Russia (behind Germany and Italy) and imports 83% of its petroleum products from Russia.[31] In addition to goods and services, in 2013 the French FDI stocks in Russia reached €19 billion and net FDI flows €1.9 billion.[32] While France has been a driving force in the context of EU sanctions on Russia following the Ukraine crisis,[33] it has not been able to exploit the economic interdependence and strategic partnership with Russia for solidarity amongst the EU Member States or for influencing Russia to agree to a rule based energy trade agreement.

As a friendly pragmatist, **Hungary** seems to have lived up to its reputation. In a meeting with President Putin, Hungarian Prime Minister Orbán stated that the EU's Energy Union is a threat to Hungary.[34] This statement came after a deal was reached with Russia, giving Hungary a major price discount for gas supplies. In addition, despite the economic crisis it is facing, Russia has agreed to a 10-billion-euro loan to Hungary so as to finance 80% of the construction cost of Paks nuclear power plant, Hungary's only atomic power station, which supplies about 40% of the country's electricity.[35] Many commentators see this investment as Russia buying influence within the EU. As in the case of the Russia–Bulgaria deal, the EU Commission has started proceedings against the deal, scrutinising the contract and its impact.[36] Those opposing the deal not only hope that Hungary's 20% contribution to the project will be considered as a subsidy, thus not allowed under EU competition rules but also argue that the Paks nuclear power plant will produce expensive energy, increase Hungarian debt, and deepen dependence on Russia.[37] The case of Hungary is yet another example of the EU's determination to bring external energy trade under the auspices of the *acquis communautaire*; a Member State's reluctance to adhere to the principle of solidarity; and Russia's geo-economic strategy to gain influence via its energy assets and investment.

There is no doubt that Nord and South Stream pipeline projects have been Russia's main instruments to promote its energy and transit interests in Europe and which it tried to exploit by affording various privileges (within these projects)

31  France Diplomatie, France and Russia, Economic Relations, <http://www.diplomatie. gouv.fr/en/country-files/russia/france-and-russia/> accessed 08 August 2017.

32  *Ibid.*

33  Cadier D, 'Russia 2030: Potential Impact on French Policies', European Council on Foreign Relations, 15 July 2016, <http://www.ecfr.eu/article/commentary_russia_ 2030_potential_impact_of_french_policies> accessed on 8 August 2017.

34  Gotev G, 'Orbán says EU's Energy Union is a threat to Hungary', *EurActive*, 20 February 2015 <www.euractiv.com/sections/eu-priorities-2020/orban-says-eus-e nergy-union-threat-hungary-312290> accessed 16 December 2016.

35  Than K, 'Inside Hungary's $10.8 billion nuclear deal with Russia' (*Reuters Special Report*, 30 March 2015) <www.reuters.com/article/2015/03/30/us-russia-europ e-hungary-specialreport-idUSKBN0MQ0MP20150330> accessed 16 December 2016.

36  Thorpe N, 'Hungary challenged on nuclear choice with Russia', *BBC news* (12 June 2015) <www.bbc.co.uk/news/world-europe-33078832> accessed 16 December 2016.

37  *Ibid.*

to select EU countries. At the same time, Russia has continuously invested in EU Member States both in energy and non-energy related sectors.[38]

These brief examples of state practices above indicate that energy policies and trade agreements among EU Member States do not always diverge when it comes to Russian energy supplies. Rather, the policies formulated are subject to complex interdependence factors which result in differing rationales and drives for energy trade relations with Russia. These complex factors determine both the terms and conditions and the cost of Russian energy.

The map in Figure 3.1 demonstrates the Russian natural gas pricing strategy across the EU. The export prices and quantities were made public for the first time in 2013 pursuant to a new EU regulation,[39] which was one of the legal instruments establishing the EU's single energy market. The requirement of such transparency in gas trade was one of the key strategic and legal issues the EU wanted to formalise for years,[40] firstly, because transparency of pricing would balance the asymmetrical economic relationships between EU Member States and

38 The stock of Russia's foreign direct investment in the EU amounted to €53 billion in 2011. The inflow of Russia's foreign direct investment in the EU totaled €265 million in 2011, while the inflows of EU foreign direct investment to Russia amounted to €6253 million in the same year. EU External Action – Delegation of the EU to Russia; Delegation of the European Union to Russia, 'Investments' (*Russia and EU*, 13 July 2016) <http://eeas.europa.eu/delegations/russia/eu_russia/trade_relation/investments/index_en.htm> accessed 16 December 2016; also see BBC, 'Russia's trade ties with Europe', *BBC News* (Europe, 4 March 2014) <www.bbc.co.uk/news/world-europe-26436291> accessed 16 December 2016.

39 Regulation (EU) No 994/2010 of the European Parliament and of the council of 20 October 2010 concerning measures to safeguard security of gas supply and repealing Council Directive 2004/67/EC [2010] OJ L295/1.

40 Establishment and regulation of the single EU energy market brought into question several pre-existing Gazprom practices, including the use of its dominant position and long-term contracts (some of them binding until the 2030s), property rights for gas transmission pipelines and their exclusive operation, numerous re-nomination rights per day, buying separate entry/exit capacity at cross border points, and others. For years, Russia used its strong allies such as Germany, managed to thwart such advances and delay the legal process. Yet, with the gradual thickening of legality in EU energy trade, a common ground was reached. While most EU energy systems are nationally focused, only those systems most open to corruption and voter manipulation and/or primarily dependent on Russian gas, such as Bulgaria, Ukraine, Hungary, firmly reject integration, transparency, and cooperation with neighbouring countries. The EU energy regulation is based on market transparency and integration in order to sustain and develop energy security and competition. See Smith C K, *Russia and European Energy Security – Divide and Dominate* (The CSIS Press, 2008) 17; Labelle M, 'The day Hungary cleaved from Europe: The true cost of Russian gas' (*The Energy SCEE Commentary*, 23 February 2015) <http://energyscee.com/2015/02/23/the-day-hungary-cleaved-from-europe-the-true-cost-of-russian-gas/> accessed 16 December 2016; for the anti-trust action taken against Gazprom by the EU Commission, see European Commission, 'Antitrust: Commission sends Statement of Objections to Gazprom for alleged abuse of dominance on Central and Eastern European gas supply markets' (*Press Release Database*, 22 April 2015) <http://europa.eu/rapid/press-release_IP-15-4828_en.htm> accessed 16 December 2016.

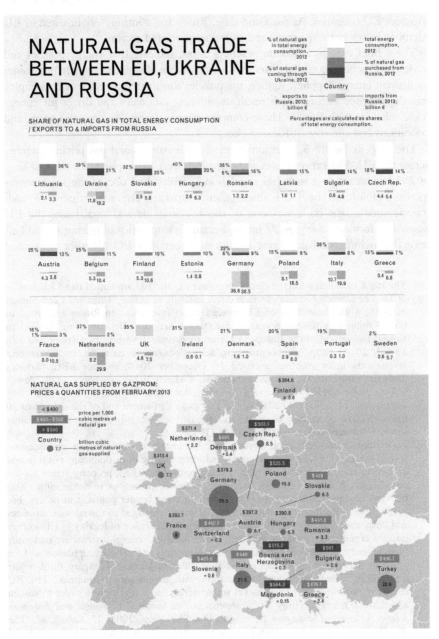

*Figure 3.1* European natural gas prices and quantities imported from Russia in 2012.[41]

41 *Turksen U and Antto V, 'The Geoeconomics of the South Stream Pipeline Project',* Columbia Journal of International Affairs, *(Special Issue on Energy Security) January, 2016. Map created by Tuomas Kortteinen.*

Russia; and secondly, it is a prerequisite for the establishment of a single energy market in which effective competitiveness can be achieved and consumer interests are protected.[42] By comparing the prices paid for 1000 cubic meters of gas by Hungary ($391) and Poland ($526), or Romania ($431) and Bulgaria ($501), it becomes clear that the differences cannot be explained by objective factors such as transportation distance or gas quantity.[43] Moreover, they are formed by competition vs. degree of dependency, and political discounts and bilateral negotiations.[44]

It is clear that it is difficult to isolate external relations of the EU Member States from affecting internal market rules of the EU. Given the various bilateral approaches undertaken towards Russia at the national, Member State level, the EU Common Energy Policy has had a limited effect in securing solidarity within the EU and a rule-based energy trade beyond the EU. Currently, there are 18 bilateral partnership agreements among 27 EU Member States[45] and around 946 bilateral agreements between the EU and non-EU states across the world.[46] A unified approach has also been hampered because the security framing of energy policy (as opposed to an economic activity) towards Russia contributed to the further legitimisation of EU member states' reluctance to cede sovereignty in the external energy policy domain. This has a direct influence on how the principle of solidarity is perceived and practised by Member States.

The EU political institutions such as the European Parliament and the Commission spoke in favour of a 'Common foreign energy policy strategy' recognising the fact that energy supply could not be dealt with only within the market sphere, but also needed a strategic, foreign policy approach, enabling the EU to maintain a unitary position in international energy relations.[47] The necessity of setting new

42  Price differentials matter greatly for the gas intensive industries in particular as they use gas as feed stock, while consuming large amounts of electricity and facing international competition; IEA, 'Energy Policies of IEA Countries: European Union, 2014 Review' (*International Energy Agency*) 6 <www.iea.org/Textbase/npsum/EU2014SUM.pdf> accessed 16 December 2016.

43  Vihma A and Turksen U, 'The Geoeconomics of the South Stream Pipeline Project' (2015 Fall/Winter Issue) 69(1) *Journal of International Affairs*.

44  Stegen S K, 'Deconstructing the "energy weapon": Russia's threat to Europe as case study' (2011) 39(10) *Energy Policy* 6505–6513. There are also differential treatments among Russia's allies. For example, in 2014, Gazprom delivered gas to Belarus at an average price of $164 per thousand cubic meters, while its European partner, Germany, paid $323.

45  Judah B, Kobzova J and Popescu N, 'Dealing with a Post-Bric Russia, European Council on Foreign Relations' (*The European Council on Foreign Relations*, 2011) 53–54 <www.ecfr.eu/page/-/ECFR44_RUSSIA_REPORT_AW.pdf> accessed 25 November 2016.

46  EU External Action, Treaties Office Database, <http://ec.europa.eu/world/agreements/searchByType.do?id=1> accessed 8 August 2017.

47  See the recent Commission Decision No 994/2012/EU of the European Parliament and of the Council of 25 October 2012 establishing an information exchange mechanism with regard to intergovernmental agreements between Member States and third countries in the field of energy [2012] OJ L 299/13.

instruments to govern energy at the EU level was also supported by dominant member states but at the same time these countries continued favouring their large national energy companies (national champions), contravening Internal Market rules and provoking intergovernmental disputes such as the Spanish-German conflict about the takeover of Endesa by E.ON that broke out at the end of 2006.[48] Member states' bilateral strategies to secure their energy supply also caused major intra-EU tensions and mutual accusations of a lack of solidarity.[49] Two particularly contentious cases in this context have been Germany's bilateral agreement with Russia to build 'Nord Stream' under the Baltic Sea without intermediaries; and Hungary and Italy's deals with Gazprom to build the 'South Stream' pipeline to the detriment of the Nabucco pipeline, one of the main European projects for diversifying the sources of gas supplies to EU countries. These countries preferred intergovernmental cooperation outside the EU framework in clear defiance of solidarity.

Both the treaties (primary) and secondary legislation (regulations and directives) of the EU are international (and supranational) legal instruments thus the legal commitments emanating from them have profoundly shaped the EU project. It is clear that the EU is based on common values as it aspires to establish collective political and legal commitment amongst its Member States. Whilst the EU legal order operates pursuant to the doctrine of supremacy of EU law, the objectives contained in the Treaties and in the acts of the EU institutions cannot realistically be achieved through the immediate assertion of legal demands alone.[50] This has been the case in regard to the principle of solidarity. In the energy field, in particular, it is clear that Member States have conducted bilateral arrangements for their energy supplies from Russia. This is neither conducive to the establishment of a strong legal framework nor does it comply with the principle of solidarity. While the consolidation and harmonisation of the EU's internal energy trade have been nearly completed, within the development of EU secondary legislation and embedding of the solidarity principle therein, there is a clear signal to Member States to coordinate and co-operate in their external energy policies. Ignoring this principle and hoping that the EU will never enforce it is wishful thinking. This principle of solidarity is likely to become enforceable at EU level as the EU energy policies develop and harmonise, and once the current economic and geopolitical crises are over. Accordingly, Member States should set clear, short-, medium- and long-term strategies in complying with and developing the solidarity doctrine in their external energy relations.

48   Milner M, 'Eon Drops out of Endesa Fight', *The Guardian*, 3 April 2007, <https://www.theguardian.com/business/2007/apr/03/spain> accessed 11 August 2017.

49   Maltby T, 'European Union energy policy integration: A case of European Commission policy entrepreneurship and increasing supranationalism' (2013) 55 *Energy Policy* 435–444 <http://dx.doi.org/10.1016/j.enpol.2012.12.031> accessed 12 December 2016.

50   Moorhead T, 'European Union Law as International Law' (2012) 5(1) *European Journal of Legal Studies*, 126–143.

It is illustrated in this chapter that owing to the state centred ownership and dominance of energy trade, coupled with the security issues connected to it, energy trade is a political undertaking and that there is a political dimension to solidarity in energy trade between the EU and Russia. State practices that emerge from these political considerations moderate the creation, reach and sustainability of the principle of solidarity. At the same time, these factors also underpin the rationale as to why the principle of solidarity needs to be articulated as a specific constitutional obligation for the Member States of the EU. As demonstrated in section 2.1.3 (above), the current legal instrument of the EU (*acquis communautaire*) possesses sufficient 'transformative capacity'[51] and the potency of solidarity clearly rests on judicial interpretation by the CJEU.

51 Ross M, 'Solidarity – A New Constitutional Paradigm for the EU?' in Ross and Borgmann-Prebil, *Promoting Solidarity in the European Union*, p. 33.

# 4 The legal framework for EU–Russian energy relations

Arguably, all inter-state trade relations must be put on a legal footing so as to enhance certainty and uphold the interests of the trading partners.[1] Among the several bilateral and multilateral legal instruments that are designed to enhance the security of energy supplies from Russia to the EU, there are number of regimes potentially capable of providing a sound basis for cooperation between the EU and Russia in the energy sector. These can be listed as follows:

- The Partnership and Cooperation Agreement 1994 (PCA);
- The Energy Charter Treaty (ECT) 1994;
- Draft Convention on Energy Security;
- The political agreements within the framework of EU-Russia Energy Dialogue;[2]
- The Treaty Establishing the Energy Community; and
- The GATT regime of the World Trade Organisation.[3]

An examination of these regimes (below) explains the degree of their effectiveness and highlights the difficulties in establishing a common ground in EU–Russia relations.

---

1 For a detailed, evidenced based study, which demonstrates the relationship between the rule of law and development see, Berg LA and Desai D, 'Overview on the Rule of Law and Sustainable Development for the Global Dialogue on Rule of Law and the Post2015 Development Agenda', United Nations Development Programme, 2013, <http://www.undp.org/content/dam/undp/library/Democratic%20Governance/Access%20to%20Justice%20and%20Rule%20of%20Law/Global%20Dialogue%20Background%20Paper%20-%20Rule%20of%20Law%20and%20Sustainable%20Developme....pdf> and *The Economist*, 'Economics – the Rule of Law, Order in the Jungle', 13 March 2008, <http://www.economist.com/node/10849115> accessed 14 August 2017.
2 *Supra* Chapter 1, note 29, Maican.
3 It should be noted that Russia was not a member of the WTO thus this agreement was not binding but could potentially be utilised. Russia is now a member of WTO – 156th member. The accession was took place in 2012; European Commission, 'EU welcomes Russia's WTO accession after 18 years of negotiations' (*Press Release Database*, 22 August 2012) <http://europa.eu/rapid/press-release_IP-12-906_en.htm?locale=en> accessed 27 November 2016.

## 4.1 The Partnership and Cooperation Agreement with Russia 1994 (PCA)[4]

The PCA with Russia was the first of its kind and is considered to be an important legal document for the relationship between the EU and Russia.[5] The agreement regulates the political, economic and cultural relations between the EU and Russia and provides a bilateral legal basis for trade, which is largely concentrated in energy and minerals sectors.[6] Its primary objectives include provisions of an overall framework for political dialogue aiming at gradual integration of Russia to market economy and creation of free trade between the EU and Russia. It was envisaged that foundations of the necessary conditions for the future establishment of companies, cross-border trade in services and capital movements,[7] and ensuring the functioning of the EU internal market would be realised by this agreement.[8]

One of the most important PCA provisions related to energy security is the express prohibition of quantitative restrictions and excessive taxation on imported goods by the parties.[9] The parties are also expected to 'provide for freedom of transit through its territory of goods originating in the customs territory or destined for the customs territory of the other Party'[10] which is considered to be essential for the achievement of the objectives of the PCA.[11] A potential problem with this commitment is that it is subject to derogations under Article 19 PCA. One of these derogations could be made on the grounds of protection of 'natural resources'.[12]

---

4 Agreement on Partnership and Cooperation Establishing a Partnership between the European Communities and Their Member States, of the One Part, and the Russian Federation, of the Other Part [1997] OJ L 327/3.

5 *Supra* Introduction, note 7, Haghighi, p. 343.

6 *Supra* Chapter 2, note 102, Leal-Arcas, pp. 337–366.

7 *Supra* Chapter 1, note 16, Seliverstov. The trade rules of the PCA are based on General Agreement on Tariffs and Trade (GATT) 1948 regime, as one of the objectives of the PCA is to facilitate the Russian accession to WTO; For information on Russia's accession to the WTO/GATT, see European Commission, 'EU welcomes Russia's WTO accession after 18 years of negotiations' (*Press Release Database*, 22 August 2012) <http://europa.eu/rapid/press-release_IP-12-906_en.htm?locale=en> accessed 27 November 2016; also see *supra* Introduction, note 7, Haghighi, p. 67; Roggenkamp M and others, *Energy Law in Europe: National, EU, and International Regulation* (2nd edn, Oxford University Press 2007).

8 Romanova T, 'The Russian Perspective on the Energy Dialogue' (2008) (16)2 *Journal of Contemporary European Studies*, 220–221.

9 PCA [1997] OJ L327/3, Article 15.

10 PCA [1997] OJ L327/3, Article 12.

11 PCA [1997] OJ L327/3, Article 12(1).

12 Complaints have been made by the EU on the inappropriate use of this article by Russia as preventing the EU from importing Middle Asia's gas through Russian pipelines, but none of it was disputed under international law. The probable reason was that the EU did not want to upset its major energy supplier – Russia; See *supra* Chapter 1, note 16, Seliverstov S; for other reservations and derogation under the PCA, see PCA [1997] OJ L 327/3 <http://trade.ec.europa.eu/doclib/docs/2003/november/tradoc_114138.pdf> accessed 12 December 2016.

Article 65 PCA is explicitly dedicated to energy.[13] It refers to a number of energy related issues, stating *inter alia* that the *cooperation* should include 'improvement of the quality and security of energy supply, in an economic and environmentally sound manner'.[14] It has been suggested that this *cooperation* strikes a balance between the security of supply and assisting Russia in overcoming its shortages in the energy sector.[15]

However, it should be pointed out[16] that unlike the PCAs with other post-Soviet republics,[17] the PCA with Russia does not make a reference to the need for diversification of supplies. This confirms the fact that Russia is the key supplier of energy for the EU and has been able to dominate the PCA terms.

It is also important to note the reference made by Article 105 PCA to the Energy Charter Treaty 1994 which states that the provisions of the PCA may be substituted by the ECT provisions only upon a formal ratification of the ECT by Russia.

The PCA between the European Communities and the Russian Federation came into force on 1 December 1997 for a period of 10 years. Under Article 106 of the PCA the agreement was automatically prolonged with mutual agreement so as to avoid a legal vacuum and uncertainty.[18]

The EU and Russia agreed to reform the PCA by initiating a New EU-Russia Agreement at Khanty-mansyisk Summit in June 2008, which was envisaged to provide the contractual basis for their energy trade relationship by the end of 2010.[19] However, after 12 full negotiation rounds, apart from a 'Memorandum on an Early Warning Mechanism in the Energy Sector within the Framework of the EU-Russia Energy Dialogue',[20] no legal or normative instrument has been created.[21] The opinions on both sides differ as to what the new PCA should look

13  PCA [1997] OJ L327/3, Article 65.
14  PCA [1997] OJ L327/3, Article 65(2).
15  *Supra* Introduction, note 7, Haghighi, p. 344.
16  *Supra* Chapter 1, note 16, Seliverstov.
17  PCA [1997] OJ L327/3, Article 53 with Kazakhstan, PCA [1997] OJ L327/3, Article 54 with Kyrgyzstan, and PCA [1997] OJ L327/3, Article 61 with Ukraine.
18  Friedrich-Elbert Stiftung, 'Partnership with Russia in Europe: Economic and Regional Topics for a Strategic Partnership' (*Fifth Roundtable Discussion Potsdam*, March 2007) <http://library.fes.de/pdf-files/id/04688.pdf> accessed 12 December 2013.
19  Council of the European Union, 'Joint Statement of the EU-Russia Summit on the Launch of Negotiations for a New EU-Russia Agreement' (*11214/08 Presse192*, 27 June 2008) <www.consilium.europa.eu/ueDocs/cms_Data/docs/pressData/en/er/101524.pdf > accessed 12 December 2016.
20  Piebalgs A and Shmatko I S, 'Memorandum on an Early Warning Mechanism in the Energy Sector within the Framework of the EU–Russia Energy Dialogue' <https://ec.europa.eu/energy/sites/ener/files/documents/2009_11_16_ewm_signed_en.pdf> accessed 25 November 2016.
21  The most recent summit (32nd EU-Russia Summit) took place on 28 January 2014 in Brussels; see Council of the European Union, 'Joint EU-Russia statement on combatting terrorism' (*5816/14 (OR en) PRESSE 40*, 28 January 2014) <http://static.kremlin.ru/media/events/eng/files/41d4b9fc4bb11a050563.pdf> accessed 25 November 2016; Permanent Mission of the Russian Federation to the European

like. The Russian side would welcome a document that is 'short, without too many details',[22] whereas the EU wants a more detailed legalistic text, with precise wording on energy security issues.[23] There are however various difficulties which have hindered the negotiations on the new PCA,[24] *inter alia* Polish objection after the Russian ban on Polish meat and vegetables,[25] Russian invasion on South Ossetia's capital,[26] and difficulties with gas supplies to Ukraine.

The issue of creation of a new PCA has been a matter of both political debate and academic discourse.[27] Konoplyanik suggested that establishing a new legal EU-Russia energy framework based on the PCA's might not be the best course of action and four specific issues have been distinguished in this regard:[28]

i  *Technical* issues – at the time of the drafting of the PCA 1994, the EC/EU consisted of only 15 Member States. Now, the EU has 28 MS, which together with Russia will have to agree on the content of the new PCA; given that most of the new MS come from the ex-communist bloc, the idea of reaching an agreement that will satisfy all 28 states and Russia is highly improbable.

Union, 'EU-Russia Summits' <https://russiaeu.ru/en/russia-eu-summits> accessed 29 November 2016.

22  Castle S, 'Medvedev makes nice with the EU', *The New York Times* (Europe, 27 June 2008) <www.nytimes.com/2008/06/27/world/europe/27iht-union.4.14050408. html> accessed 29 November 2016.

23  House of Lords European Union Committee, *The EU and Russia: before and beyond the crisis in Ukraine* (HL 2014–15, 115–16); also see European Commission, 'The EU-Russia Partnership – basic facts and figures' (*Press Release Database MEMO/11/104*, 22 February 2011) <http://europa.eu/rapid/press-release_MEMO-11-104_en. htm?locale=en> accessed 29 November 2016.

24  An interesting opinion was presented by one of the Polish MEP's Janusz Onyszkiewicz, who stated that the new PCA should incorporate, amongst other provisions, the principles of the ECT and its Transit Protocol; EurActiv, 'EU-Russia welcome "new page" in relationship' (*EU news and policy debates across languages*, 30 June 2008) < www.euractiv.com/section/global-europe/news/eu-russia-welcome-new-page-in-rela tionship/ > accessed 25 November 2016; the issue of the ECT and its transit protocol is discussed below.

25  Leonard M and Popescu N, 'A Power Audit of EU-Russia Relations' (*Policy Paper, European Council on Foreign Relations*, 2 November 2007) 50 <http://fride.org/up loads/file/A_power_audit_of_relations_eu-russia.pdf> accessed 12 December 2012.

26  EU authorities decided to postpone the talks until Russian troops withdraw completely; see Euractiv, 'EU contemplates "common market" with Russia' (*EU news and policy debates across languages*, 22 October 2008) <www.euractiv.com/section/globa l-europe/news/eu-contemplates-common-market-with-russia/> accessed 29 November 2016.

27  For a broader analysis of the issues related to the development of a new PCA, see Emerson M, Tassinari F and Vahl M, 'A New Agreement between the EU and Russia: Why, what and when?' (May 2006) No 103 CEPS Policy Brief.

28  Konoplyanik A, 'A Common Russia-EU Energy Space (The new EU-Russia Partnership Agreement, acquis communautaire, the Energy Charter and the new Russian initiative)' (2009) 2 *Oil Gas and Energy Law*.

ii *Legal* issues – the PCA 1994 with Russia was negotiated on the basis of the existing *acquis communautaire*[29] which was less liberalised in the early 1990s.[30] Currently, it is evident that there is a growing 'liberalisation gap' between EU and Russian trade systems, which is likely to create difficulties in reaching a compromise.

iii *Political* issues – in the early 1990s shortly after the end of the Cold War and dissolution of COMECON[31] the political window for negotiations between the EU and Russia was much wider than today. After more than 20 years, this enthusiasm and willingness have diminished.

iv *Operational* issues – given the length of the EU-Russia negotiations on the Transit Protocol to the ECT,[32] it is likely that negotiations on a more complex document (new PCA) will be even lengthier.

According to some commentators it is more desirable 'to build a common Russia-EU energy space on the basis of the already existing common legal denominator in energy between Russia and the European Union – the multilateral Energy Charter Treaty.'[33] To some extent, this seemed to be the intention of

29 I.e. the whole body of EU laws; see European Commission, 'Glossary: Acquis communautaire' (*Agriculture and Rural Development*) <http://ec.europa.eu/agriculture/glossary/acquis-communautaire_en> accessed 28 November 2016. Also see European Commission, Communication from the Commission to the European Parliament and the Council - Codification of the Acquis communautaire (Communication) COM (2001) 645 final <http://eur-lex.europa.eu/legal-content/EN/TXT/?qid=1480360248874&uri=CELEX:52001DC0645> accessed 29 November 2016.

30 Owing to the development of the Internal Energy Market; *supra* Chapter 2, note 4, Belyi; the liberalisation of the gas market in particular was advanced through a number of directives, i.e. Council Directive 98/30/EC of the European Parliament and of the Council of 22 June 1998 concerning common rules for internal market in natural gas [1998] OJ L204/1 (First Directive); Council Directive 2003/55EC of the European Parliament and of the Council of 26 June 2003 concerning common rules for the internal market in natural gas and repealing Directive 98/30/EC [2003] OJ L176/57 (Second Directive); Third Liberalisation Package which is due to come into force in 3/3/2011, see European Commission, Questions and Answers on the third legislative package for an internal EU gas and electricity market (*Press Release Database MEMO/11/125*, 2 March 2011) <http://europa.eu/rapid/press-release_MEMO-11-125_en.htm?locale=en> accessed 26 November 2016.

31 A communistic economic union comprising former Soviet Satellite States; see, Comecon International Organization, 'Comecon' *Encyclopaedia Britannica* (Last updated: 17 April 2003) <www.britannica.com/topic/Comecon> accessed 26 November 2016.

32 Negotiations on Transit Protocol began in 2000 and ended unsuccessfully in 2009; see International Energy Charter (IEC), 'Transit Protocol' <www.energycharter.org/what-we-do/trade-and-transit/transit-protocol/> accessed 26 November 2016; also see Konoplyanik A, 'Energy Charter Plus – Russia to Take the Lead Role in Modernizing ECT?' (2009) 4 *Oil Gas & Energy Law*.

33 Shtilkind I T, 'Energy Charter Treaty: A critical Russian Perspective' (2005) 3(1) *Oil Gas & Energy Law*.

Russia as the 2009 Memorandum on an Early Warning Mechanism in the Energy Sector between the EU and Russia[34] and the Joint Statement on the Partnership for Modernisation,[35] during the EU-Russia Summit indicate. It could be argued however, that Russia does not want to extend the legal scope or give any binding character to these initiatives.[36] Russian President Medvedev seemingly supports a document that is 'short, without too many details'[37] which suggests that Russia wants to prevent the thickening of legality and independent dispute settlement in its energy agreements with the EU.

## 4.2 The Energy Charter Treaty (ECT)[38]

With the end of the Cold War two groups of countries emerged:

i   Those who are energy rich but in need of investment, i.e. Eastern countries of the Former Soviet Union[39] (e.g. Russia, Azerbaijan); and
ii  Those who are energy poor but rich in cash such as the countries of Western Europe.[40]

The nature of rights and obligations under international law regarding the transit of energy materials (e.g. natural gas) from Eastern to Western Europe was uncertain. Perhaps the only commonly accepted international principle was the principle of 'good faith'.[41]

---

34 European Commission, 'The EU and Russia reinforce the Early Warning Mechanism to improve prevention and management in case of an energy crisis' (*Press Release Database Doc IP/09/1718*, 16 November 2009) <http://europa.eu/rapid/press-release_ IP-09-1718_en.htm> accessed 10 December 2016; also see Piebalgs A and Shmatko I S, 'Memorandum on an Early Warning Mechanism in the Energy Sector within the Framework of the EU-Russia Energy Dialogue' (24 February 2016) <https://ec.europa. eu/energy/sites/ener/files/documents/2009_11_16_ewm_signed_en.pdf> accessed 7 December 2016.
35 The Council of the European Union, Joint Statement on the Partnership for Modernisation EU-Russia Summit, 31 May-1 June 2010, 1 June 2010, <https://www. google.com.tr/url?sa=t&rct=j&q=&esrc=s&source=web&cd=1&cad=rja&uact=8& ved=0ahUKEwiNzN2ezdbVAhUBbFAKHUIEAzoQFgglMAA&url=http%3A%2F% 2Feuropa.eu%2Frapid%2Fpress-release_PRES-10-154_en.pdf&usg=AFQjCNGLq win245tXgH_RyVh69dUjqdx0w> accessed on 14 August 2017.
36 *Ibid* Section 13 states that, 'this memorandum does not constitute an international agreement or other legally binding document and does not establish rights and obligations governed by international law'.
37 *Supra* Introduction, note 4, De Jong et al. p. 516.
38 International Energy Charter, 'Latest News' <www.encharter.org/> accessed 18 December 2016.
39 Uzbekistan, Kazakhstan and Ukraine.
40 Such as France, Austria, West Germany, Italy and Spain.
41 UNGA Res 2625 (XXV) (24 October 1970). But the operation of this principle alone was not sufficiently reassuring for the parties involved in the energy trade, especially where the large volumes of energy were traded; see *supra* Chapter 1, note 31, Flynn.

The need for combining Western European concerns and interests regarding the security of energy supplies with Eastern energy assets through facilitation of investment gave the impetus for the creation of the European Energy Charter in 1991. The EU's main aims were to increase the interdependence between East and West in terms of both energy and investment flows as well as to provide greater diversification of the energy sources and routes.[42]

The European Energy Charter 1991 provided the political direction for more important and legally binding agreement – Energy Charter Treaty 1994 (ECT), which entered into force in 1998. So far, the ECT has been signed by 52 European and Asian countries plus the European Communities (EC and EURATOM)[43] and ratified by 54 of them.[44]

The ECT is a binding multilateral legal instrument – the only one of its kind dealing specifically with cooperation in the energy sector that includes governments and private parties.[45] The ECT has also the largest geographical coverage in the energy field thus is argued to be the best device for improving international energy security.[46]

The basic elements of the ECT are the following:

- Investment protection (e.g. by granting investors non-discriminatory treatment[47] – national treatment and most-favoured nation treatment[48] – compensation in case of expropriation and other losses, free transfer of capital);[49]
- Trade in energy, energy products and energy related equipment, based on WTO rules;[50]
- Freedom of energy transit;[51]
- Improvement of energy efficiency;[52]

---

42  Konoplyanik A and Wälde W T, 'Energy Charter Treaty and its Role in International Energy' (2006) 4 Journal of Energy and Natural Resources Law.

43  Since 01 December 2009 – the European Union.

44  International Energy Charter(IEC), Consolidated Energy Charter Treaty (ECT), with Related Documents (17 December 1994: Last Updated 15 January 2016) <www.energycharter.org/fileadmin/DocumentsMedia/Legal/ECTC-en.pdf>; and <www.energycharter.org/process/energy-charter-treaty-1994/energy-charter-treaty/> accessed 26 November 2016.

45  For a comprehensive legal and economic analysis of the ECT, its historical roots, see Wälde W T, *The Energy Charter Treaty: An East-West Gateway for Investment and Trade* (Kluwer 1996).

46  *Supra* note 42, Konoplyanik and Wälde.

47  Particularly, see ECT [1994] Part III, Articles 10(1), 13 and 26.

48  ECT [1994] Articles 21, 22, 23.

49  ECT [1994] Article 12.

50  ECT [1994] Article 29.

51  ECT [1994] Article 7, discussed below.

52  ECT [1994] Article 19 and Protocol on Energy Efficiency and Related Environmental Aspects (PEREEA) <www.energycharter.org/what-we-do/energy-efficiency/overview/> accessed 28 November 2016.

- International dispute settlement, including investor-state arbitration and inter-state arbitration;[53] and
- Improved legal transparency.[54]

### 4.2.1 The ECT and Russia

The ECT is open to any party that follows the application procedure and is ready to take on the obligations stipulated by the Treaty.[55] The first step for a state wanting to join the ECT is to sign the European Energy Charter 1991. The applicant state then becomes an observer to the Energy Charter and can access all meetings and documents. If the applicant still wishes to join the Treaty, it will have to assess the compatibility of its domestic legislation with the provisions of the Treaty. Once the relevant reports from the applicant country are submitted and approved by the Energy Charter Conference, the Party is invited to accede to the Treaty.[56]

For the original ECT signatories, one of the options was the 'provisional application' of the Treaty under Article 45 ECT. This provision allowed the signatories to apply the ECT provisions to the extent that such application is not inconsistent with their domestic law.[57] Following its accession to the ECT in 1994,[58] Russia was applying the Treaty provisionally, i.e. as long as 'national Russian laws and regulations [did] not prohibit the provisional application of the entire Treaty or certain clauses of it'.[59]

Article 15(4) of the 1993 Russian Constitution provides that the principles and norms of international law and international treaties of the Russian Federation are an integral part of Russia's legal system.[60] Therefore through a provisional application under Article 45 ECT Russia could keep this 'domestic exception' alive and

---

53 Baltag C (Associate ed.), 'What's New with the Energy Charter Treaty?' (*Kluwer Arbitration Blog*, 13 June 2015) <http://kluwerarbitrationblog.com/2015/06/13/whats-new-with-the-energy-charter-treaty/> accessed 22 December 2016; IEC, 'List of all Investment Dispute Settlement Cases' <www.energycharter.org/what-we-do/dispute-settlement/all-investment-dispute-settlement-cases/> accessed 22 December 2016.

54 Energy Charter Secretariat, 'The Energy Charter Treaty: The Reader's Guide' <www.energycharter.org/fileadmin/DocumentsMedia/Legal/ECT_Guide_en.pdf> accessed 12 December 2016.

55 See IEC, 'The Energy Charter Treaty' <www.energycharter.org/process/energy-charter-treaty-1994/energy-charter-treaty/> accessed 26 November 2016.

56 Roche P, Abraham S and Petit S, 'Russia's withdrawal from the Energy Charter Treaty' (*Norton Rose Fulbright*, August 2009) <www.nortonrosefulbright.com/knowledge/publications/22691/russias-withdrawal-from-the-energy-charter-treaty> accessed 26 November 2016.

57 Nappert S, 'EU-Russia Relations in the Energy Field: The Continuing Role of International Law' (2009) 2 *Oil Gas & Energy Law*.

58 The ECT [1994] came into force in 1998.

59 *Supra* Chapter 2, note 4, Belyi, p. 205.

60 Butler E W, *Russian Foreign Relations and Investment Law* (Oxford University Press 2006) 49; adoption of the international law without a need for its prior translation into the domestic legislation is termed 'monist'; see *Morgan and Baker v Hinton Organics (Wessex) Ltd and CAJE* [2009] EWCA Civ 107 CA.

invoke the incompatibility of the ECT provisions with its domestic law as a defence when required.

On 20 August 2009 Russia officially informed the Depository of the Energy Charter Secretariat of its wish to terminate its provisional application, which became effective on 18 October 2009.[61] Since then Russia's status remained somewhat ambiguous as it is still one of the Contracting Parties, although it no longer applies the Treaty. Before the analysis of the reasons given by Russia for its withdrawal it is important to consider the Russian concerns that had accumulated over the years and led to its final decision.

### 4.2.2 EU vs. Russia – *Transit Dispute*

One of the crucial provisions of the ECT in the context of security of supply is the freedom of transit provision under Article 7. This provision is based on Article V of the GATT,[62] and creates an open-ended obligation to authorise and facilitate energy transit.[63] The freedom of transit operates on a non-discriminatory basis when it comes to access to the pipeline network[64] and rights to construct new transit capacities.[65] It also ensures no interruption or reduction of the flow of energy materials and products[66] and in the case of a dispute, provides a conciliator who can recommend a solution or a procedure to resolve the problems in order to secure the existing agreement.[67] As energy and related products are transported across multiple national boundaries the issue of a secure transit had become more pertinent to energy security.[68]

For that reason, in 2000 it was decided that the subject of transit had to be addressed, which later resulted in a Transit Protocol (TP), a separate legal document complementary to the ECT which is only open to countries which have already signed and ratified[69] the ECT first.[70] The TP reinforces and clarifies

---

61  This procedure was allowed under ECT [1994] Article 45(3)(a); for further explanation see, ECT, 'What is Russia's status with the Energy Charter?' www.encharter.org/ index.php?id=18> accessed 12 December 2016; Mironova I, 'Russia and the Energy Charter Treaty' (*IEC*, 7 August 2014) <www.energycharter.org/what-we-do/knowl edge-centre/occasional-papers/russia-and-the-energy-charter-treaty/> accessed 26 November 2016. According to the Vienna Convention of the Law of Treaties [1969] Article 25(2) provisional application may be terminated at any time.

62  For a discussion on the implications of the similarity between GATT [1947] Article V and ECT [1994] Article 7, see Konoplyanik A, 'Russia-EU summit: WTO, the Energy Charter Treaty and the Issue of Transit Energy', (2005) *International Energy Law and Taxation Review*, 2, 30–35..

63  *Supra* note 42, Konoplyanik A and Wälde W T.

64  ECT [1994] Article 7(1).

65  ECT [1994] Article 7(2).

66  ECT [1994] Article 7(7).

67  *Supra* Chapter 2, note 4, Belyi; *supra* Chapter 1, note 31, Flynn.

68  *Supra* note 42, Konoplyanik and Wälde.

69  Russia only signed but not ratified ECT [1994]: *supra* Chapter 1, note 16, Seliverstov.

70  Konoplyanik A, 'Russia-EU, G-8, ECT and Transit Protocol' (2006) 3 *Russian/CIS Energy & Mining Law Journal*; see also IEC, Transit Protocol <www.energycharter. org/what-we-do/trade-and-transit/transit-protocol/> accessed 25 November 2016.

various aspects of Article 7 ECT.[71] Only three outstanding issues were left to be finalised:[72]

i  the EU's proposal of Regional Economic Integration Clause (REIO clause);
ii  the Russian proposal for a so-called 'Right of First Refusal' for existing transit shippers; and
iii  the issue of methodology of transit tariffs calculations, when using the transport congestion management mechanism such as 'auctions', specifically.[73]

While it seems that both the EU and Russia are prepared to meet each other half way with respect to the last two issues, both sides have no desire to compromise on the first one. The first issue relates to the interpretation of the term 'transit' within the context of Article 7 ECT and the operation of 'exemption clause' proposed by Article 20 TP. According to Article 7 ECT, transit should be understood as the situation when the energy goods are crossing at least two borders before they reach their destination.[74] The European Union and its Members have ratified the ECT in two capacities: as individual Member States and the EU as a whole – adhering to the REIO. Article 20 TP, the so called 'REIO clause' is designed to limit the definition of 'transit' only to a carriage across the territory of the EU as a whole. It means that the 'transit' will end once the energy reaches the external border of the EU, regardless of how many individual MS's borders it crosses. Therefore, there could be no 'transit'[75] within the EU, only the 'transportation' unless the energy merely travels across the EU's territory from one non-MS to another.[76]

This problem has been one of the major obstacles to Russia's full ratification of the ECT. One of the solutions that have been suggested is the possibility of inserting a provision into the Transit Protocol requiring that once Russia signs and ratifies TP, Article 20 TP will be automatically deleted. However, prior to the ratification of the TP, Russia will need to ratify the ECT first.[77]

---

71  For example, draft TP [2003] Article 1 defines major terms used in transit of energy; TP [2003] Article 6 prohibits unlawful taking of energy by transit country or its network operator; TP [2003] Article 8 stipulates the use of available capacity and regulates situations of a denial of access by transit state; TP [2003] Article 8.4 deals with the situations where a transit agreement does not match a supply agreement; and TP [2003] Article 10 guarantees non-discrimination in Tariffs; see *supra* Chapter 2, note 4, Belyi, p. 205.
72  Konoplyanik A, 'The evolution of contractual structure of Russian gas supplies to Europe' (2006) 10 *Perspectives in Energy* 16.
73  The last issue is related to the price and is beyond the scope of this monologue.
74  Liesen R, 'Transit Under the 1994 Energy Charter Treaty' (1999) 17 *Journal of Energy and Natural Resources Law*.
75  This principle stems from the idea of common market and free movement of goods; thus, when a product/good enters the EU then that product is considered to be a good in free circulation.
76  *Supra* note 28, Konoplyanik, 'A Common Russia-EU Energy Space...'
77  *Ibid.*

One solution that has been also offered by the EU is the introduction of the 'equal treatment' in Article 20.2 TP. The party affected by the transit measure would be able to invoke the ECT transit rules from the Transit Protocol that will apply to the EU as a whole, but not to the individual Member States. Any remedies could be enforced by the Court of Justice of the European Union. Russia however is not in favour of this idea.[78]

### 4.2.3 Russian Concerns about the ECT

Russia expressed various concerns about the ECT which could be grouped into three categories: political concerns; concerns as 'negotiating tools'; and well-founded concerns.[79] Political concerns include the Russian reaction (usually negative) to outside political pressure, for example to ratify the ECT. Concerns as 'negotiating tools' include all artificial and unsubstantiated claims, which can be endlessly created and used as leverage to negotiate the substantial concerns. Only the last group of fair and well-founded *legal* concerns will be discussed here.

The first two problems in this category relate to the controversial interpretation of the *transit* provisions under Article 7(3) ECT, i.e. the correlation of the levels of transit tariffs and tariffs of domestic transport and the mechanism for recalculating interim transit tariffs as final tariffs. Russia fears that ECT will demand transit tariffs equal to domestic transit tariffs which in combination with the alleged mandatory third party access provided by the ECT, would result in an unfair advantage for the Russian competitors.[80] This however is not an accurate interpretation of Article 7.3 ECT which in dealing with cross-border energy flows, requires each contracting Party to treat its and other external energy materials and products in a non-discriminatory manner. It was agreed that this matter would be addressed in the course of negotiations on the TP.

Other problems directly relate to the contractual structure of gas supply from Russia to the EU. These include:

i   an accusation by Russia that the ECT stands against long-term contracts by supporting open and competitive energy markets;

ii   a Russian allegation that the ECT obliges the contracting Parties to introduce mandatory-third party access to the gas transportation systems; and

iii   the issue of so called 'contractual mismatch'[81] between the long-term supply contracts and short-term transit/transportation contracts.

---

78  Belyi A., Nappert S. and Pogoretskyy V., 'Modernising the Energy Charter Process? The Energy Charter Conference Road Map and the Russian Draft Convention on Energy Security' (2011) 29(3) *Journal of Energy and Natural Resources Law*.

79  *Supra* note 28, Konoplyanik.

80  It is worth noting here that Russia sells its gas domestically for a third of the price it charges the EU.

81  For instance, the situations where the duration and volume of long-term export supply contracts do not match the duration and volume of the transit agreements; see Konoplyanik A, 'Gas Transit in Eurasia: Transit Issues between Russia and the

The first issue is unsubstantiated as there is nothing in the ECT suggesting express or implied opposition to the use of the long-term contracts. On the contrary, the ECT is designed to protect the existing contractual structures of the energy markets.[82] The second issue is specifically addressed in the Preamble of the TP, which clearly states that 'the provisions of the Treaty and this Protocol do not oblige any Contracting Party to introduce mandatory third party access ...'[83] The third problem concerning the 'contractual mismatch' has also been addressed in the Transit Protocol by Article 8 which deals with the situations of a denial of access by the transit State.[84]

The biggest concern for Russia is that the operation of the ECT as a whole will enable Central Asian gas producers to use Russian pipelines, to transport cheaper gas to the EU. However, this fear is also groundless as, on the contrary, the ECT provides a number of transit-related safeguards that Russia will benefit from. For example, Article 7.1 ECT provides that 'each contracting party shall take necessary measures to facilitate the transit' and this relates only to the existing transit (not a new one) and would therefore protect Russian existing interests. Article 7.2 ECT states that ECT should encourage relevant entities to cooperate in the sphere of transit. Article 7.4 ECT stipulates that 'the Contracting Parties shall not place obstacles in the way of new capacity being established, except as may be otherwise provided in applicable legislation...' – therefore if Russia was to continue applying the Treaty provisionally, the national legislation would take precedence over the ECT provisions in case of incompatibility. If Russia ever wished to become a transit country and become a full ECT member, it would not have to permit the construction or modification of its existing transit systems or to allow new or additional transit, a move which would provide safeguards for the efficiency of Russian energy systems, including the security of supply. In addition to these legal protections it is not economically feasible for Central Asian countries to sell their gas directly to the EU (transited through Russia) because it is more profitable to sell the gas to Russia which can then re-sell it to the EU, as it is the current practice.[85] Furthermore, Russia's current monopoly over major Central Asian oil export routes[86] means that it can exercise strong economic and political leverage to demand high transit fees. However, it is worth noting that the expanding

European Union and the European Union and the Role of the Energy Charter' (2009) (27)3 *Journal of Energy and Natural Resources Law*.

82  The above is a combined analysis from *supra* note 28, Konoplyanik, 'A Common Russia-EU Energy Space', pp, 277–280 and *supra* note 42, Konoplyanik and Wälde, pp. 540–541.

83  Energy Charter Secretariat, 'Final Act of the Energy Charter Conference with Respect to the Energy Charter Protocol on Transit (draft)' (31 October 2003) <www.energy charter.org/fileadmin/DocumentsMedia/CC_251_ENG.pdf> accessed 27 November 2016.

84  The issue of 'contractual mismatch' is discussed later.

85  Konoplyanik A, 'Energy Charter and the Russian initiative – future prospects of the legal base of international cooperation' (2009) 2 *Oil Gas & Energy Law*.

86  Namely, the Atyrau-Samara and Caspian Pipeline Consortium pipelines.

project of the Aktau-Baku-Tbilisi-Ceyhan oil export route[87] will become a critical component of the East-West energy corridor and will deliberately side line Russia in the energy market.[88]

### 4.2.4 Reasons for the termination of the provisional application of the ECT by Russia

A number of reasons for the termination of the provisional application of the ECT have been given by the Russian officials. Overall assessment was that the ECT 'has not worked' and there is a need for a new document regulating the sphere of energy dealings between Russia and other countries. In addition to the 'concerns' outlined above, Russia regards the dispute resolution mechanism under the ECT as not efficient, and claims that it 'failed' on the occasion of the last Russian-Ukrainian conflict in 2009.[89] However, Russia did not use the settlement mechanism provided by Article 7(7) ECT despite the fact that this option was available.[90] It has been suggested that the real reason for Russia's refusal to use this mechanism was 'its political unwillingness to accept an "EU-sponsored Treaty"'.[91]

Another reason for Russia's withdrawal is the multimillion proceedings against it by the former Yukos company executives.[92] Russia sought to avoid liability by withdrawing from the ECT. However, Article 45(3) (b) ECT clearly states that Russia's obligations regarding the investments already made will remain in effect for twenty years after Russia's notification of the termination, a fact confirmed in

---

87  Abbasova N., 'Kazakhstan eager to join huge oil transportation systems via Azerbaijan', AzerNews, 06 October 2016, <https://www.azernews.az/oil_and_gas/103321.html> accessed on 14 August 2017.

88  The 1,768 km Aktau-Baku-Tbilisi-Ceyhan oil pipeline will run from Aktau region of West Kazakhstan through the capital of Azerbaijan – Baku – to the Georgian port of Supsa on the Black Sea and finally reach the Turkish Mediterranean port of Ceyhan and from there en route to the EU. The potential capacity of this pipeline is 1.8mb/d; see Galpin R, 'Russia loses ground in central Asian energy battle' *BBC News* (Moscow, 2 June 2010) < www.bbc.co.uk/news/10131641 > accessed 11 December 2016; Roberts J, 'Will Central Asia's Oil and Gas go East or West?' *BBC News* (Asia-Pacific, 1 June 2010) <www.bbc.co.uk/news/10185429 > accessed 12 December 2016.

89  *Supra* note 32, Konoplyanik, 'Energy Charter Plus'.

90  Belyi V A, 'A Russian Perspective on the Energy Charter Treaty' (*Real Institute Elcano, ARI 98/2009*, 16 June 2009) <www.realinstitutoelcano.org/wps/portal/web/rielcano_en/contenido?WCM_GLOBAL_CONTEXT=/elcano/Elcano_in/Zonas_in/ARI98-2009> accessed 27 November 2016.

91  Belyi V A and Nappert S, 'A New Charter: Myth or Reality?' (2009) 2 *Oil Gas & Energy Law*.

92  Rankin J., 'Russia ordered to pay $50bn in damages to Yukos shareholders', *The Guardian*, 24 July 2014, <https://www.theguardian.com/business/2014/jul/28/russia-order-pay-50bn-yukos-shareholders-khodorkovsky-court> accessed 21 June 2017; *Yukos Universal Limited v Russian Federation* Arbitration(2), Final Arbitration Award [18 July 2014] PCA Case No AA227 <www.khodorkovsky.com/resources/yukos-shareholders-vs-russia-arbitration-award/ > accessed 27 November 2016.

the case of *Hulley Enterprises Ltd (Cyprus) v Russian Federation*.[93] Even though the ruling may not be enforced in Russia,[94] applicants have secured recovery from a number of Russian state-owned business assets across Europe and North America.

## 4.3 Draft Convention on Energy Security

In 2009 Russian President Dmitry Medvedev published a document titled 'Conceptual Approach to the New Legal Framework for Energy Cooperation (Goals and Principles)'[95] which was subsequently embodied in a legal text – the 'Draft Convention on Ensuring International Energy Security'.[96] Both the *Conceptual Approach* and the *Convention Approach* have been interpreted by experts as either new material on the modernisation of the ECT or a proposition for a complete replacement of the ECT by the Russia.[97] A strong resemblance to the ECT suggests that the second scenario is more plausible. The *Draft Convention* is not only similar to the ECT in regards to its structure but also on areas of investment, trade and transit; protection of long contracts and legitimacy of dual pricing of energy and security.

However, the main focal point of the *Draft Convention* is *Russian* energy security. It aims to:

- reserve the energy transit capacity in the existing contractual relations[98] (which may hinder the EU's diversification plans);
- bring the issue of construction of new pipelines solely under national legislation and avoid multilateral arrangements;[99] and
- 'resolve' the issue of the REIO clause in a way favourable to Russia where the *Draft Convention* would apply to both – the REIO as well as to individual Member States.[100]

These attributes do not provide a mutual benefit for all and hinder potential unified EU stance towards Russia. In addition, the *Draft Convention* provides a

---

93 *Hulley Enterprises Limited (Cyprus) v The Russian Federation*, Final Arbitral Award [18 July 2014] PCA Case No AA226.
94 For detailed analysis of enforcement of arbitration awards in Russia see, Turksen U, 'Investment Disputes in the Russian Federation', (2016) Vol. 14 Issue 4, *Oil, Gas and Energy Law*.
95 Kremlin, 'Conceptual Approach to the New Legal Framework for Energy Cooperation (Goals and Principles)' (21 April 2009) <http://en.kremlin.ru/supplement/258> accessed 27 November 2016.
96 'Draft Convention on Ensuring International Energy Security' (CEIES) <http://ua-energy.org/upload/files/Convention-engl1.pdf> accessed 12 December 2016.
97 *Supra* note 78, Belyi A and others.
98 CEIES Article II.2 (e) which may have adverse effect on freedom of transit provision in ECT [1994] Article 7.
99 This diminishes the possibilities of international investment in pipelines.
100 CEIES Article V. 4.

simplified dispute settlement mechanism, a new investment regime based on WTO rules and new obligations for the Parties in relation to the Law of the Sea.[101]

The *Draft Convention* does not provide a feasible framework for securing the energy supply to the EU and contradicts the EU's interests. Therefore, it should not be adopted by the EU in its current form. In the light of the current EU diversification plans[102] and its rather uncompromising stance on the REIO treatment, it is inconceivable that the Convention could serve as a legal basis for EU-Russia energy relations. Moreover, the Russian stance on these contentious issues illustrates a dichotomy in perceiving energy security by Russia and the EU which is likely to hinder any future compromise. At its best, the *Draft Convention* may function as a Russian motion to initiate a discussion on the modernisation of the ECT.

## 4.4 The EU–Russia Energy Dialogue

With the sixth EU-Russia Summit on 30 October 2000 a formal Energy Dialogue has started, establishing the EU-Russia energy partnership between the European Commission and the Russian Ministry of Energy.[103] The energy sector has been considered by both parties as too important to be dealt with only on the basis of one small section in the PCA.[104] The objective of the dialogue is to 'enhance the energy security of the European continent by binding Russia and the EU into a closer relationship'.[105] The ultimate aims of this energy partnership are the integration of EU and Russian energy markets, reform of the Russian energy industry and the incorporation of the existing rules of the European energy market[106] in Russia.[107] The key elements of the energy dialogue revolve around issues such as investments, market access, and infrastructure and energy efficiency.[108]

In 2005 the EU-Russia Energy Dialogue created the Permanent Partnership Council that comprises of the Russian Minister Responsible for Energy, the EU Energy Commissioner and the Minister Responsible for Energy from the current

101  *Supra* note 78, Belyi A and others.
102  Euractiv, 'Europe's Southern Gas Corridor: The Great Pipeline Race' (*EU News and Policy Debates across Languages*, 11 October 2010) <www.euractiv.com/section/m ed-south/linksdossier/europe-s-southern-gas-corridor-the-great-pipeline-race/> accessed 27 November 2016.
103  *Supra* Chapter 2, note 4, Belyi, p. 216.
104  PCA [1997] OJ L327/3, Article 65; *supra* Introduction, note 7, Haghighi, p. 344.
105  Espuny F T, 'EU-Russia Energy Dialogue at the Origins of the European Foreign Energy Policy' (2009) 2 *Oil Gas & Energy Law*.
106  For example, export of the EU *acquis communautaire*; for details, see Konoplyanik A, 'A Common Russia-EU Energy Space: The New EU Russia Partnership Agreement, *Acquis Communautaire* and the Energy Charter' (2009) (27) 2 *Journal of Energy and Natural Resources Law*.
107  Putin V V and Aznar J M, 'Joint Statement on energy dialogue in Russia-European Union Summit, annex 2' (*Moscow, Presse 171*, 29 May 2002) <www.consilium.europa. eu/uedocs/cms_data/docs/pressdata/en/er/70903.pdf> accessed 28 November 2016.
108  *Supra* note 105, Espuny.

EU Presidency and the next Presidency. The regular contacts are maintained through the Coordinators of the Energy Dialogue – the EU Commissioner and Russian Energy Minister, who meet twice a year. At technical level the Dialogue is structured in Thematic Groups[109] that involve experts nominated by the MS and Russia from the European Industrial Federation and from the Commission. In addition, the Dialogue occasionally takes the form of 'round tables' where various issues are discussed.[110]

The practical results of the EU-Russia Energy Dialogue are published annually as 'Progress Reports'.[111] Except for the friendly declarations and warm assurances on both sides, there are some tangible achievements of the Dialogue that add to the security of the energy supply from Russia. One of the examples was the creation of the EU-Russia Technology Centre in November 2002 which strengthened cooperation in development of advanced energy technologies.[112] In addition, a Memorandum on Early Warning Mechanism was signed in 2007 to deal with and solve the trade problems before they turn into a conflict.[113]

There are also a number of matters that are 'in progress' such as the creation of an 'Observation System for Oil and Gas Supply'[114] which is meant to assist in 'designing and properly applying Community legislation regarding oil supplies, monitoring the application of this legislation and helping to evaluate the effectiveness of the measures in force, as well as monitoring more closely the changes with regard to the security of oil supplies in the framework of the internal market'.[115]

It should be noted that the EU has been a major advocate for Russia to join major international trade and investment regimes – the ECT,[116] Encom,[117] and

109 Energy Strategies, Forecasts and Scenarios, Market Developments and Energy Efficiency.
110 December 2002 – gas, October 2003 – energy strategies, October 2003 – electricity; It is important to note that although in this Dialogue the bulk of energy negotiations is conducted by the Commission, it is not meant to replace the negotiations of the private sector companies with the Commission's ones. The Commission's role is merely to 'prepare the ground' for the actual energy contract negotiations between EU and Russian energy companies; see *supra* Introduction, note 7, Haghighi.
111 European Commission, 'Russia' (Europa Energy) <http://ec.europa.eu/energy/en/ topics/international-cooperation/russia> accessed 29 November 2016.
112 'Technology Centre' <www.technologycentre.org> accessed 22 December 2016.
113 *Supra* note 105, Espuny; note that Section 13 of the Memorandum explicitly states that the MoU does not constitute an international agreement or other legally binding document thus does not create rights and/or obligations governed by international law. Such MoUs between the EU and Russia do not therefore create any legal certainty.
114 Proposal for Directive of the European Parliament and the Council concerning the Alignment of Measures with regard to Security of Supply for Petroleum Products, COM (2002) 488 Final, Article 12.
115 *Supra* Introduction, note 7, Haghighi, p. 347.
116 Discussed above.
117 Encom (Energy Community) was created by the Treaty Establishing Energy Community which has been signed by all EU Member States and nine non-EU countries in 2005.

the WTO.[118] The successes of any progress with respect to these two as well as the success of consultations on the new PCA 1994 are somewhat questionable. Nevertheless, the Dialogue is an important part of the EU-Russia energy relations which exist as a potential pathway to rule based energy trade between the EU and Russia.

## 4.5 Energy Community (Encom)[119]

As stated in the Treaty establishing the Energy Community (2005), Encom's mission is to extend the EU's energy *acquis* to South-East Europe on the basis of a legally binding framework on energy trade. One of the key aims is an enhancement of the security of supply in line with relevant EU legislation. The concept of the security of supply encompasses reduction of external dependence, enforcement of transport infrastructure and gas storage facilities and diversification of supply of gas and electricity. The EU Commission stated that 'Energy Community is about *investments, economic development, security of energy supply* and *social stability*, but – more than this – the Energy Community is also about *solidarity, mutual trust* and *peace*. The very existence of the Energy Community, only ten years after the end of the Balkan conflict, is a success in itself, as it stands as the first common institutional project undertaken by the non-European Union countries of South East Europe.'[120]

The Treaty provides for three measures in respect of the energy security. Firstly, pursuant to Title III, Chapter III of the Treaty each contracting party is under an obligation to issue a statement on its energy security every two years. Secondly, Article 36 provides standardised measures in the event of sudden supply disturbances. Thirdly, in accordance with Article 3(c) the contracting parties should cooperate in the event of a sudden crisis in one of the parties. In addition, the Procedural Act[121] outlines the Rules of Operation for the Mutual Assistance Obligations which were designed to set up legal control mechanisms to deal with deficient *acquis* implementation.[122]

The Energy Community is also an observer to the EU Security of Supply Group which plays the instrumental role in improving the security of supply. The main tasks of this Group – as specified in the Procedural Act – are to facilitate the

118 Selivanova Y, 'World Trade Organization and Energy Pricing: Russia's Case' (2004) (38) 4 *Journal of World Trade* 559–602; *supra* Introduction, note 7, Haghighi; *supra* note 7, Roggenkamp M and others.
119 'Energy Community' <www.energy-community.org> accessed 12 December 2016.
120 European Commission, 'Report from the Commission to the European Parliament and the Council under Article 7 of Decision 2006/500/EC' (Energy Community Treaty) COM (2011) 105 Final.
121 Procedural Act of the Ministerial Council of the Energy Community, 2015, PA/2015/04/MC-EnC, on amending Procedural Act of the Ministerial Council 2008/01/MC- EnC of 27 June 2008 on Rules of Procedure for Dispute Settlement under the Treaty.
122 European Parliament Resolution of 23 October 2013 on the European Neighbourhood Policy: towards a strengthening of the partnership, (2013/2621(RSP)).

coordination of security of supply measures and advise the Energy Community institutions on issues relating to gas and electricity security of supply *as well as to* regularly monitor the state of security of supply of network energy within the Energy Community, share experience on security of supply mechanisms and develop comprehensive risk analysis. While, the Group has no legal powers and is only responsible for co-ordination tasks, the Treaty provides a dispute settlement mechanism. The complaints might be brought before the Ministerial Council either by the Party to the Treaty, Regulatory Board or the Secretariat. The Council's Decisions are of a binding nature and if the breach is serious and persistent the Council has the power to impose one of the sanctions outlined by Article 92 of the Treaty.

While the Energy Community undoubtedly contributes to the security of the EU's energy supply and fosters solidarity, it lacks one important element – Russian Membership. Subsequently, the Encom regime cannot offer a rule based platform for EU-Russia energy trade and disputes arising therein.

## 4.6 World Trade Organisation (WTO)

One of the options for the EU-Russia Energy Framework could be through the WTO. The thickening of legality and effective dispute settlement under the WTO can be seen as the main reason for its success[123] and legitimacy of this regime[124] albeit WTO agreements do not address energy as a distinctive sector. Nevertheless, it is argued that fundamental principles[125] of the WTO are applicable to all forms of trade thus they also apply to trade in energy goods and services even though these rules were not initially created with the energy sector in mind.[126] It is also true that the WTO rules on energy are only a fraction of international legal instruments pertaining to energy yet it is the only international trade organisation that has an adjudication regime with an automatic and compulsory jurisdiction.[127]

It should be also noted that owing to the increase in the number of energy exporting countries in the WTO, the topics of energy goods and services have

---

123 Petersmann E-U, *The GATT/WTO Dispute Settlement System: International Law, International Organisations and Dispute Settlement* (Kluwer 1997) 85.

124 Currently (as of 29 July 2016) there are 164 member states in the WTO; WTO, 'Understanding the WTO, the organisation, members and observers' <www.wto.org/english/thewto_e/whatis_e/tif_e/org6_e.htm> accessed 16 December 2016.

125 Fundamental principles of the WTO can be listed as 'most favoured nation' (MFN), 'national treatment', 'liberation of trade and reduction in trade barriers', fair competition, ensuring development and equitable share of trade benefits and 'predictable trade' through transparency and rule of law; World Trade Organization, 'Understanding the WTO – Principles of the Trading System', <www.wto.org/english/thewto_e/whatis_e/tif_e/fact2_e.htm> accessed 16 December 2016.

126 Lamy P, 'Doha Round will benefit energy trade' (*20th World Energy Congress, Rome*, 16 November 2007), <www.wto.org/english/news_e/sppl_e/sppl80_e.htm> and Cottier T. *et al.*, 'Energy in WTO law and policy' (*WTO Publications*, 7 May 2010) <www.wto.org/english/res_e/publications_e/wtrl0_forum_e/wtrl0_7may10_e.pdf> accessed 16 December 2016.

127 WTO, Dispute Settlement Understanding, <https://www.wto.org/english/tratop_e/dispu_e/dsu_e.htm> accessed on 15 August 2017.

dominated the negotiations agenda in recent years. In addition, liberalisation and privatisation of the energy sector coupled with increase in the demand for energy have led to concerns about energy security, competition and consumer rights and resulted in market reform and a need for a distinct legal framework. Given the fact that energy has direct impact on development, environment and climate change, multilateral trade negotiations have inevitably included energy policy initiatives also.

While the distinction between energy goods and energy-related services did not exist in the past, it can be argued that the production of energy goods comes within the scope of the General Agreement on Tariffs and Trade (GATT), while energy-related services, including transmission and distribution, fall under the scope of the General Agreement on Trade in Services (GATS).[128] However, the diverse and fragmented nature of energy regulation worldwide as well as various forms of energy (e.g. bio fuels, electricity, gas, oil, coal, solar power) not only make it difficult to create a global regulatory framework but also establish which of the existing WTO Covered Agreements would apply to energy. For example, are subsidies provided for agricultural goods destined for biofuel production subject to Agreement on Agriculture, the Agreement on Subsidies and Countervailing Measures or the GATT? It is clear that the WTO does not systematically address energy regulation thus there is a need for an integrated policy, which would set the international standards in energy trade. Rule-based energy regulation and ensuring open and competitive energy markets are particularly important in the context of the current global economic recession and of efforts aimed at stimulating global economic recovery and development.[129] The WTO rules require operations of market mechanisms through non-discrimination (meaning national and most-favoured-nation treatment), regulatory transparency and provide access to fair, open and impartial adjudicative processes. Because of these attributes, the WTO and the interests of the energy sector converge.[130]

After nearly two decades of accession negotiations the Russian Federation became the 156th member of the WTO on 22 August 2012. This is a significant development for the international community in general and for the energy sector in particular. Whilst there may be a degree of uncertainty as to if and how energy is regulated under the WTO rules, it is indicated that 97% per cent of Russian trade will be subject to WTO rules.[131] Having said that, in terms of Russia's Schedule of Commitments, Russia was able to become a member of the WTO with virtually no 'WTO-plus' commitments in the energy sector which means that

128 WTO, 'Energy Services' (09 September 1998) Background Note by the Secretariat, S/C/W/52, para 36.
129 Richards T and Herman L, 'Relationship between International Trade and Energy, WTO – Research and Analysis' (*World Trade Report*, 2010) <www.wto.org/english/res_e/publications_e/wtr10_richards_herman_e.htm> accessed 15 August 2017.
130 *Ibid.*
131 Kerr W A, 'Taming the Bear: The WTO after the Accession of Russia' (2012) (13) 2 *The Estey Centre Journal of International Law and Trade Policy* 150.

the state owned energy exporter, Gazprom, is free from trade barriers and can apply export taxes when exporting its energy products.[132]

One of the commitments which can be found in Russia's accession agreement was that: 'Producers and distributors of natural gas in the Russian Federation would operate on the basis of normal commercial considerations, based on recovery of costs and profit.'[133] The real impact of this membership will need to be seen because the General Agreement on Tariffs and Trade (GATT) regime under WTO does not provide such a comprehensive protection as the one available under the ECT[134] nor is there anything the WTO can do if Russia continues to employ its energy for political purposes and/or makes use of the (national security) exception clauses under Article XXI GATT and/or Article XIV of the General Agreement on Trade in Services (GATS) respectively. In addition, there are other exception clauses such as Article XI:2, Articles XII, XX and XXI of the GATT 1994 which can be utilised to restrict trade in the energy sector.

One of the major issues for delaying the Russian accession had been (similar to the ECT) disagreement regarding 'dual pricing'[135] based on the EU's interpretation of Article 3 of the WTO Agreement on Subsidies and Countervailing Measures prohibiting the state from subsidising the energy trade in all forms between the nations.[136] The EU argues that the Russian practice of having extremely low tariffs on its domestic sales of energy in comparison to the external ones amounts to an unfair subsidy[137] despite the huge amount of subsidies the EU provides to its farmers under its Common Agricultural Policy.[138] Furthermore, the EU perceives these practices as unfair competition under the EU Competition Law and Policy.[139] However, the EU Commission has not pursued Gazprom (Russian state

132 Marhold A, The World Trade Organization and Energy: Fuel for Debate, (2013) Vol. 2, Issue 8, *European Society of International Law* – ESIL Reflections, p. 5, <http://www.esil-sedi.eu/sites/default/files/Marhold%20-%20ESIL%20Reflections.pdf> accessed 15 August 2017.
133 WTO, 'Working Party Seals Deal on Russia's Membership Negotiations' (*WTO News Items*, 10 November 2011) <www.wto.org/english/news_e/news11_e/acc_rus_10nov11_e.htm> accessed 16 December 2016.
134 For the analysis of the WTO regime, see *supra* Introduction, note 7, Haghighi.
135 It has been argued that the 'dual pricing' practices were the main reason why Russia was able to accede to the WTO without any specific commitments on energy trade. *Supra* note 132, Marhold, p. 5.
136 Selivanova J, *Energy Dual Pricing in WTO Law* (Cameron, 2008); also, see WTO, 'Agreement on Subsidies and Countervailing Measures (SCM Agreement)' <www.wto.org/english/docs_e/legal_e/24-scm.pdf> accessed 31 December 2016.
137 *Supra* Chapter 2, note 4, Belyi.
138 For main elements of the EU Common Agricultural Policy, see *Eur-lex*, 'Agriculture' (*Access to European Union Law*) <http://europa.eu/legislation_summaries/agriculture/general_framework/index_en.htm> accessed 16 December 2016.
139 For details, see Selivanova J and Ratliff J, 'Major Events and Policy Issues in EC Competition Law, 2009–2010: Part 1' (2011) (22)3 *International Company and Commercial Law Review*, 67–95.

owned gas company) which is a monopolist undertaking[140] and owns nearly 80 entities across Europe including in key EU Member States.[141] Russia on the other hand stated that adoption of the Transit Protocol or any other provision deriving from the GATT is not a viable option.[142] In spite of the limited action against Russian energy firms under EU law, the EU Trade Commissioner has already indicated that there could be legal action taken against Russia pursuant to the WTO Dispute Settlement Understanding[143] as Russia has been accused of putting in place protectionist measures in total disregard for obligations which it has committed to under its Schedule of WTO Commitments.[144]

Similar to other legalisation initiatives such as the ECT and Transit Protocol, Russia's behaviour under the WTO trading regime will be interesting to observe given the fact that trade disputes under the WTO Covered Agreements[145] are depoliticised and put under a rule of law via an independent adjudication mechanism. However, there is scepticism about the potential success of this regime, owing to a number of factors:

i   the use of commodities, particularly energy, as a weapon to achieve political objectives;
ii  corruption and weak democratic governance; and
iii crony capitalism and an absence of well-functioning market institutions.

Accordingly, as some commentators argue, the Russian membership of the WTO may hinder the WTO's long-term objectives[146] and it will be difficult to create 'solidarity' in the confines of the WTO trading regime. On the other hand, it is argued that Russia possesses a number of positive attributes that warrant recognition. For example, Brill argues that Russia ought to be a G20 member owing to its strong economy, adherence to the rule of law and its financial inter-connectedness or the size of its financial services sector and the volume of its

---

140 Gray C B, 'Europe should tackle Gazprom Monopoly' (2009) Nos. 1–2 *European Affairs*, 45.
141 Steurmer M, *Putin and the Rise of Russia* (Pegasus Books 2009) 134–139.
142 IEC, 'Transit Protocol, Background to the Negotiations' <www.energycharter.org/what-we-do/trade-and-transit/transit-protocol/> accessed 27 November 2016.
143 Chaffin J, 'Europe cools on Russia's WTO Accession', *Financial Times* (5 December 2012)    <www.ft.com/cms/s/0/ff524424-3eff-11e2-9214-00144feabdc0.html> accessed 16 December 2016.
144 *Ibid*. For the Schedule of Commitments, see WTO, 'Member Information: Russian Federation and the WTO' (Russian Federation) <www.wto.org/english/thewto_e/countries_e/russia_e.htm> accessed 16 December 2016.
145 The Dispute Settlement Understanding (DSU) [1995] Article 1 provides that 'The rules and procedures of this Understanding shall apply to disputes brought pursuant to the consultation and dispute settlement provisions of the agreements listed in Appendix 1 to this Understanding (referred to in this Understanding as the "covered agreements")'; WTO, 'Dispute Settlement System Training Module (Chapter 4): Legal basis for a Dispute' <www.wto.org/english/tratop_e/dispu_e/disp_settlement_cbt_e/c4s1p1_e.htm> accessed 16 December 2016.
146 *Supra* note 131, Kerr.

financial transactions.[147] This is rather a weak argument because Russia's economic deficit,[148] its reliance on oil exports, rampant corruption[149] and huge shadow economy (approximately between 30% and 43% of its GDP)[150] and the serious human rights abuses[151] and disregard for the rule of law by the state authorities are well documented.[152] A full integration to the international/multilateral trade regime does not solely depend on economic power and success, thus some fundamental improvements and reforms need to be executed by Russia so as to gain the trust of the international community.

At the same time, it can be argued that whilst the WTO membership is unlikely to provide a magic solution to energy trade problems with Russia, it is certainly a step in the right direction as the WTO provides a dispute settlement mechanism with a compulsory jurisdiction[153] and its vast membership endorses the gravity and legitimacy of its Covered Agreements.

Importantly, any future initiative in regards to energy trade within the WTO legal framework ought to recognise both composition and structural factors unique to the energy sector. Some commentators opine that because of this uniqueness the WTO ought to allow for flexible application of its rules to the

---

147 Brill A, 'A Modest Approach for Effective Multilateral Institutions' (32)2 *The SAIS Review of International Affairs* < https://muse.jhu.edu/article/493416 > accessed 12 December 2016; Brill A and Glassman K J, 'Who Should the Twenty Be? A New Membership System to Boost the Legitimacy of the G20 at a Critical Time for the Global Economy' (*National Taxpayers Union*, 14 June 2012) <https://papers.ssrn.com/sol3/papers.cfm?abstract_id=2235636> accessed 27 November 2016; For a critique of Brill, see Anand A, 'Russia in the G20: "Bearly" fitting in?' (2012) XXXII(2) *SAIS Review* (Summer/Fall 2012) 27 <https://muse.jhu.edu/article/493417/summary> accessed 27 November 2016.
148 World Bank, 'Russian Economic Report 28: Reinvigorating the Economy' (*Press Release*, 8 October 2012) <www.worldbank.org/en/news/press-release/2012/10/08/russian-economic-report-28> accessed 11 December 2016.
149 Balcer A, 'Corruption is not just endemic to the Russian system, it is the system. It is in the EU's interest to increase its engagement with Russian society' (*LSE European Politics and Policy (EUROPP) Blog*, 7 June 2012) <http://eprints.lse.ac.uk/46228/> accessed 11 December 2016.
150 *Supra* note 147, Anand, p. 29; also see Schneider F, Buehn A and Montenegro E C, 'Shadow Economies All over the World: New Estimates for 162 Countries from 1999 to 2007' (*The World Bank*, July 2010) <http://documents.worldbank.org/curated/en/311991468037132740/pdf/WPS5356.pdf> accessed 27 November 2016.
151 See the jurisprudence of the European Court of Human Rights pertaining to the European Convention on Human Rights to which the Russian Federation is a signatory; Council of Europe, European Court of Human Rights, <www.echr.coe.int/ECHR/EN/Header/Case-Law/Decisions+and+judgments/HUDOC+database/> accessed 16 December 2016.
152 European Parliament, 'Rule of law in Russia' – European Parliament Resolution of 13 June 2013 on the rule of law in Russia (2013/2667(RSP)) <http://www.europarl.europa.eu/document/activities/cont/201306/20130620ATT68114/20130620ATT68114EN.pdf> accessed on 15 August 2017.
153 WTO, Dispute Settlement Understanding [1995] Article 6(2) <www.wto.org/english/tratop_e/dispu_e/dsu_e.htm> accessed 16 December 2016.

energy sector.[154] The rationale for this special treatment stems from the fact that 'energy resources typically belong to a State and that many energy exporting countries have structured their energy sectors around state owned enterprises. State ownership and sovereignty interests differentiate energy goods from typical goods and services in international trade. This affects any consideration of an enlarged role of the WTO in this area'.[155] Whilst such an approach may be a pragmatic response to the current state of affairs it is unlikely to provide an effective mechanism for liberalisation and adjudication of energy trade.

## Conclusion

The analysis of existing legal frameworks and platforms above indicates that a comprehensive and effective legal energy framework between the EU and Russia is nearly non-existent. Although the EU-Russia negotiations on the new PCA have been underway, these initiatives are unlikely to deliver any tangible results anytime soon. Even if these negotiations would eventually come to an end, the result is unlikely to be satisfactory for two reasons. Firstly, it will be a matter of an uneasy compromise between the 28 EU Member States, specifically the compromise between the 'Old' Western bloc and 'New' Central and Eastern bloc of countries, the interests of which diverge considerably. Secondly, the new PCA will only bind the EU and Russia and will not include any other relevant states, such as Transit States (e.g. Ukraine). It means that the important transit issues are likely to remain unresolved.

The situation with the ECT is even less promising. More than a decade of negotiations on the Transit Protocol resulted in nothing more than a termination of the provisional application by Russia. This is a major drawback as the ECT is probably the best mechanism for providing stability and security for energy trade between Russia and the EU.

The only successful avenue albeit without a legal footing appears to be the EU-Russia Energy Dialogue. Its importance should not however be overstated because of its non-binding nature and therefore limited effectiveness. Nevertheless, continuing dialogue and diplomacy may prepare the grounds for discussions on introducing legally binding measures in future EU-Russia relations. While one may choose to be optimistic about the future of EU-Russia energy trade, if we were to use history as evidence, Russia is unlikely to engage in a legally binding (rule based) system of energy trade relations.

While Russia has shied away from energy trade agreement based in the rule of law, there has been an increase in the number of the EU's legal instruments pertaining to external energy supply. However, these do not add up to a functional and effective legal framework for EU-Russia relations, which can provide security of energy supplies or legal remedies in the event of a dispute. The current legal regime does not have Russia's consent, thus puts the EU at significant energy risk.

---

154 *Supra* note 129, Richards and Herman.
155 *Ibid.*

# 5 Future prospects

In the interest of energy security and predictability of energy trade, all inter-state trade relations ought to be put on a legal footing so as to enhance certainty and protection of the interests of the trading partners and other stakeholders and end users. Among the several bilateral and multilateral legal instruments that are designed to enhance the security of energy supplies from Russia to the EU, there are number of legal and/or institutional regimes (as explored above) potentially capable of providing a sound basis for cooperation between the EU and Russia in the energy sector. These include:

- The Partnership and Cooperation Agreement 1994 (PCA);
- The Energy Charter Treaty (ECT) 1994;
- Draft Convention on Energy Security;
- The political agreements within the framework of EU-Russia Energy Dialogue;[1]
- The Treaty Establishing the Energy Community; and
- The World Trade Organisation.[2]

Even with the cursory examination of these regimes it is possible to see that there are difficulties in establishing a common ground in EU-Russia relations within these international trade agreements. These difficulties stem from the fact that the majority of these regimes are not based on the rule of law as they lack a number of essential elements, *inter alia* specific and explicit commitments, an independent adjudication, effective and predictable legal redress and enforcement mechanisms.[3] While the EU has endeavoured to create a legalistic regime for its

---

1 *Supra* Chapter 1, note 29, Maican.
2 For a detailed study of WTO and Energy Charter Treaty, see Selivanova Y, *Regulation of Energy in International Trade Law* (Kluwer Law International 2011).
3 While the WTO Dispute Settlement Understanding has automatic jurisdiction with independent adjudication and a good record of ensuring compliance, the WTO agreements do not systematically address energy regulation as a distinctive sector; see Richards T and Herman L, 'Relationship between International Trade and Energy' (*WTO – Research and Analysis, World Trade Report*, 2010) <www.wto.org/english/res_e/publications_e/wtr10_richards_herman_e.htm> accessed 16 December 2016.

internal (single market) and external (international) energy trade, the Russian Federation has shied away from such legal frameworks. For example, the recent International Energy Charter 2015, which maps out common principles for international cooperation in the field of energy and promotes mutually beneficial energy cooperation among nations for the sake of energy security and sustainability, has not been signed by the Russian Federation.[4]

The current situation indicates that the EU is facing a monopolistic and quasi-statist energy supplier, which is not willing to embed the energy trade in a predictable and independent legal framework. The situation is even more complex because the rule of law is not only problematic in Russia's external energy trade relations but also in its domestic sphere, affecting both Russian and foreign investors. For example, by utilising the military, law enforcement, and security agencies (*siloviki*), the Russian bureaucratic elite achieved the *de facto* nationalisation of YUKOS (the largest oil company in Russia) while securing the imprisonment of its former owners.[5] Furthermore, the recent Panama Papers indicate that some of the Russian energy companies and banks were involved in international 'off-shore' money laundering schemes.[6] It can be argued therefore, that in addition to creating a more predictable energy policy, the future of Russia depends on whether and to what extent the elites within Russia can agree on and comply with new rules of international trade.[7] In an environment where any dissent is quashed brutally, it is not clear if and how much alternative opinions other than what the Kremlin dictates will be heard.[8] It has also been observed that thanks to huge sums of revenue generated by its energy resources, the Russian political elite 'pursue[s] energy development strategies that are politically rational, but not necessarily economically optimal'.[9] In turn, the political entities have secured the support of the general populace within Russia.

The fact that the Member States of the EU are not able to create solidarity and speak with one voice helps Russia's political and economic power in energy trade

4 International Energy Charter 2015 currently has 79 Signatories (updated 23 June 2016) <www.energycharter.org/process/international-energy-charter-2015/> accessed 10 December 2016.
5 Yakovlev A, 'In Search for a New Social Base or Why the Russian Authorities Are Changing Their Relations with Business' (21 December 2012) No 121 *Russian Analytical Digest* 10.
6 Thompson D, 'Panama Papers: Putin associates linked to "money laundering"', *BBC News*, 3 April 2016, <http://www.bbc.com/news/world-europe-35918845> accessed 7 August 2017.
7 *Ibid.*; Yakovlev opines 'Russia's highest officials recognize that in order to preserve the political regime, it is necessary to change the model of relations with business. However, the lack of correct stimuli for bureaucrats at the middle level continues to be a serious obstacle for development'.
8 BBC, 'Russia opposition politician Boris Nemtsov shot dead', *BBC News* (Europe, 28 February 2015) <www.bbc.co.uk/news/world-europe-31669061> accessed 19 December 2016.
9 Luong P J and Weinthal E, 'Prelude to the resource curse – explaining oil and gas development strategies in the Soviet successor states and beyond' (2001) 34 *Comparative Political Studies*, 367–399.

in which the EU remains the weaker party. A number of suggestions have been made to improve the security of EU-Russia energy relations. For example, Konoplyanik proposed three possible ways of creating a 'common EU-Russia' energy space.[10] The first option is the export of the EU *acquis communautaire* directly through geographic expansion of the EU or indirectly through a new bilateral EU–Russia Agreement. He opines that this is the least feasible option as Russia never expressed its willingness either to join the EU or to adopt its *acquis* in any way or through a bilateral agreement. The second option is the creation of the PCA either on principles of ECT or via a new agreement. The creation of a new PCA clearly faces a number of obstacles that may be impossible to circumvent. The third option that is advocated is Russia's accession to the ECT. Although this option would be the best way forward to improve security in EU–Russia energy relations, it has become less feasible in light of the recent Russian withdrawal of its provisional application to the ECT.

In addition, it is feasible to create a single energy market and ensure EU competition rules are enforced in the energy sector.[11] This is one of the priorities of the EU Commission.[12] Once an integrated energy sector is established, it will be easier to achieve energy security and regulate internal and external suppliers (including Gazprom) effectively. In fact, on 3 October 2013, the EU Commission instigated an anti-trust case against Gazprom, which could have led to a £9.26bn fine.[13] The EU Commission alleged that Gazprom was:

i   Hindering cross-border gas sales in the Baltic States, Bulgaria, Czech Republic, Poland, Hungary and Slovakia, by imposing territorial restrictions in supply agreements with wholesalers and industrial customers;
ii  Charging unfair prices in the Baltic States, Bulgaria and Poland, by applying territorial restrictions in relevant contracts;

10  Konoplyanik A, 'A Common Russia-EU Energy Space: The New EU Russia Partnership Agreement, *Acquis Communautaire* and the Energy Charter' (2009) 27(2) *Journal of Energy and Natural Resources Law.*
11  European Union Commission, 'Communication from the Commission to the European Parliament, the Council, the European Economic and Social Committee and the Committee of the Regions: Making the internal energy market work' COM (2012) 663 final.
12  European Union Commission, 'Single Market Act II: Twelve priority actions for new growth' (*Press Release Database IP/12/1054*, 3 October 2012) <http://europa.eu/rapid/press-release_IP-12-1054_en.htm> accessed 18 December 2016; for example, Article 36 of the Directive 2009/73/EC could be applied vigorously to control and check investment by dominant companies such as Gazprom. For a detailed analysis of the implications of the Gas Directive, see Yafimava K, 'The EU Third Package for Gas and the Gas Target Model: major contentious issues inside and outside the EU' [April 2013] NG 75 Oxford Institute for Energy Studies <www.oxfordenergy.org/wpcms/wp-content/uploads/2013/04/NG-75.pdf> accessed 18 December 2016.
13  The initial investigation was started in September 2012. If found in breach of anti-trust rules of the EU (EU's antitrust Regulation 1/2003), the EU Commission can impose a fine up to 10% of the company's worldwide turnover.

iii  Making gas supplies conditional on obtaining unrelated commitments from wholesalers concerning gas transport infrastructure, such as the South Stream project in Bulgaria and the Yamal pipeline in Poland.

Subsequently in February 2014, despite the initial resistance to cooperate with the Commission's investigation, it was reported that Gazprom would implement European Union market rules and would not 'question (implementation) of the EU's Third Energy Package'.[14] In particular, Gazprom expressed its commitment to:

i   Remove all contractual barriers to the free flow of gas in Central and Eastern European gas markets and to take active steps to enable their better integration (e.g. by removing export bans and destination clauses). Gazprom also committed to facilitate interconnection agreements between Bulgaria and Greece, and to create opportunities for more gas flows to the Baltic States and Bulgaria;

ii  Introduce competitive benchmarks, including Western European hub prices, into its price review clauses in contracts with customers in the Baltic States, Bulgaria and Poland. By giving the customers an explicit contractual right to trigger a price review when the prices they pay diverge from competitive price benchmarks, this should ensure competitive gas prices in these regions. Gazprom also committed to more frequent and efficient price reviews;

iii Not to seek any damages from its Bulgarian partners following the termination of the South Stream project.[15]

On 13 March 2017, it was announced by the EU Commission that a compromise was reached with Gazprom.[16] Willingness by Russia to comply should not come as a surprise because some of the long-term Russian gas supply contracts expired in 2015[17] and the maintenance and the cost of energy production is a major concern for Russia.[18] Gazprom has strong incentives to comply with the

14 Adomaitis N, 'Russia's Gazprom agrees to adopt EU market rules in Lithuania – PM' *Reuters Oil Report* (7 February 2014) <http://uk.reuters.com/article/2014/02/07/lithuania-gazprom-idUKL5N0LC2HU20140207> accessed 18 December 2016.

15 Tagliapietra S, 'The EU antitrust case: no big deal for Gazprom', Bruegel, 15 March 2017, <http://bruegel.org/2017/03/the-eu-antitrust-case-no-big-deal-for-gazprom/> accessed 15 August 2017.

16 European Commission, Press Release, 'Antitrust: Commission invites comments on Gazprom commitments concerning Central and Eastern European gas markets', 13 March 2017, <http://europa.eu/rapid/press-release_IP-17-555_en.htm> accessed 15 August 2017.

17 Alternative buyers of Russian energy could be China and India. However, they are unlikely to accept and pay the lucrative prices the European consumers pay.

18 Hanson P, 'The Russian Budget: Why So Much Fuss?' (21 December 2012) No 121 *Russian Analytical Digest* 1–2, demonstrating that 'When oil prices fell steeply in 2008–09, its GDP in Russia fell by 7.8% (2009 over 2008); This was the largest percentage fall among G-20 nations'. Russia's other customers are the Commonwealth of

EU rules. According to Riley, developments in the energy markets are rendering Gazprom's existing business model irrelevant and it is that business model which is being substantially challenged in the antitrust case. In addition, reputational damage and liability that would be created as a consequence of an actual anti-competition ruling against the company would be devastating for Gazprom and the Russian Federation.[19]

Despite the EU Commission flexing its muscles and enforcing EU Single Market trading rules, because of the ongoing crisis in Ukraine and Crimea and subsequent EU sanctions on Russia, it is not clear whether the compliance with the EU rules will make a significant difference to future conduct and strategic decisions of Russia.

The current Ukrainian crisis is subject to geopolitics and its implications go to the very heart of the energy sector and security within the EU and Russia. In this context, the EU has shown its solidarity and imposed sanctions against Russia, which went into force in July 2014[20] and had a devastating effect on Russia's economy.[21] The sanctions block loans for five big Russian state banks and curb EU business with oil and defence firms. They also block the export of services and deep-water technology for Russia's oil industry and three major Russian state oil firms are targeted: Rosneft, Transneft and Gazprom Neft, the oil unit of gas giant Gazprom. The access of these firms to financial markets is restricted – a serious matter for Rosneft, which last August asked the Russian government for a $42bn

Independent States (CIS), which include Armenia, Azerbaijan, Belarus, Kazakhstan, Kyrgyzstan, Moldova, Russia, Tajikistan, and Uzbekistan with Turkmenistan and Ukraine having unofficial status. These states however have been unreliable in paying what they owe and/or receive natural gas at subsidised, lower prices; Paltsev S, 'Russian Natural Gas Export Potential Up to 2050' (July 2011) MIT Center for Energy and Environmental Policy Research.

19 Riley A, 'Commission v Gazprom: Time to do a deal? The Russian energy giant has strong incentives to do a deal' (*Natural Gas World*, 3 August 2015) <www.naturalga seurope.com/european-commission-vs-gazprom-time-to-do-a-deal-24881> accessed 18 December 2016.

20 For an overview of the EU sanctions regime, see EU News Room, 'Highlights' (December 2016) <http://europa.eu/newsroom/highlights/specialcoverage/eu_sa nctions/index_en.htm> accessed 18 December 2016; for legal instruments, see Council Regulation (EU) No 1351/2014 of 18 December 2014 amending Regulation (EU) No 692/2014 concerning restrictive measures in response to the illegal annexation of Crimea and Sevastopol [2014] OJ L365/46; Council Regulation (EU) No 692/2014 of 23 June 2014 concerning restrictions on the import into the Union of goods originating in Crimea or Sevastopol, in response to the illegal annexation of Crimea and Sevastopol [2014] OJ L183/9; Council Decision 2014/386/CFSP of 23 June 2014 concerning restrictions on goods originating in Crimea or Sevastopol, in response to the illegal annexation of Crimea and Sevastopol [2014] OJ L183/70; and Council Regulation (EU) No 833/2014 of 31 July 2014 concerning restrictive measures in view of Russia's actions destabilising the situation in Ukraine [2014] OJ L229/1.

21 Picardo E, 'How US & European Union Sanctions Impact Russia' (*Investopedia*, 15 January 2015) <www.investopedia.com/articles/investing/011515/how-us-europea n-union-sanctions-impact-russia.asp> accessed 18 December 2016.

(£25.2bn) loan. Big Russian state-owned banks are also barred from getting loans with maturity longer than one month, and from getting other financial services in the EU.[22] It is clear that the sanctions were drafted carefully with key strategic priorities and weaknesses of the EU in mind. Some big economic sectors are unaffected by the sanctions: Russian gas exports, the space industry and nuclear energy. Many EU countries rely heavily on Russian deliveries of gas and nuclear technology thus it is not surprising that these sectors have been spared by the sanctions.

As a countermeasure, Russia has scrapped the plans for the South Stream Pipeline[23] and adopted a number of sanctions mainly in the form of trade restrictions on EU, US and Canadian goods. Russia has a wide-ranging embargo on food imports from the EU, banning fruit, vegetables, meat, dairy produce and other important foods. Similar measures also apply to food from the US, Canada, Australia and Norway, which have imposed sanctions similar to the EU's. Following the sanctions imposed on Russia and nearly 40% fall in petrol prices since July 2014, the Russian currency, the ruble, fell to a new low against the US dollar and the euro.[24]

After informing the EU Commission that within a few years, Gazprom would stop delivering gas to the EU via Ukraine, and would only make an amount of gas available at the Greek-Turkish border, Russia signed a Memorandum of Understanding with Turkey in 2015 for the building of a $12 billion Turkish Stream pipeline.[25] Subsequently, the parties negotiated prices and quantities,[26] which was approved by the Council of Ministers of Turkey.[27] It has been argued that this

22 For the latest guidance on the EU sanctions on Russia, see 'The EU Commission Guidance Note on the implementation of certain provisions of Regulation (EU) No 833/2014 C(2015)6477 final'; the sanctions have been extended by Council Decision (CFSP) 2015/1524 amending Council Decision 2014/145/CFSP [2015] OJ L239/157, until March 2016, along with Council Implementing Regulation (EU) 2015/1514 implementing Council Regulation 269/2014 [2015] OJ L239/30.

23 Bierman S, Arkhipov I and Mazneva E, 'Putin scraps South Stream Pipeline after EU pressure' (*Bloomberg*, 1 December 2014) <www.bloomberg.com/news/articles/2014-12-01/putin-halts-south-stream-gas-pipeline-after-pressure-from-eu> accessed 18 December 2016.

24 For an overview of the fall of ruble against the USD, see XE, 'Currency Charts: RUB to USD' <www.xe.com/currencycharts/?from=RUB&to=USD> accessed 18 December 2016; Galouchko K, 'Ruble slides most in emerging markets on sanctions, Brent' (*Bloomberg*, 13 November 2014) <www.bloomberg.com/news/2014-11-13/ruble-slides-most-in-emerging-markets-on-sanctions-brent.html> accessed 18 December 2016 and Hille K and Weaver C, 'Rouble suffers worst fall since 1998 crisis', *Financial Times* (4 December 2014) <https://www.ft.com/content/4bb50fcc-7937-11e4-9567-00144feabdc0> accessed 15 August 2017.

25 Gotev G, 'Russia says it will shift gas transit from Ukraine to Turkey' (*EurActiv*, 15 January 2015) <www.euractiv.com/section/energy/news/russia-says-it-will-shift-gas-transit-from-ukraine-to-turkey/> accessed 18 December 2016.

26 Gurbanov I, 'In Search of New Partners: Putin's Turkish Stream for Turkey' (*Energy Corridors Review*, 25 December 2014) <https://www.naturalgasworld.com/new-partners-putin-turkish-stream-turkey> accessed 15 August 2017.

27 Guzeloglu A. and Guzeloglu F. E., 'TurkStream Gas Pipeline Project is approved by the Council of Ministers of the Republic of Turkey', 25 December 2016, <http://www.lex

new development reinforces Russia's reputation as an unreliable trading partner.[28] More importantly, the cancellation and potential replacement of SSPP with pipelines across the Black Sea to Turkey ought to be seen as a significant event for the European gas industry in particular.

Market analysts have expressed doubt about the prospects of gas exports to the EU via Turkey, which would require substantial investment in new infrastructure in South-Eastern Europe by many of the same countries that are still smarting over the demise of the SSPP.[29] Turkey's own gas market is growing, but not nearly fast enough to accommodate gas imports on a scale comparable to those SSPP was intended to mobilise.[30]

Current circumstances suggest that there is no comprehensive solution to these problems. Arguably, the most appropriate solution is the exploitation of the existing avenue of EU-Russia energy relations via the EU-Russia Energy Dialogue and other international legal forums to which both parties belong.[31] Although these platforms, apart from the WTO DSU, are not capable of delivering legally binding measures, it provides a forum where political, legal and technical opinions of both sides could be confronted and addressed with the intention that perhaps, one day, a legal consensus can be reached.

The most recent developments in regards to the EU–Russian Energy relations are articulated in the 2013 Energy Dialogue Roadmap (EDR)[32] initiative following the Common Understanding on the Preparation of the Roadmap of the EU-Russia Energy Cooperation until 2050.[33] The initiative serves as a generalised Terms of Reference for the future EU-Russia Energy Dialogue. The EDR sets out an ambitious strategic target of creating a Pan-European Energy space and there is a clear emphasis on 'improvement of the legal framework governing the relations,

ology.com/library/detail.aspx?g=0200a112-b285-4838-a5c2-98d3b6e0c924&utm_
source=Lexology+Daily+Newsfeed&utm_medium=HTML+email+-+Body+-+General
+section&utm_campaign=Lexology+subscriber+daily+feed&utm_content=Lexology+Da
ily+Newsfeed+2016-12-30&utm_term> accessed on 7 August 2017.

28 Gregory R P, 'Putin's Gas Problem' (*Project Syndicate*, 26 February 2015) <www.
project-syndicate.org/commentary/russia-ukraine-gas-pipeline-by-paul-r–
gregory-2015-02#YJZP0vsfOeFMCa3v.99> accessed 18 December 2016.

29 Chow C E, 'Russian Gas Stream or Dream' (*Center for Strategic & International
Studies Commentary*, February 2015) <www.csis.org/analysis/russian-gas-stream
-or-dream> accessed 19 December 2016.

30 *Ibid.*

31 For example, Rafael Leal-Arcas suggests that the Kyoto Protocol could depoliticise the
EU-Russia energy debate and take the pressure off the gas and oil agenda and
encourage parties to concentrate on issues with global significance. Russia, the EU and
its Member States are signatories to the Kyoto Protocol, 1997; Leal-Arcas R, *International Trade and Investment Law: Multilateral, Regional and Bilateral Governance*
(Edward-Elgar 2010) 156.

32 European Union and Russia, 'Roadmap – EU Russia Energy Cooperation until 2050'
(March 2013) <https://ec.europa.eu/energy/sites/ener/files/documents/2013_
03_eu_russia_roadmap_2050_signed.pdf> accessed 27 November 2016.

33 European Commission and Russia, 'Common Understanding on the Preparation of
the Roadmap of the EU-Russia Energy Cooperation until 2050' (24 February 2011).

which should contain strong provisions on energy to lay a firm basis to permit the gradual approximation of rules, standards and markets in the field of energy which could be the basis for greater reciprocal investments and technology exchange'. The Road Map also sets out objectives for information exchange to 'reduce uncertainty to [...] a "tolerable level"'.[34] However, it is unlikely in the immediate future that the current energy EU-Russia trade environment will be set against a legalistic framework.

In the immediate future, it is likely that the EU will intensify the diversification of its energy supply whilst limiting investment by Russian companies in the single market. This could mean turning to North Africa (e.g. Algeria and Libya) and to other EEA energy exporting countries such as Norway;[35] and exploring and investing in alternative supplies (e.g. renewables) and enhancing existing extraction of fossil fuels (e.g. coal and gas); increasing its liquefied natural gas imports as an additional alternative to Russian natural gas; and using unconventional extraction methods such as hydraulic fracturing (a.k.a. fracking for shale gas).[36] The Nabucco project, which was once seen as a cornerstone for the EU's energy diversification has been replaced by a project with significantly less capacity. According to current plans, the TANAP pipeline project, beginning in 2018, will initially transport 565 bcf of Azerbaijan gas from the Shah Deniz field with further potential supply from Turkmenistan via Turkey, Georgia, Azerbaijan and the Caspian Sea.[37] It is asserted that the capacity of the Turkmenistan gas is between 100 million and 200 million cubic meters a year. This amount would be more than the entire Russian gas supply to the EU. While it is technically straightforward to establish the pipeline for this gas supply, there are significant political obstacles. Russia and Iran oppose such plans. Russia argues that the continental shelf of the Caspian Sea is not legally regulated, such a project would have implications for the preservation of the environmental integrity of the Caspian Sea, and therefore such a project cannot go ahead without the approval of all Caspian countries.[38] Russia however, does not

---

34  *Ibid.*
35  It is worth noting that Norway is *de facto* and *de jure* included in the Internal Market, as the European Economic Area agreement, signed in 1994, obliges Norway to adopt all Internal Market legislation.
36  European Commission, 'Environment: European Commission recommends minimum principles for shale gas, European Commission' (*Press Release Database IP/14/55*, 22 January 2014) <http://europa.eu/rapid/press-release_IP-14-55_en.htm> accessed 19 December 2016; the Communication and the Recommendation by the EU Commission in this regard can be found at: European Commission, 'Environment and Energy' <http://ec.europa.eu/environment/integration/energy/unconventional_en.htm> accessed 19 December 2016. For the current status of fracking in the EU see, Osterath B, 'What ever happened with Europe's fracking boom?', DW, Environment <http://www.dw.com/en/what-ever-happened-with-europes-fracking-boom/a-18589660> accessed 15 August 2017.
37  Cohen A, 'Energy Security in the Caspian Basin' in Luft G and Korin A (eds), *Energy Security Challenges in the 21st Century* (Greenwood Publishing Group 2009).
38  Roberts J, 'Turkmenistan key to EU energy needs?' *BBC News* (Asia, 20 November 2014) <www.bbc.co.uk/news/world-asia-30125544> accessed 19 December 2016.

voice such concerns when it comes to its own pipelines to be built in the Baltic and Black Seas.

While the EU has been trying to secure its energy supply, Russia has not been idle in protecting its interests. Russia is aware of its energy power and officially recognises this as a foreign policy and political tool. In its 'National Security Strategy to 2020', which was published in 2009, it is stated that 'the resource potential of Russia' is one of the factors that has 'expanded the possibilities of the Russian Federation to strengthen its influence in the world arena'.[39] In tandem with the EU's efforts to diversify its energy supply, Russia has been trying to diversify its customer base. For instance, Russia intends to increase gas exports to Asian countries such as China, South Korea, and Japan until they make up 19%-20% of the total by 2030.[40] It has been reported that Gazprom and the Chinese government have completed a multi-billion dollar, 30-year gas deal.[41] While this long-term project has been presented as a major breakthrough in Russian-Chinese energy trade and investment, the envisaged supply of 38bn cubic meters of gas (in 2018) to China is only a quarter of the volume of gas Russia exported to Europe in 2013 alone.[42] Furthermore, the gas aimed for the Chinese market will derive from Siberia thus will not compete with resources destined for Europe. Accordingly, this new initiative will not replace the revenues available under the current EU-Russian energy trade.

In addition, Russia has either attempted to prevent alternative pipeline projects for energy supply to the EU or created competing pipeline projects as well as trying to dissuade potential suppliers (especially those in Central Asia) from participating in European-supported plans.[43] The Russian government has also raised environmental concerns (e.g. potential impact of fracking) in order to hinder other alternatives to its supplies.[44]

Sovereignty and sovereign control of energy resources and trade are at the heart of the current tension among the EU Member States. When the internal market

39 Russian National Security Council (SCRF), 'The Russian Federation National Security Strategy 2009 until 2020' (*Approved decree of the President of Russian Federation of May 12 2009 No 537*) <https://www.files.ethz.ch/isn/154909/RusNatSecStra tegyto2020.pdf> accessed 21 June 2017.

40 Ministry of Energy of the Russian Federation, 'The Energy Strategy of Russia for the Period up to 2030' (Russian Government 2010) <www.energystrategy.ru/projects/ docs/ES-2030_(Eng).pdf> accessed 19 December 2016.

41 Farchy J, Hille K and Mitchell T, 'Russia – Putin courts China as west turns away: gas deal centrepiece of Russian President's Beijing visit', *Financial Times* (19 May 2014) <www.google.co.uk/amp/s/amp.ft.com/content/0344dc50-df44-11e3-86a 4-00144feabdc0> accessed 20 December 2016; also, see BBC, 'Russia signs 30-year gas deal with China', *BBC News* (21 May 2014) <www.bbc.co.uk/news/busi ness-27503017> accessed 20 December 2016.

42 Granholm N, Malminen J and Persson G (eds), *A Rude Awakening – Ramification of Russian Aggression towards Ukraine* (FOI June 2014) 75.

43 Ratner M and others, 'Europe's Energy Security: Options and Challenges to Natural Gas Supply Diversification' (*US Congressional Research Service No 7–5700*, 20 August 2013) <www.fas.org/sgp/crs/row/R42405.pdf > accessed 20 December 2016.

44 *Ibid.*

of the EU is concerned, there is an additional pressure on this sovereignty because firstly, the interests at stake do not belong to a single country but are shared by many; and secondly, Member States of the EU have created a supranational legal regime in which solidarity is a legal requirement and the exercise of unilateral action in the context of energy security is prohibited. However, until now there has been no enforcement of this principle, thus creating a grey area within the *acquis.*[45]

It is worth remembering that President Putin came into power as a war president and continued in office during various conflicts involving Russia (Chechnya, Georgia and now Ukraine) and does not want another territorial separation. The majority of the Russian population believes in nationalism, a strong Russian empire, and wants Russia as a major actor and power internationally. Putin could not and cannot ignore this and has no possibility of getting out from this game because he will immediately lose support if he does so. One opinion poll gave Putin an 82% percent approval rate at the height of the Ukrainian conflict[46] and in another poll in 2015, Putin enjoyed an approval rate of 89%.[47] While Russia is turning East (e.g. the Chinese gas pipeline project from Siberia) the current problems Putin is facing with the EU are not seen as an economic issue. We are deep in geo-politics and the prospect of democratic change in Russia does not exist anymore.

With the escalation of the EU and US sanctions in the context of the Ukraine–Russia crisis, the energy trade has been forced into the geo-politics further, thus will inevitably continue to be a contentious issue. Subsequently, any effort to instil a rule-based energy trade between the EU and Russia also counters this political arena.

45  Braun J F, 'EU Energy Policy under the Treaty of Lisbon Rules: Between a New Policy and Business as Usual' (CEPS/EPIN Working Paper 3 2011) <www.ceps.eu/system/files/book/2011/02/EPIN%20WP31%20Braun%20on%20EU%20Energy%20Policy%20under%20Lisbon.pdf> accessed 20 December 2016.
46  Levada Center 2014, <http://www.levada.ru/en/2014/11/05/levada-center-and-kiis-about-crisis-in-ukraine/> accessed 21 June 2017.
47  Sputnik News, 'Putin's Performance Hits Record 89% Approval Rating – Independent Poll', 24 June 2016, https://sputniknews.com/russia/201506241023791005/ accessed 21 June 2017.

# 6  Conclusion

Having explored the evolution of the current state of energy trade and relations between the EU and Russia it is evident that there is no comprehensive legal framework that governs the EU's external energy trade and security. Accordingly, the EU has sought to establish a 'rule-based market approach' to energy trade[1] and it is possible to conclude that the attempts by the EU to secure its energy supplies have been twofold.

Firstly, the EU has taken internal steps and reformed both its institutional framework and competences of its agents (e.g. the Commission and High Representative for Foreign Affairs and Security) in the realm of international energy trade and security. In tandem with these changes the principle of solidarity has been acknowledged in the Treaty so as to enhance the political and economic power of the EU. The latter initiative however has been hampered by different interests and at times conflicting priorities and strategies of the EU Member States. It could be argued that although the principle of solidarity features persistently in a number of legal provisions, its application has been diverse and has not been effective in regards to EU energy policy.

Secondly, the EU has endeavoured to engage with Russia at bilateral and multilateral legal platforms so as to place its energy trade with Russia on a legal footing. However, Russia continually resisted such initiatives and such stance has been perceived as 'a signal to the international community that Russia refuses to live by its international commitments and is not interested in protecting future energy investments.'[2] To a certain extent, it is possible to assert that at the end of the Cold War, Russia's and Europe's paths had failed to converge both in terms of politics and trade relations.[3]

Russia owns and the EU needs an invaluable commodity – energy – for their economic development and security. This mutual reliance however has not been

1 Kochenov D and Amtenbrink F, *The European Union's Shaping of the International Legal Order* (Cambridge 2014) 236.
2 Gaillard E, 'Russia cannot walk away from its legal obligations', *Financial Times* (18 August 2009).
3 John Sawers, speaking at an interview with the BBC, 'Sir John Sawers, ex-MI6 chief, warns of Russia "danger"' *BBC News* (UK, 28 February 2015) <www.bbc.co.uk/news/uk-31669195> accessed 20 December 2016.

reflected on the legal framework as the demand for Russian energy is great and the EU has not managed to diversify its energy sources or suppliers so far. In a similar vein, it is clear that Russia has done very little to diversify its economy. Until these aspects of the EU-Russia energy relations change, it will be challenging to create solidarity between Member States and to convince Russia to commit to legal obligations.

State practices reveal that unilateral and bilateral action and agreements also undermine the EU's overall normative and institutionalist approach to international energy relations as well as its credibility because of its underlying contradictions to the main principles of the Energy Charter Treaty. Importantly, such bilateral policies and practices pursued by the key EU member states (namely, Germany, France, Italy, etc.) put smaller economies in a predicament as they have to either continue to call for a stronger common EU energy security policy which ensures solidarity (which is hindered by the stronger Member States via the bilateral deals with Russia), or with the limited bargaining power they have, they end up negotiating bilateral deals with Russia.

This monograph illustrates that the energy order which Russia envisages fundamentally differs from the EU's vision of energy trade internally and externally. Russia has always sought bilateral energy trade agreements and instead of open competition and fluid price formation subject to market conditions, it prefers fixed long-term contracts based on 'take-or-pay' clauses and restrictive resale options.[4] Furthermore, state owned Russian companies have not been shy to exploit the asymmetrical EU energy market whereby the on-going privatisation and unbundling of energy assets offer these companies further market share and profits at the end market of energy sales. As aptly summarised by Haukkala, 'where the EU sees mutual interdependence and tries to optimise it through market principles, Russia sees varying layers of segmentation and dependence that it wants to cultivate, control and use to its own advantage'.[5] In other words, Russia uses its energy as a tool for its geo-political and geo-economic interests.[6]

The EU has sufficient legal scope to create a common energy policy both internally and externally. This makes sense both strategically and economically. However, the Member States do not seem to be ready to give up their competences to the EU Commission in the external energy policy and practice. The principle of solidarity is not only found in various constitutions of the EU Member States (e.g. Spain, Italy and France) but also expressed in primary and secondary legislation of the EU. Accordingly, it can be argued that solidarity is an important element of the EU's legal culture.[7] The doctrine of solidarity is still developing and is likely to become a permanent feature of external energy policy as the

---

4 See Haukkala H, 'Towards a Pan-European energy order? Energy as an object of contention in EU-Russia relations' (2014) 12(4) *Oil, Gas & Energy Law* 1–26.
5 *Ibid.*
6 Vihma A and Turksen U, 'The Geoeconomics of the South Stream Pipeline Project' (2015) 69(1) *Columbia Journal of International Affairs.*
7 Gessner V and Nelken D, *European Ways of Law – Towards a European Sociology of Law* (Hart 2007).

internal (EU) energy market is harmonised and regulated effectively with the enforcement of competition and anti-trust rules. At the same time, in order to realise and reinforce solidarity in practice, the EU needs to take into account the various positions of its Members. This is a priority for the EU as integrated energy infrastructure is a precondition for economic integration and growth.[8] The EU has achieved solidarity internationally and regionally on a number of fronts pertaining to economic, security and humanitarian spheres[9] (including the free movement of goods and EU citizens in the single market). However, particularly in the external energy trade context, the EU Member States have continuously preferred to pursue bilateral trade agreements ('every country for itself' strategy) and this in turn has weakened the potency and spirit of solidarity. It is clear that energy is the basis of economic growth, which can also be translated into political power. Therefore, it is essential that energy trade must be conducted within a robust, transparent platform based on the rule of law.

8 Commission, 'Single Market Act II – Together for New Growth' COM (2012) 573 final.
9 European Commission, 'European Solidarity in Action' (*Humanitarian Aid and Civil Protection*) <http://ec.europa.eu/echo/files/core_achievements/solidarity_in_action/index_en.htm> accessed 20 December 2016.

# Appendix
## (Legal Instruments in the order they appear in the book)

### Treaty on the Functioning of the European Union 2009

#### Article 2

1   When the Treaties confer on the Union exclusive competence in a specific area, only the Union may legislate and adopt legally binding acts, the Member States being able to do so themselves only if so empowered by the Union or for the implementation of Union acts.

2   When the Treaties confer on the Union a competence shared with the Member States in a specific area, the Union and the Member States may legislate and adopt legally binding acts in that area. The Member States shall exercise their competence to the extent that the Union has not exercised its competence. The Member States shall again exercise their competence to the extent that the Union has decided to cease exercising its competence.

3   The Member States shall coordinate their economic and employment policies within arrangements as determined by this Treaty, which the Union shall have competence to provide.

4   The Union shall have competence, in accordance with the provisions of the Treaty on European Union, to define and implement a common foreign and security policy, including the progressive framing of a common defence policy.

5   In certain areas and under the conditions laid down in the Treaties, the Union shall have competence to carry out actions to support, coordinate or supplement the actions of the Member States, without thereby superseding their competence in these areas.

   Legally binding acts of the Union adopted on the basis of the provisions of the Treaties relating to these areas shall not entail harmonisation of Member States' laws or regulations.

6   The scope of and arrangements for exercising the Union's competences shall be determined by the provisions of the Treaties relating to each area.

#### Article 3

1   The Union shall have exclusive competence in the following areas:

   a   customs union;

b the establishing of the competition rules necessary for the functioning of the internal market;

c monetary policy for the Member States whose currency is the euro;

d the conservation of marine biological resources under the common fisheries policy;

e common commercial policy.

2 The Union shall also have exclusive competence for the conclusion of an international agreement when its conclusion is provided for in a legislative act of the Union or is necessary to enable the Union to exercise its internal competence, or in so far as its conclusion may affect common rules or alter their scope.

## Article 4

1 The Union shall share competence with the Member States where the Treaties confer on it a competence which does not relate to the areas referred to in Articles 3 and 6.

2 Shared competence between the Union and the Member States applies in the following principal areas:

a internal market;

b social policy, for the aspects defined in this Treaty;

c economic, social and territorial cohesion;

d agriculture and fisheries, excluding the conservation of marine biological resources;

e environment;

f consumer protection;

g transport;

h trans-European networks;

i energy;

j area of freedom, security and justice;

k common safety concerns in public health matters, for the aspects defined in this Treaty.

3 In the areas of research, technological development and space, the Union shall have competence to carry out activities, in particular to define and implement programmes; however, the exercise of that competence shall not result in Member States being prevented from exercising theirs.

4 In the areas of development cooperation and humanitarian aid, the Union shall have competence to carry out activities and conduct a common policy; however, the exercise of that competence shall not result in Member States being prevented from exercising theirs.

## Article 6

The Union shall have competence to carry out actions to support, coordinate or supplement the actions of the Member States. The areas of such action shall, at European level, be:

a   protection and improvement of human health;
b   industry;
c   culture;
d   tourism;
e   education, vocational training, youth and sport
f   administrative cooperation.

## Article 17

1   The Union respects and does not prejudice the status under national law of churches and religious associations or communities in the Member States.
2   The Union equally respects the status under national law of philosophical and non-confessional organisations.
3   Recognising their identity and their specific contribution, the Union shall maintain an open, transparent and regular dialogue with these churches and organisations.

## Article 36

The provisions of Articles 34 and 35 shall not preclude prohibitions or restrictions on imports, exports or goods in transit justified on grounds of public morality, public policy or public security; the protection of health and life of humans, animals or plants; the protection of national treasures possessing artistic, historic or archaeological value; or the protection of industrial and commercial property. Such prohibitions or restrictions shall not, however, constitute a means of arbitrary discrimination or a disguised restriction on trade between Member States.

## Article 47

Member States shall, within the framework of a joint programme, encourage the exchange of young workers.

## Article 63

1   Within the framework of the provisions set out in this Chapter, all restrictions on the movement of capital between Member States and between Member States and third countries shall be prohibited.
2   Within the framework of the provisions set out in this Chapter, all restrictions on payments between Member States and between Member States and third countries shall be prohibited.

## Article 64

1   The provisions of Article 63 shall be without prejudice to the application to third countries of any restrictions which exist on 31 December 1993 under

national or Union law adopted in respect of the movement of capital to or from third countries involving direct investment – including in real estate – establishment, the provision of financial services or the admission of securities to capital markets. In respect of restrictions existing under national law in Bulgaria, Estonia and Hungary, the relevant date shall be 31 December 1999.

2  Whilst endeavouring to achieve the objective of free movement of capital between Member States and third countries to the greatest extent possible and without prejudice to the other Chapters of the Treaties, the European Parliament and the Council, acting in accordance with the ordinary legislative procedure, shall adopt the measures on the movement of capital to or from third countries involving direct investment – including investment in real estate – establishment, the provision of financial services or the admission of securities to capital markets.

3  Notwithstanding paragraph 2, only the Council, acting in accordance with a special legislative procedure, may unanimously, and after consulting the European Parliament, adopt measures which constitute a step backwards in Union law as regards the liberalisation of the movement of capital to or from third countries.

## Article 65

1  The provisions of Article 63 shall be without prejudice to the right of Member States:

  a  to apply the relevant provisions of their tax law which distinguish between taxpayers who are not in the same situation with regard to their place of residence or with regard to the place where their capital is invested;

  b  to take all requisite measures to prevent infringements of national law and regulations, in particular in the field of taxation and the prudential supervision of financial institutions, or to lay down procedures for the declaration of capital movements for purposes of administrative or statistical information, or to take measures which are justified on grounds of public policy or public security.

2  The provisions of this Chapter shall be without prejudice to the applicability of restrictions on the right of establishment which are compatible with the Treaties.

3  The measures and procedures referred to in paragraphs 1 and 2 shall not constitute a means of arbitrary discrimination or a disguised restriction on the free movement of capital and payments as defined in Article 63.

4  In the absence of measures pursuant to Article 64(3), the Commission or, in the absence of a Commission decision within three months from the request of the Member State concerned, the Council, may adopt a decision stating that restrictive tax measures adopted by a Member State concerning one or more third countries are to be considered compatible with the Treaties in so far as they are justified by one of the objectives of the Union and compatible

with the proper functioning of the internal market. The Council shall act unanimously on application by a Member State.

### *Article 66*

Where, in exceptional circumstances, movements of capital to or from third countries cause, or threaten to cause, serious difficulties for the operation of economic and monetary union, the Council, on a proposal from the Commission and after consulting the European Central Bank, may take safeguard measures with regard to third countries for a period not exceeding six months if such measures are strictly necessary.

### *Article 114*

1  Save where otherwise provided in the Treaties, the following provisions shall apply for the achievement of the objectives set out in Article 26. The European Parliament and the Council shall, acting in accordance with the ordinary legislative procedure and after consulting the Economic and Social Committee, adopt the measures for the approximation of the provisions laid down by law, regulation or administrative action in Member States which have as their object the establishment and functioning of the internal market.

2  Paragraph 1 shall not apply to fiscal provisions, to those relating to the free movement of persons nor to those relating to the rights and interests of employed persons.

3  The Commission, in its proposals envisaged in paragraph 1 concerning health, safety, environmental protection and consumer protection, will take as a base a high level of protection, taking account in particular of any new development based on scientific facts. Within their respective powers, the European Parliament and the Council will also seek to achieve this objective.

4  If, after the adoption of a harmonisation measure by the European Parliament and the Council, by the Council or by the Commission, a Member State deems it necessary to maintain national provisions on grounds of major needs referred to in Article 36, or relating to the protection of the environment or the working environment, it shall notify the Commission of these provisions as well as the grounds for maintaining them.

5  Moreover, without prejudice to paragraph 4, if, after the adoption of a harmonisation measure by the European Parliament and the Council, by the Council or by the Commission, a Member State deems it necessary to introduce national provisions based on new scientific evidence relating to the protection of the environment or the working environment on grounds of a problem specific to that Member State arising after the adoption of the harmonisation measure, it shall notify the Commission of the envisaged provisions as well as the grounds for introducing them.

6  The Commission shall, within six months of the notifications as referred to in paragraphs 4 and 5, approve or reject the national provisions involved after

having verified whether or not they are a means of arbitrary discrimination or a disguised restriction on trade between Member States and whether or not they shall constitute an obstacle to the functioning of the internal market.

In the absence of a decision by the Commission within this period the national provisions referred to in paragraphs 4 and 5 shall be deemed to have been approved.

When justified by the complexity of the matter and in the absence of danger for human health, the Commission may notify the Member State concerned that the period referred to in this paragraph may be extended for a further period of up to six months.

7 When, pursuant to paragraph 6, a Member State is authorised to maintain or introduce national provisions derogating from a harmonisation measure, the Commission shall immediately examine whether to propose an adaptation to that measure.

8 When a Member State raises a specific problem on public health in a field which has been the subject of prior harmonisation measures, it shall bring it to the attention of the Commission which shall immediately examine whether to propose appropriate measures to the Council.

9 By way of derogation from the procedure laid down in Articles 258 and 259, the Commission and any Member State may bring the matter directly before the Court of Justice of the European Union if it considers that another Member State is making improper use of the powers provided for in this Article.

10 The harmonisation measures referred to above shall, in appropriate cases, include a safeguard clause authorising the Member States to take, for one or more of the non-economic reasons referred to in Article 36, provisional measures subject to a Union control procedure.

## Article 122

1 Without prejudice to any other procedures provided for in the Treaties, the Council, on a proposal from the Commission, may decide, in a spirit of solidarity between Member States, upon the measures appropriate to the economic situation, in particular if severe difficulties arise in the supply of certain products, notably in the area of energy.

2 Where a Member State is in difficulties or is seriously threatened with severe difficulties caused by natural disasters or exceptional occurrences beyond its control, the Council, on a proposal from the Commission, may grant, under certain conditions, Union financial assistance to the Member State concerned. The President of the Council shall inform the European Parliament of the decision taken.

## Article 192

1 The European Parliament and the Council, acting in accordance with the ordinary legislative procedure and after consulting the Economic and Social

Committee and the Committee of the Regions, shall decide what action is to be taken by the Union in order to achieve the objectives referred to in Article 191.

2   By way of derogation from the decision-making procedure provided for in paragraph 1 and without prejudice to Article 114, the Council acting unanimously in accordance with a special legislative procedure and after consulting the European Parliament, the Economic and Social Committee and the Committee of the Regions, shall adopt:

a   provisions primarily of a fiscal nature;
b   measures affecting:

   – town and country planning,
   – quantitative management of water resources or affecting, directly or indirectly, the availability of those resources,
   – land use, with the exception of waste management;

c   measures significantly affecting a Member State's choice between different energy sources and the general structure of its energy supply.

   The Council, acting unanimously on a proposal from the Commission and after consulting the European Parliament, the Economic and Social Committee and the Committee of the Regions, may make the ordinary legislative procedure applicable to the matters referred to in the first subparagraph.

3   General action programmes setting out priority objectives to be attained shall be adopted by the European Parliament and the Council, acting in accordance with the ordinary legislative procedure and after consulting the Economic and Social Committee and the Committee of the Regions.

   The measures necessary for the implementation of these programmes shall be adopted under the terms of paragraph 1 or 2, as the case may be.

4   Without prejudice to certain measures adopted by the Union, the Member States shall finance and implement the environment policy.

5   Without prejudice to the principle that the polluter should pay, if a measure based on the provisions of paragraph 1 involves costs deemed disproportionate for the public authorities of a Member State, such measure shall lay down appropriate provisions in the form of:

   – temporary derogations, and/or
   – financial support from the Cohesion Fund set up pursuant to Article 177.

### Article 194

1   In the context of the establishment and functioning of the internal market and with regard for the need to preserve and improve the environment, Union policy on energy shall aim, in a spirit of solidarity between Member States, to:

a   ensure the functioning of the energy market;
b   ensure security of energy supply in the Union;

c  promote energy efficiency and energy saving and the development of new and renewable forms of energy; and

d  promote the interconnection of energy networks.

2  Parliament and the Council, acting in accordance with the ordinary legislative procedure, shall establish the measures necessary to achieve the objectives in paragraph 1. Such measures shall be adopted after consultation of the Economic and Social Committee and the Committee of the Regions.

Such measures shall not affect a Member State's right to determine the conditions for exploiting its energy resources, its choice between different energy sources and the general structure of its energy supply, without prejudice to Article 192(2)(c).

3  By way of derogation from paragraph 2, the Council, acting in accordance with a special legislative procedure, shall unanimously and after consulting the European Parliament, establish the measures referred to therein when they are primarily of a fiscal nature.

### Article 207

1  The common commercial policy shall be based on uniform principles, particularly with regard to changes in tariff rates, the conclusion of tariff and trade agreements relating to trade in goods and services, and the commercial aspects of intellectual property, foreign direct investment, the achievement of uniformity in measures of liberalisation, export policy and measures to protect trade such as those to be taken in the event of dumping or subsidies. The common commercial policy shall be conducted in the context of the principles and objectives of the Union's external action.

2  The European Parliament and the Council, acting by means of regulations in accordance with the ordinary legislative procedure, shall adopt the measures defining the framework for implementing the common commercial policy.

3  Where agreements with one or more third countries or international organisations need to be negotiated and concluded, Article 218 shall apply, subject to the special provisions of this Article.

The Commission shall make recommendations to the Council, which shall authorise it to open the necessary negotiations. The Council and the Commission shall be responsible for ensuring that the agreements negotiated are compatible with internal Union policies and rules.

The Commission shall conduct these negotiations in consultation with a special committee appointed by the Council to assist the Commission in this task and within the framework of such directives as the Council may issue to it. The Commission shall report regularly to the special committee and to the European Parliament on the progress of negotiations.

4  For the negotiation and conclusion of the agreements referred to in paragraph 3, the Council shall act by a qualified majority.

For the negotiation and conclusion of agreements in the fields of trade in services and the commercial aspects of intellectual property, as well as foreign direct investment, the Council shall act unanimously where such agreements include provisions for which unanimity is required for the adoption of internal rules.

The Council shall also act unanimously for the negotiation and conclusion of agreements:

a   in the field of trade in cultural and audiovisual services, where these agreements risk prejudicing the Union's cultural and linguistic diversity;
b   in the field of trade in social, education and health services, where these agreements risk seriously disturbing the national organisation of such services and prejudicing the responsibility of Member States to deliver them.

5   The negotiation and conclusion of international agreements in the field of transport shall be subject to Title VI of Part Three and to Article 218.

6   The exercise of the competences conferred by this Article in the field of the common commercial policy shall not affect the delimitation of competences between the Union and the Member States, and shall not lead to harmonisation of legislative or regulatory provisions of the Member States in so far as the Treaties exclude such harmonisation.

### Article 222

1   The Union and its Member States shall act jointly in a spirit of solidarity if a Member State is the object of a terrorist attack or the victim of a natural or man-made disaster. The Union shall mobilise all the instruments at its disposal, including the military resources made available by the Member States, to:

a   prevent the terrorist threat in the territory of the Member States;

    –   protect democratic institutions and the civilian population from any terrorist attack;
    –   assist a Member State in its territory, at the request of its political authorities, in the event of a terrorist attack;

b   assist a Member State in its territory, at the request of its political authorities, in the event of a natural or man-made disaster.

2   Should a Member State be the object of a terrorist attack or the victim of a natural or man-made disaster, the other Member States shall assist it at the request of its political authorities. To that end, the Member States shall coordinate between themselves in the Council.

3   The arrangements for the implementation by the Union of the solidarity clause shall be defined by a decision adopted by the Council acting on a joint proposal by the Commission and the High Representative of the Union for Foreign Affairs and Security Policy. The Council shall act in accordance with

Article 31(1) of the Treaty on European Union where this decision has defence implications. The European Parliament shall be informed.

For the purposes of this paragraph and without prejudice to Article 240, the Council shall be assisted by the Political and Security Committee with the support of the structures developed in the context of the common security and defence policy and by the Committee referred to in Article 71; the two committees shall, if necessary, submit joint opinions.

4   The European Council shall regularly assess the threats facing the Union in order to enable the Union and its Member States to take effective action

## Art 258

If the Commission considers that a Member State has failed to fulfil an obligation under the Treaties, it shall deliver a reasoned opinion on the matter after giving the State concerned the opportunity to submit its observations.

If the State concerned does not comply with the opinion within the period laid down by the Commission, the latter may bring the matter before the Court of Justice of the European Union.

## Article 347

Member States shall consult each other with a view to taking together the steps needed to prevent the functioning of the internal market being affected by measures which a Member State may be called upon to take in the event of serious internal disturbances affecting the maintenance of law and order, in the event of war, serious international tension constituting a threat of war, or in order to carry out obligations it has accepted for the purpose of maintaining peace and international security.

## Article 352

1   If action by the Union should prove necessary, within the framework of the policies defined in the Treaties, to attain one of the objectives set out in the Treaties, and the Treaties have not provided the necessary powers, the Council, acting unanimously on a proposal from the Commission and after obtaining the consent of the European Parliament, shall adopt the appropriate measures. Where the measures in question are adopted by the Council in accordance with a special legislative procedure, it shall also act unanimously on a proposal from the Commission and after obtaining the consent of the European Parliament.

2   Using the procedure for monitoring the subsidiarity principle referred to in Article 5(3) of the Treaty on European Union, the Commission shall draw national Parliaments' attention to proposals based on this Article.

3   Measures based on this Article shall not entail harmonisation of Member States' laws or regulations in cases where the Treaties exclude such harmonisation.

4   This Article cannot serve as a basis for attaining objectives pertaining to the common foreign and security policy and any acts adopted pursuant to this Article shall respect the limits set out in Article 40, second paragraph, of the Treaty on European Union.

## Consolidated Version of the Treaty on European Union 2009

### Article 2

The Union is founded on the values of respect for human dignity, freedom, democracy, equality, the rule of law and respect for human rights, including the rights of persons belonging to minorities.

These values are common to the Member States in a society in which pluralism, non-discrimination, tolerance, justice, solidarity and equality between women and men prevail.

### Article 3

1   The Union's aim is to promote peace, its values and the well-being of its peoples.
2   The Union shall offer its citizens an area of freedom, security and justice without internal frontiers, in which the free movement of persons is ensured in conjunction with appropriate measures with respect to external border controls, asylum, immigration and the prevention and combating of crime.
3   The Union shall establish an internal market. It shall work for the sustainable development of Europe based on balanced economic growth and price stability, a highly competitive social market economy, aiming at full employment and social progress, and a high level of protection and improvement of the quality of the environment. It shall promote scientific and technological advance.

It shall combat social exclusion and discrimination, and shall promote social justice and protection, equality between women and men, solidarity between generations and protection of the rights of the child.

It shall promote economic, social and territorial cohesion, and solidarity among Member States.

It shall respect its rich cultural and linguistic diversity, and shall ensure that Europe's cultural heritage is safeguarded and enhanced.
4   The Union shall establish an economic and monetary union whose currency is the euro.
5   In its relations with the wider world, the Union shall uphold and promote its values and interests and contribute to the protection of its citizens. It shall contribute to peace, security, the sustainable development of the Earth, solidarity and mutual respect among peoples, free and fair trade, eradication of poverty and the protection of human rights, in particular the rights of the child, as well as to the strict observance and the development of international law, including respect for the principles of the United Nations Charter.

6   The Union shall pursue its objectives by appropriate means commensurate with the competences which are conferred upon it in the Treaties.

## Article 4

1   In accordance with Article 5, competences not conferred upon the Union in the Treaties remain with the Member States.

2   The Union shall respect the equality of Member States before the Treaties as well as their national identities, inherent in their fundamental structures, political and constitutional, inclusive of regional and local self-government. It shall respect their essential State functions, including ensuring the territorial integrity of the State, maintaining law and order and safeguarding national security. In particular, national security remains the sole responsibility of each Member State.

3   Pursuant to the principle of sincere cooperation, the Union and the Member States shall, in full mutual respect, assist each other in carrying out tasks which flow from the Treaties.

   The Member States shall take any appropriate measure, general or particular, to ensure fulfilment of the obligations arising out of the Treaties or resulting from the acts of the institutions of the Union.

   The Member States shall facilitate the achievement of the Union's tasks and refrain from any measure which could jeopardise the attainment of the Union's objectives.

## Article 13

1   The Union shall have an institutional framework which shall aim to promote its values, advance its objectives, serve its interests, those of its citizens and those of the Member States, and ensure the consistency, effectiveness and continuity of its policies and actions.
   The Union's institutions shall be:

   – the European Parliament,
   – the European Council,
   – the Council,
   – the European Commission (hereinafter referred to as 'the Commission'),
   – the Court of Justice of the European Union,
   – the European Central Bank,
   – the Court of Auditors.

2   Each institution shall act within the limits of the powers conferred on it in the Treaties, and in conformity with the procedures, conditions and objectives set out in them. The institutions shall practice mutual sincere cooperation.

3   The provisions relating to the European Central Bank and the Court of Auditors and detailed provisions on the other institutions are set out in the Treaty on the Functioning of the European Union.

4   The European Parliament, the Council and the Commission shall be assisted by an Economic and Social Committee and a Committee of the Regions acting in an advisory capacity

## Article 21

1   The Union's action on the international scene shall be guided by the principles which have inspired its own creation, development and enlargement, and which it seeks to advance in the wider world: democracy, the rule of law, the universality and indivisibility of human rights and fundamental freedoms, respect for human dignity, the principles of equality and solidarity, and respect for the principles of the United Nations Charter and international law.

　　The Union shall seek to develop relations and build partnerships with third countries, and international, regional or global organisations which share the principles referred to in the first subparagraph. It shall promote multilateral solutions to common problems, in particular in the framework of the United Nations.

2   The Union shall define and pursue common policies and actions, and shall work for a high degree of cooperation in all fields of international relations, in order to:

a   safeguard its values, fundamental interests, security, independence and integrity;

b   consolidate and support democracy, the rule of law, human rights and the principles of international law;

c   preserve peace, prevent conflicts and strengthen international security, in accordance with the purposes and principles of the United Nations Charter, with the principles of the Helsinki Final Act and with the aims of the Charter of Paris, including those relating to external borders;

d   foster the sustainable economic, social and environmental development of developing countries, with the primary aim of eradicating poverty;

e   encourage the integration of all countries into the world economy, including through the progressive abolition of restrictions on international trade;

f   help develop international measures to preserve and improve the quality of the environment and the sustainable management of global natural resources, in order to ensure sustainable development;

g   assist populations, countries and regions confronting natural or man-made disasters; and

h   promote an international system based on stronger multilateral cooperation and good global governance.

3   The Union shall respect the principles and pursue the objectives set out in paragraphs 1 and 2 in the development and implementation of the different areas of the Union's external action covered by this Title and by Part Five of the Treaty on the Functioning of the European Union, and of the external aspects of its other policies.

4    The Union shall ensure consistency between the different areas of its external action and between these and its other policies. The Council and the Commission, assisted by the High Representative of the Union for Foreign Affairs and Security Policy, shall ensure that consistency and shall cooperate to that effect.

## *Article 24*

1    The Union's competence in matters of common foreign and security policy shall cover all areas of foreign policy and all questions relating to the Union's security, including the progressive framing of a common defence policy that might lead to a common defence.

The common foreign and security policy is subject to specific rules and procedures. It shall be defined and implemented by the European Council and the Council acting unanimously, except where the Treaties provide otherwise. The adoption of legislative acts shall be excluded. The common foreign and security policy shall be put into effect by the High Representative of the Union for Foreign Affairs and Security Policy and by Member States, in accordance with the Treaties. The specific role of the European Parliament and of the Commission in this area is defined by the Treaties. The Court of Justice of the European Union shall not have jurisdiction with respect to these provisions, with the exception of its jurisdiction to monitor compliance with Article 40 of this Treaty and to review the legality of certain decisions as provided for by the second paragraph of Article 275 of the Treaty on the Functioning of the European Union.

2    Within the framework of the principles and objectives of its external action, the Union shall conduct, define and implement a common foreign and security policy, based on the development of mutual political solidarity among Member States, the identification of questions of general interest and the achievement of an ever-increasing degree of convergence of Member States' actions.

3    The Member States shall support the Union's external and security policy actively and unreservedly in a spirit of loyalty and mutual solidarity and shall comply with the Union's action in this area.

The Member States shall work together to enhance and develop their mutual political solidarity. They shall refrain from any action which is contrary to the interests of the Union or likely to impair its effectiveness as a cohesive force in international relations.

The Council and the High Representative shall ensure compliance with these principles.

## *Article 31*

1    Decisions under this Chapter shall be taken by the European Council and the Council acting unanimously, except where this Chapter provides otherwise. The adoption of legislative acts shall be excluded.

When abstaining in a vote, any member of the Council may qualify its abstention by making a formal declaration under the present subparagraph. In that case, it shall not be obliged to apply the decision, but shall accept that the decision commits the Union. In a spirit of mutual solidarity, the Member State concerned shall refrain from any action likely to conflict with or impede Union action based on that decision and the other Member States shall respect its position. If the members of the Council qualifying their abstention in this way represent at least one third of the Member States comprising at least one third of the population of the Union, the decision shall not be adopted.

2    By derogation from the provisions of paragraph 1, the Council shall act by qualified majority:

–    when adopting a decision defining a Union action or position on the basis of a decision of the European Council relating to the Union's strategic interests and objectives, as referred to in Article 22(1),

–    when adopting a decision defining a Union action or position, on a proposal which the High Representative of the Union for Foreign Affairs and Security Policy has presented following a specific request from the European Council, made on its own initiative or that of the High Representative,

–    when adopting any decision implementing a decision defining a Union action or position,–when appointing a special representative in accordance with Article 33.

If a member of the Council declares that, for vital and stated reasons of national policy, it intends to oppose the adoption of a decision to be taken by qualified majority, a vote shall not be taken. The High Representative will, in close consultation with the Member State involved, search for a solution acceptable to it. If he does not succeed, the Council may, acting by a qualified majority, request that the matter be referred to the European Council for a decision by unanimity.

3    The European Council may unanimously adopt a decision stipulating that the Council shall act by a qualified majority in cases other than those referred to in paragraph 2.

4    Paragraphs 2 and 3 shall not apply to decisions having military or defence implications.

5    For procedural questions, the Council shall act by a majority of its members.

## Charter of Fundamental Rights of the European Union 2010

*Chapter IV Solidarity*

*Article 27*

*Workers' right to information and consultation within the undertaking*

Workers or their representatives must, at the appropriate levels, be guaranteed information and consultation in good time in the cases and under the conditions provided for by Union law and national laws and practices.

*Article 28*

### Right of collective bargaining and action

Workers and employers, or their respective organisations, have, in accordance with Union law and national laws and practices, the right to negotiate and conclude collective agreements at the appropriate levels and, in cases of conflicts of interest, to take collective action to defend their interests, including strike action.

*Article 29*

### Right of access to placement services

Everyone has the right of access to a free placement service.

*Article 30*

### Protection in the event of unjustified dismissal

Every worker has the right to protection against unjustified dismissal, in accordance with Union law and national laws and practices.

*Article 31*

### Fair and just working conditions

1   Every worker has the right to working conditions which respect his or her health, safety and dignity.
2   Every worker has the right to limitation of maximum working hours, to daily and weekly rest periods and to an annual period of paid leave.

*Article 32*

### Prohibition of child labour and protection of young people at work

The employment of children is prohibited. The minimum age of admission to employment may not be lower than the minimum school-leaving age, without prejudice to such rules as may be more favourable to young people and except for limited derogations.

Young people admitted to work must have working conditions appropriate to their age and be protected against economic exploitation and any work likely to harm their safety, health or physical, mental, moral or social development or to interfere with their education.

*Article 33*

*Family and professional life*

1  The family shall enjoy legal, economic and social protection.
2  To reconcile family and professional life, everyone shall have the right to protection from dismissal for a reason connected with maternity and the right to paid maternity leave and to parental leave following the birth or adoption of a child.

*Article 34*

*Social security and social assistance*

1  The Union recognises and respects the entitlement to social security benefits and social services providing protection in cases such as maternity, illness, industrial accidents, dependency or old age, and in the case of loss of employment, in accordance with the rules laid down by Union law and national laws and practices.
2  Everyone residing and moving legally within the European Union is entitled to social security benefits and social advantages in accordance with Union law and national laws and practices.
3  In order to combat social exclusion and poverty, the Union recognises and respects the right to social and housing assistance so as to ensure a decent existence for all those who lack sufficient resources, in accordance with the rules laid down by Union law and national laws and practices.

*Article 35*

*Health care*

Everyone has the right of access to preventive health care and the right to benefit from medical treatment under the conditions established by national laws and practices. A high level of human health protection shall be ensured in the definition and implementation of all the Union's policies and activities.

*Article 36*

*Access to services of general economic interest*

The Union recognises and respects access to services of general economic interest as provided for in national laws and practices, in accordance with the Treaties, in order to promote the social and territorial cohesion of the Union.

*Article 37*

*Environmental protection*

A high level of environmental protection and the improvement of the quality of the environment must be integrated into the policies of the Union and ensured in accordance with the principle of sustainable development.

*Article 38*

*Consumer protection*

Union policies shall ensure a high level of consumer protection.

## Council Directive 2004/67/EC

*Para 13*

The establishment of genuine solidarity between Member States in major emergency supply situations is essential, even more so as Member States become increasingly interdependent regarding security of supply.

## Treaty Establishing the European Coal and Steel Community 1951

*Article 3*

Within the framework of their respective powers and responsibilities and in the common interest, the institutions of the Community shall:

a   see that the common market is regularly supplied, taking account of the needs of third countries;
b   assure to all consumers in comparable positions within the common market equal access to the sources of production;
c   seek the establishment of the lowest prices which are possible without requiring any corresponding rise either in the prices charged by the same enterprises in other transactions or in the price-level as a whole in another period, while at the same time permitting necessary amortization and providing normal possibilities of remuneration for capital invested;
d   see that conditions are maintained which will encourage enterprises to expand and improve their ability to produce and to promote a policy of rational development of natural resources, avoiding inconsiderate exhaustion of such resources;
e   promote the improvement of the living and working conditions of the labour force in each of the industries under its jurisdiction so as to make possible the equalization of such conditions in an upward direction;

f　further the development of international trade and see that equitable limits are observed in prices charged on external markets;

g　promote the regular expansion and the modernization of production as well as the improvement of its quality, under conditions which preclude any protection against competing industries except where justified by illegitimate action on the part of such industries or in their favour.

### Article 95

In all cases not expressly provided for in the present Treaty in which a decision or a recommendation of the High Authority appears necessary to fulfil, in the operation of the common market for coal and steel and in accordance with the provisions of Article 5 above, one of the purposes of the Community as defined in Articles 2, 3 and 4, such decision or recommendation may be taken subject to the unanimous concurrence of the Council and after consultation with the Consultative Committee. The same decision or recommendation, taken in the same manner, shall fix any sanctions to be applied.

If, following the expiration of the transition period provided for by the Convention containing the transitional provisions, unforeseen difficulties which are brought out by experience in the means of application of the present Treaty, or a profound change in the economic or technical conditions which affects the common coal and steel market directly, should make necessary an adaptation of the rules concerning the exercise by the High Authority of the powers which are conferred upon it, appropriate modifications may be made provided that they do not modify the provisions of Articles 2, 3 and 4, or the relationship among the powers of the High Authority and the other institutions of the Community.

These modifications will be proposed jointly by the High Authority and the Council acting by a five-sixths majority. They shall then be submitted to the opinion of the Court. In its examination, the Court may look into all elements of law and fact. If the Court should recognize that they conform to the provisions of the preceding paragraph, such proposals shall be transmitted to the Assembly. They will enter into force if they are approved by the Assembly acting by a majority of three-quarters of the members present and voting comprising two-thirds of the total membership.

## The European Atomic Energy Community Treaty 1957

### Article 64

The Agency, acting where appropriate within the framework of agreements concluded between the Community and a third State or an international organization, shall, subject to the exceptions provided for in this Treaty, have the exclusive right to enter into agreements or contracts whose principal aim is the supply of ores, source materials or special fissile materials coming from outside the Community.

*Article 66*

Should the Commission find, on application by the users concerned, that the Agency is not in a position to deliver within a reasonable period of time all or part of the supplies ordered, or that it can only do so at excessively high prices, the users shall have the right to conclude directly contracts relating to supplies from outside the Community, provided that such contracts meet in essential respects the requirements specified in their orders.

This right shall be granted for a period of one year; it may be extended if the situation which justified its granting continues.

Users who avail themselves of the right provided for in this Article shall communicate to the Commission the direct contracts which they propose to conclude. The Commission may, within one month, object to the conclusion of such contracts if they are contrary to the objectives of this Treaty.

## European Economic Community Treaty 1957

*Article 103*

1    Member States shall consider their policy relating to economic trends as a matter of common interest. They shall consult with each other and with the Commission on measures to be taken in response to current circumstances.
2    Without prejudice to any other procedures provided for in this Treaty, the Council may, by means of a unanimous vote on a proposal of the Commission, decide on measures appropriate to the situation.
3    The Council, acting by means of a qualified majority vote on a proposal of the Commission, shall, where necessary, issue any requisite directives concerning the particulars of application of the measures decided upon under the terms of paragraph 2.
4    The procedures provided for in this Article shall apply also in the event of difficulties arising in connection with the supply of certain products.

*Article 228*

1    Where this Treaty provides for the conclusion of agreements between the Community and one or more States or an international organisation, such agreements shall be negotiated by the Commission. Subject to the powers conferred upon the Commission in this field, such agreements shall be concluded by the Council after the Assembly has been consulted in the cases provided for by this Treaty.

The Council, the Commission or a Member State may, as a preliminary, obtain the opinion of the Court of Justice as to the compatibility of the contemplated agreements with the provisions of this Treaty. An agreement which is the subject of a negative opinion of the Court of Justice may only enter into force under the conditions laid down, according to the case concerned, in Article 236.

2   Agreements concluded under the conditions laid down above shall be binding on the institutions of the Community and on Member States.

## Treaty Establishing the European Community 1957

### Article 3

1   For the purposes set out in Article 2, the activities of the Community shall include, as provided in this Treaty and in accordance with the timetable set out therein:

a   the prohibition, as between Member States, of customs duties and quantitative restrictions on the import and export of goods, and of all other measures having equivalent effect;

b   a common commercial policy;

c   an internal market characterised by the abolition, as between Member States, of obstacles to the free movement of goods, persons, services and capital;

d   measures concerning the entry and movement of persons as provided for in Title IV;

e   a common policy in the sphere of agriculture and fisheries;

f   a common policy in the sphere of transport;

g   a system ensuring that competition in the internal market is not distorted;

h   the approximation of the laws of Member States to the extent required for the functioning of the common market;

i   the promotion of coordination between employment policies of the Member States with a view to enhancing their effectiveness by developing a coordinated strategy for employment;

j   a policy in the social sphere comprising a European Social Fund;

k   the strengthening of economic and social cohesion;

l   a policy in the sphere of the environment;

m   the strengthening of the competitiveness of Community industry;

n   the promotion of research and technological development;

o   encouragement for the establishment and development of trans-European networks;

p   a contribution to the attainment of a high level of health protection;

q   a contribution to education and training of quality and to the flowering of the cultures of the Member States;

r   a policy in the sphere of development cooperation;

s   the association of the overseas countries and territories in order to increase trade and promote jointly economic and social development;

t   a contribution to the strengthening of consumer protection;

u   measures in the spheres of energy, civil protection and tourism.

2   In all the activities referred to in this Article, the Community shall aim to eliminate inequalities, and to promote equality, between men and women.

*Article 4*

1  For the purposes set out in Article 2, the activities of the Member States and the Community shall include, as provided in this Treaty and in accordance with the timetable set out therein, the adoption of an economic policy which is based on the close coordination of Member States' economic policies, on the internal market and on the definition of common objectives, and conducted in accordance with the principle of an open market economy with free competition.

2  Concurrently with the foregoing, and as provided in this Treaty and in accordance with the timetable and the procedures set out therein, these activities shall include the irrevocable fixing of exchange rates leading to the introduction of a single currency, the ecu, and the definition and conduct of a single monetary policy and exchange-rate policy the primary objective of both of which shall be to maintain price stability and, without prejudice to this objective, to support the general economic policies in the Community, in accordance with the principle of an open market economy with free competition.

3  These activities of the Member States and the Community shall entail compliance with the following guiding principles: stable prices, sound public finances and monetary conditions and a sustainable balance of payments.

*Article 5*

The Community shall act within the limits of the powers conferred upon it by this Treaty and of the objectives assigned to it therein.

In areas which do not fall within its exclusive competence, the Community shall take action, in accordance with the principle of subsidiarity, only if and in so far as the objectives of the proposed action cannot be sufficiently achieved by the Member States and can therefore, by reason of the scale or effects of the proposed action, be better achieved by the Community.

Any action by the Community shall not go beyond what is necessary to achieve the objectives of this Treaty.

*Article 30*

The provisions of Articles 28 and 29 shall not preclude prohibitions or restrictions on imports, exports or goods in transit justified on grounds of public morality, public policy or public security; the protection of health and life of humans, animals or plants; the protection of national treasures possessing artistic, historic or archaeological value; or the protection of industrial and commercial property. Such prohibitions or restrictions shall not, however, constitute a means of arbitrary discrimination or a disguised restriction on trade between Member States.

*Article 95*

1  By way of derogation from Article 94 and save where otherwise provided in this Treaty, the following provisions shall apply for the achievement of the

objectives set out in Article 14. The Council shall, acting in accordance with the procedure referred to in Article 251 and after consulting the Economic and Social Committee, adopt the measures for the approximation of the provisions laid down by law, regulation or administrative action in Member States which have as their object the establishment and functioning of the internal market.

2  Paragraph 1 shall not apply to fiscal provisions, to those relating to the free movement of persons nor to those relating to the rights and interests of employed persons.

3  The Commission, in its proposals envisaged in paragraph 1 concerning health, safety, environmental protection and consumer protection, will take as a base a high level of protection, taking account in particular of any new development based on scientific facts. Within their respective powers, the European Parliament and the Council will also seek to achieve this objective.

4  If, after the adoption by the Council or by the Commission of a harmonisation measure, a Member State deems it necessary to maintain national provisions on grounds of major needs referred to in Article 30, or relating to the protection of the environment or the working environment, it shall notify the Commission of these provisions as well as the grounds for maintaining them.

5  Moreover, without prejudice to paragraph 4, if, after the adoption by the Council or by the Commission of a harmonisation measure, a Member State deems it necessary to introduce national provisions based on new scientific evidence relating to the protection of the environment or the working environment on grounds of a problem specific to that Member State arising after the adoption of the harmonisation measure, it shall notify the Commission of the envisaged provisions as well as the grounds for introducing them.

6  The Commission shall, within six months of the notifications as referred to in paragraphs 4 and 5, approve or reject the national provisions involved after having verified whether or not they are a means of arbitrary discrimination or a disguised restriction on trade between Member States and whether or not they shall constitute an obstacle to the functioning of the internal market.

In the absence of a decision by the Commission within this period the national provisions referred to in paragraphs 4 and 5 shall be deemed to have been approved.

When justified by the complexity of the matter and in the absence of danger for human health, the Commission may notify the Member State concerned that the period referred to in this paragraph may be extended for a further period of up to six months.

7  When, pursuant to paragraph 6, a Member State is authorised to maintain or introduce national provisions derogating from a harmonisation measure, the Commission shall immediately examine whether to propose an adaptation to that measure.

8  When a Member State raises a specific problem on public health in a field which has been the subject of prior harmonisation measures, it shall bring it to

the attention of the Commission which shall immediately examine whether to propose appropriate measures to the Council.

9 By way of derogation from the procedure laid down in Articles 226 and 227, the Commission and any Member State may bring the matter directly before the Court of Justice if it considers that another Member State is making improper use of the powers provided for in this Article.

10 The harmonisation measures referred to above shall, in appropriate cases, include a safeguard clause authorising the Member States to take, for one or more of the non-economic reasons referred to in Article 30, provisional measures subject to a Community control procedure.

## *Article 100*

1 Without prejudice to any other procedures provided for in this Treaty, the Council, acting by a qualified majority on a proposal from the Commission, may decide upon the measures appropriate to the economic situation, in particular if severe difficulties arise in the supply of certain products.

2 Where a Member State is in difficulties or is seriously threatened with severe difficulties caused by natural disasters or exceptional occurrences beyond its control, the Council, acting by a qualified majority on a proposal from the Commission, may grant, under certain conditions, Community financial assistance to the Member State concerned. The President of the Council shall inform the European Parliament of the decision taken.

## *Article 111*

1 By way of derogation from Article 300, the Council may, acting unanimously on a recommendation from the ECB or from the Commission, and after consulting the ECB in an endeavour to reach a consensus consistent with the objective of price stability, after consulting the European Parliament, in accordance with the procedure in paragraph 3 for determining the arrangements, conclude formal agreements on an exchange-rate system for the ecu in relation to non-Community currencies. The Council may, acting by a qualified majority on a recommendation from the ECB or from the Commission, and after consulting the ECB in an endeavour to reach a consensus consistent with the objective of price stability, adopt, adjust or abandon the central rates of the ecu within the exchange-rate system. The President of the Council shall inform the European Parliament of the adoption, adjustment or abandonment of the ecu central rates.

2 In the absence of an exchange-rate system in relation to one or more non-Community currencies as referred to in paragraph 1, the Council, acting by a qualified majority either on a recommendation from the Commission and after consulting the ECB or on a recommendation from the ECB, may formulate general orientations for exchange-rate policy in relation to these

currencies. These general orientations shall be without prejudice to the primary objective of the ESCB to maintain price stability.

3   By way of derogation from Article 300, where agreements concerning mone- tary or foreign-exchange regime matters need to be negotiated by the Com- munity with one or more States or international organisations, the Council, acting by a qualified majority on a recommendation from the Commission and after consulting the ECB, shall decide the arrangements for the negotia- tion and for the conclusion of such agreements. These arrangements shall ensure that the Community expresses a single position. The Commission shall be fully associated with the negotiations.

Agreements concluded in accordance with this paragraph shall be binding on the institutions of the Community, on the ECB and on Member States.

4   Subject to paragraph 1, the Council, acting by a qualified majority on a pro- posal from the Commission and after consulting the ECB, shall decide on the position of the Community at international level as regards issues of particular relevance to economic and monetary union and on its representation, in compliance with the allocation of powers laid down in Articles 99 and 105.

5   Without prejudice to Community competence and Community agreements as regards economic and monetary union, Member States may negotiate in international bodies and conclude international agreements.

## Article 133

1   The common commercial policy shall be based on uniform principles, parti- cularly in regard to changes in tariff rates, the conclusion of tariff and trade agreements, the achievement of uniformity in measures of liberalisation, export policy and measures to protect trade such as those to be taken in the event of dumping or subsidies.

2   The Commission shall submit proposals to the Council for implementing the common commercial policy.

3   Where agreements with one or more States or international organisations need to be negotiated, the Commission shall make recommendations to the Council, which shall authorise the Commission to open the necessary negotiations. The Council and the Commission shall be responsible for ensuring that the agree- ments negotiated are compatible with internal Community policies and rules.

The Commission shall conduct these negotiations in consultation with a special committee appointed by the Council to assist the Commission in this task and within the framework of such directives as the Council may issue to it. The Commission shall report regularly to the special committee on the progress of negotiations.

The relevant provisions of Article 300 shall apply.

4   In exercising the powers conferred upon it by this Article, the Council shall act by a qualified majority.

5   Paragraphs 1 to 4 shall also apply to the negotiation and conclusion of agreements in the fields of trade in services and the commercial aspects of

intellectual property, in so far as those agreements are not covered by the said paragraphs and without prejudice to paragraph 6.

By way of derogation from paragraph 4, the Council shall act unanimously when negotiating and concluding an agreement in one of the fields referred to in the first subparagraph, where that agreement includes provisions for which unanimity is required for the adoption of internal rules or where it relates to a field in which the Community has not yet exercised the powers conferred upon it by this Treaty by adopting internal rules.

The Council shall act unanimously with respect to the negotiation and conclusion of a horizontal agreement insofar as it also concerns the preceding subparagraph or the second subparagraph of paragraph 6.

This paragraph shall not affect the right of the Member States to maintain and conclude agreements with third countries or international organisations in so far as such agreements comply with Community law and other relevant international agreements.

6　An agreement may not be concluded by the Council if it includes provisions which would go beyond the Community's internal powers, in particular by leading to harmonisation of the laws or regulations of the Member States in an area for which this Treaty rules out such harmonisation.

In this regard, by way of derogation from the first subparagraph of paragraph 5, agreements relating to trade in cultural and audio-visual services, educational services, and social and human health services, shall fall within the shared competence of the Community and its Member States. Consequently, in addition to a Community decision taken in accordance with the relevant provisions of Article 300, the negotiation of such agreements shall require the common accord of the Member States. Agreements thus negotiated shall be concluded jointly by the Community and the Member States.

The negotiation and conclusion of international agreements in the field of transport shall continue to be governed by the provisions of Title V and Article 300.

7　Without prejudice to the first subparagraph of paragraph 6, the Council, acting unanimously on a proposal from the Commission and after consulting the European Parliament, may extend the application of paragraphs 1 to 4 to international negotiations and agreements on intellectual property in so far as they are not covered by paragraph 5.

### *Article 154*

1　To help achieve the objectives referred to in Articles 14 and 158 and to enable citizens of the Union, economic operators and regional and local communities to derive full benefit from the setting-up of an area without internal frontiers, the Community shall contribute to the establishment and development of trans-European networks in the areas of transport, telecommunications and energy infrastructures.

2   Within the framework of a system of open and competitive markets, action by the Community shall aim at promoting the interconnection and interoperability of national networks as well as access to such networks. It shall take account in particular of the need to link island, landlocked and peripheral regions with the central regions of the Community.

### Article 174

1   Community policy on the environment shall contribute to pursuit of the following objectives:

- preserving, protecting and improving the quality of the environment,
- protecting human health,
- prudent and rational utilisation of natural resources,
- promoting measures at international level to deal with regional or worldwide environmental problems.

2   Community policy on the environment shall aim at a high level of protection taking into account the diversity of situations in the various regions of the Community. It shall be based on the precautionary principle and on the principles that preventive action should be taken, that environmental damage should as a priority be rectified at source and that the polluter should pay.

   In this context, harmonisation measures answering environmental protection requirements shall include, where appropriate, a safeguard clause allowing Member States to take provisional measures, for non-economic environmental reasons, subject to a Community inspection procedure.

3   In preparing its policy on the environment, the Community shall take account of:

- available scientific and technical data,
- environmental conditions in the various regions of the Community,
- the potential benefits and costs of action or lack of action,
- the economic and social development of the Community as a whole and the balanced development of its regions.

4   Within their respective spheres of competence, the Community and the Member States shall cooperate with third countries and with the competent international organisations. The arrangements for Community cooperation may be the subject of agreements between the Community and the third parties concerned, which shall be negotiated and concluded in accordance with Article 300.

   The previous subparagraph shall be without prejudice to Member States' competence to negotiate in international bodies and to conclude international agreements.

### Article 175

1   The Council, acting in accordance with the procedure referred to in Article 251 and after consulting the Economic and Social Committee and the

Committee of the Regions, shall decide what action is to be taken by the Community in order to achieve the objectives referred to in Article 174.

2 By way of derogation from the decision-making procedure provided for in paragraph 1 and without prejudice to Article 95, the Council, acting unanimously on a proposal from the Commission and after consulting the European Parliament, the Economic and Social Committee and the Committee of the Regions, shall adopt:

    a   provisions primarily of a fiscal nature;

    b   measures affecting:

- town and country planning,
- quantitative management of water resources or affecting, directly or indirectly, the availability of those resources,
- land use, with the exception of waste management;

    c   measures significantly affecting a Member State's choice between different energy sources and the general structure of its energy supply.

The Council may, under the conditions laid down in the first subparagraph, define those matters referred to in this paragraph on which decisions are to be taken by a qualified majority.

3 In other areas, general action programmes setting out priority objectives to be attained shall be adopted by the Council, acting in accordance with the procedure referred to in Article 251 and after consulting the Economic and Social Committee and the Committee of the Regions.

The Council, acting under the terms of paragraph 1 or paragraph 2 according to the case, shall adopt the measures necessary for the implementation of these programmes.

4 Without prejudice to certain measures of a Community nature, the Member States shall finance and implement the environment policy.

5 Without prejudice to the principle that the polluter should pay, if a measure based on the provisions of paragraph 1 involves costs deemed disproportionate for the public authorities of a Member State, the Council shall, in the act adopting that measure, lay down appropriate provisions in the form of:

- temporary derogations, and/or
- financial support from the Cohesion Fund set up pursuant to Article 161.

### Article 181

Within their respective spheres of competence, the Community and the Member States shall cooperate with third countries and with the competent international organisations. The arrangements for Community cooperation may be the subject of agreements between the Community and the third parties concerned, which shall be negotiated and concluded in accordance with Article 300.

The previous paragraph shall be without prejudice to Member States' competence to negotiate in international bodies and to conclude international agreements.

## Article 228

1  If the Court of Justice finds that a Member State has failed to fulfil an obligation under this Treaty, the State shall be required to take the necessary measures to comply with the judgment of the Court of Justice.

2  If the Commission considers that the Member State concerned has not taken such measures it shall, after giving that State the opportunity to submit its observations, issue a reasoned opinion specifying the points on which the Member State concerned has not complied with the judgment of the Court of Justice.

   If the Member State concerned fails to take the necessary measures to comply with the Court's judgment within the time limit laid down by the Commission, the latter may bring the case before the Court of Justice. In so doing it shall specify the amount of the lump sum or penalty payment to be paid by the Member State concerned which it considers appropriate in the circumstances.

   If the Court of Justice finds that the Member State concerned has not complied with its judgment it may impose a lump sum or penalty payment on it.

   This procedure shall be without prejudice to Article 227.

## Article 281

The Community shall have legal personality.

## Article 308

If action by the Community should prove necessary to attain, in the course of the operation of the common market, one of the objectives of the Community, and this Treaty has not provided the necessary powers, the Council shall, acting unanimously on a proposal from the Commission and after consulting the European Parliament, take the appropriate measures.

## Article 310

The Community may conclude with one or more States or international organisations agreements establishing an association involving reciprocal rights and obligations, common action and special procedure.

# EU Directive 2009/73/EC

## Article 6

### Regional solidarity

1  In order to safeguard a secure supply on the internal market in natural gas, Member States shall cooperate in order to promote regional and bilateral solidarity.

2    Such cooperation shall cover situations resulting or likely to result in the short term in a severe disruption of supply affecting a Member State. It shall include:

a    co-ordination of national emergency measures referred to in Article 8 of Council Directive 2004/67/EC of 26 April 2004 concerning measures to safeguard security of natural gas supply
b    identification and, where necessary, development or upgrading of electricity and natural gas interconnections; and
c    conditions and practical modalities for mutual assistance.

3    The Commission and the other Member States shall be kept informed of such cooperation.
4    The Commission may adopt Guidelines for regional cooperation in a spirit of solidarity. Those measures, designed to amend non-essential elements of this Directive by supplementing it, shall be adopted in accordance with the regulatory procedure with scrutiny referred to in Article 51(3).

## Article 36

### New infrastructure

1    Major new gas infrastructure, i.e. interconnectors, LNG and storage facilities, may, upon request, be exempted, for a defined period of time, from the provisions of Articles 9, 32, 33 and 34 and Article 41(6), (8) and (10) under the following conditions:

a    the investment must enhance competition in gas supply and enhance security of supply;
b    the level of risk attached to the investment must be such that the investment would not take place unless an exemption was granted;
c    the infrastructure must be owned by a natural or legal person which is separate at least in terms of its legal form from the system operators in whose systems that infrastructure will be built;
d    charges must be levied on users of that infrastructure; and
e    the exemption must not be detrimental to competition or the effective functioning of the internal market in natural gas, or the efficient functioning of the regulated system to which the infrastructure is connected.

2    Paragraph 1 shall also apply to significant increases of capacity in existing infrastructure and to modifications of such infrastructure which enable the development of new sources of gas supply.
3    The regulatory authority referred to in Chapter VIII may, on a case-by-case basis, decide on the exemption referred to in paragraphs 1 and 2.
4    Where the infrastructure in question is located in the territory of more than one Member State, the Agency may submit an advisory opinion to the regulatory authorities of the Member States concerned, which may be used as a

basis for their decision, within two months from the date on which the request for exemption was received by the last of those regulatory authorities.

Where all the regulatory authorities concerned agree on the request for exemption within six months of the date on which it was received by the last of the regulatory authorities, they shall inform the Agency of their decision.

The Agency shall exercise the tasks conferred on the regulatory authorities of the Member States concerned by the present Article:

a   where all regulatory authorities concerned have not been able to reach an agreement within a period of six months from the date on which the request for exemption was received by the last of those regulatory authorities; or

b   upon a joint request from the regulatory authorities concerned.

All regulatory authorities concerned may, jointly, request that the period referred to in point (a) of the third subparagraph is extended by up to three months.

5   Before taking a decision, the Agency shall consult the relevant regulatory authorities and the applicants.

6   An exemption may cover all or part of the capacity of the new infrastructure, or of the existing infrastructure with significantly increased capacity.

In deciding to grant an exemption, consideration shall be given, on a case-by-case basis, to the need to impose conditions regarding the duration of the exemption and non-discriminatory access to the infrastructure. When deciding on those conditions, account shall, in particular, be taken of the additional capacity to be built or the modification of existing capacity, the time horizon of the project and national circumstances.

Before granting an exemption, the regulatory authority shall decide upon the rules and mechanisms for management and allocation of capacity. The rules shall require that all potential users of the infrastructure are invited to indicate their interest in contracting capacity before capacity allocation in the new infrastructure, including for own use, takes place. The regulatory authority shall require congestion management rules to include the obligation to offer unused capacity on the market, and shall require users of the infrastructure to be entitled to trade their contracted capacities on the secondary market. In its assessment of the criteria referred to in points (a), (b) and (e) of paragraph 1, the regulatory authority shall take into account the results of that capacity allocation procedure.

The exemption decision, including any conditions referred to in the second subparagraph of this paragraph, shall be duly reasoned and published.

7   Notwithstanding paragraph 3, Member States may provide that their regulatory authority or the Agency, as the case may be, shall submit, for the purposes of the formal decision, to the relevant body in the Member State its opinion on the request for an exemption. That opinion shall be published together with the decision.

8   The regulatory authority shall transmit to the Commission, without delay, a copy of every request for exemption as of its receipt. The decision shall be

notified, without delay, by the competent authority to the Commission, together with all the relevant information with respect to the decision. That information may be submitted to the Commission in aggregate form, enabling the Commission to reach a well-founded decision. In particular, the information shall contain:

a  the detailed reasons on the basis of which the regulatory authority, or Member State, granted or refused the exemption together with a reference to paragraph 1 including the relevant point or points of that paragraph on which such decision is based, including the financial information justifying the need for the exemption;

b  the analysis undertaken of the effect on competition and the effective functioning of the internal market in natural gas resulting from the grant of the exemption;

c  the reasons for the time period and the share of the total capacity of the gas infrastructure in question for which the exemption is granted;

d  in case the exemption relates to an interconnector, the result of the consultation with the regulatory authorities concerned; and

e  the contribution of the infrastructure to the diversification of gas supply.

9  Within a period of two months from the day following the receipt of a notification, the Commission may take a decision requiring the regulatory authority to amend or withdraw the decision to grant an exemption. That two-month period may be extended by an additional period of two months where further information is sought by the Commission. That additional period shall begin on the day following the receipt of the complete information.

The initial two-month period may also be extended with the consent of both the Commission and the regulatory authority. Where the requested information is not provided within the period set out in the request, the notification shall be deemed to be withdrawn unless, before the expiry of that period, either the period has been extended with the consent of both the Commission and the regulatory authority, or the regulatory authority, in a duly reasoned statement, has informed the Commission that it considers the notification to be complete.

The regulatory authority shall comply with the Commission decision to amend or withdraw the exemption decision within a period of one month and shall inform the Commission accordingly.

The Commission shall preserve the confidentiality of commercially sensitive information.

The Commission's approval of an exemption decision shall lose its effect two years from its adoption in the event that construction of the infrastructure has not yet started, and five years from its adoption in the event that the infrastructure has not become operational unless the Commission decides that any delay is due to major obstacles beyond control of the person to whom the exemption has been granted.

10  The Commission may adopt Guidelines for the application of the conditions
laid down in paragraph 1 of this Article and to set out the procedure to be
followed for the application of paragraphs 3, 6, 8 and 9 of this Article. Those
measures, designed to amend non-essential elements of this Directive by supplementing it, shall be adopted in accordance with the regulatory procedure
with scrutiny referred to in Article 51(3).

## Council Directive 2009/119/EC

### Recital 13

In view of what is required in connection with setting up emergency policies,
bringing about convergence in the standards secured by national stockholding
mechanisms and ensuring a better overview of stock levels, particularly in the
event of a crisis, Member States and the Community should have the means for
reinforced control of those stocks. Stocks held under bilateral agreements, or
contractual rights to purchase certain volumes of stocks (tickets) that fulfil all
obligations set by the current Directive, should form useful instruments compatible
with this aim of greater convergence.

### Recital 28

The Member States concerned should be allowed to fulfil any obligations they
may be subject to as a result of a decision to release stocks taken pursuant to
the IEA Agreement or its implementing measures. A proper and timely
execution of IEA decisions is a key factor for efficient response to cases of
supply difficulties. In order to ensure this, Member States should release part
of their emergency stocks to the extent provided for in the IEA decision in
question. The Commission should cooperate closely with IEA and base action
at Community level on the IEA methodology. In particular, the Commission
should be in a position to recommend stock releases by all Member States, as
appropriate to complement, and facilitate the implementation of, the IEA decision inviting its members to release stocks. It is appropriate for Member States
to respond positively to such Commission recommendations in the interest of a
strong Community-wide solidarity and cohesion, between those Member States
that are members of the IEA and those that are not, in response to a supply
disruption.

### Recital 33

Since the objective of this Directive, namely to maintain a high level of security of
oil supply in the Community through reliable and transparent mechanisms based
on solidarity amongst Member States while complying with the internal market
and competition rules, cannot be sufficiently achieved by the Member States and
can therefore, by reason of its scale and effects, be better achieved at Community

level, the Community may adopt measures in accordance with the principle of subsidiarity as set out in Article 5 of the Treaty. In accordance with the principle of proportionality, as set out in that Article, this Directive does not go beyond what is necessary in order to achieve that objective.

### Article 1Objective

This Directive lays down rules aimed at ensuring a high level of security of oil supply in the Community through reliable and transparent mechanisms based on solidarity amongst Member States, maintaining minimum stocks of crude oil and/ or petroleum products and putting in place the necessary procedural means to deal with a serious shortage.

## Directive 2009/72/EC

### Recital 24

Fully effective separation of network activities from supply and generation activities should apply throughout the Community to both Community and non-Community undertakings. To ensure that network activities and supply and generation activities throughout the Community remain independent from each other, regulatory authorities should be empowered to refuse certification to transmission system operators that do not comply with the unbundling rules. To ensure the consistent application of those rules across the Community, the regulatory authorities should take utmost account of the Commission's opinion when the former take decisions on certification. To ensure, in addition, respect for the international obligations of the Community, and solidarity and energy security within the Community, the Commission should have the right to give an opinion on certification in relation to a transmission system owner or a transmission system operator which is controlled by a person or persons from a third country or third countries.

## EU Directive 2006/67/EC, 24 July 2006, L 217/8

### Recital 18

Since the objective of the action to be taken, namely the maintenance of a high level of security in the supply of crude oil within the Community, by means of reliable and transparent arrangements based on solidarity between Member States, while complying with the rules of the internal market and the competition rules, may be better achieved at Community level, the Community may adopt measures, in accordance with the principle of subsidiarity as set out in Article 5 of the Treaty. In accordance with the principle of proportionality, as set out in that Article, this Directive does not go beyond what is necessary in order to achieve that objective.

# EU Directive 2004/67/EC, 26 April 2004, L 127/92

## *Recital 13*

The establishment of genuine solidarity between Member States in major emergency supply situations is essential, even more so as Member States become increasingly interdependent regarding security of supply.

## Partnership and Cooperation Agreement with Russia 1994

### *Article 15*

1  Goods originating in Russia shall be imported into the Community free of quantitative restrictions without prejudice to the provisions of Articles 17, 20 and 21 of this Agreement and to the provisions of Articles 77, 81, 244, 249 and 280 of the Act of Accession of Spain and Portugal to the Community.
2  Goods originating in the Community shall be imported into Russia free of quantitative restrictions without prejudice to the provisions of Articles 17, 20 and 21 and Annex 2 to this Agreement.

### *Article 12*

1  The Parties agree that the principle of freedom of transit is an essential condition of attaining the objectives of this Agreement.
2  In this connection, each Party shall provide for freedom of transit through its territory of goods originating in the customs territory or destined for the customs territory of the other Party.
3  The rules described in Article V, paragraphs 2, 3, 4 and 5 of the GATT shall be applicable between the Parties.

### *Article 19*

The Agreement shall not preclude prohibitions or restrictions on imports, exports or goods in transit justified on grounds of public morality, public policy or public security; the protection of health and life of humans, animals or plants; the protection of natural resources; the protection of national treasures of artistic, historic or archaeological value or the protection of intellectual, industrial and commercial property or rules relating to gold and silver. Such prohibitions or restrictions shall not, however, constitute a means of arbitrary discrimination or a disguised restriction on trade between the Parties.

### *Article 65*

### *Energy*

1  Cooperation shall take place within the principles of the market economy and the European Energy Charter, against a background of the progressive integration of the energy markets in Europe.

2   The cooperation shall include among others the followings areas:

- improvement of the quality and security of energy supply, in an economic and environmentally sound manner,
- formulation of energy policy,
- improvement in management and regulation of the energy sector in line with a market economy,
- the introduction of a range of institutional, legal, fiscal and other conditions necessary to encourage increased energy trade and investment,
- promotion of energy saving and energy efficiency,
- modernization of energy infrastructure including interconnection of gas supply and electricity networks,
- the environmental impact of energy production, supply and consumption, in order to prevent or minimize the environmental damage resulting from these activities,
- improvement of energy technologies in supply and end use across the range of energy types,
- management and technical training in the energy sector.

## Article 53

### Competition

1   The Parties agree to work to remedy or remove through the application of their competition laws or otherwise, restrictions on competition by enterprises or caused by State intervention in so far as they may affect trade between the Community and Russia.

2   In order to attain the objectives mentioned in paragraph 1:

2.1. The Parties shall ensure that they have and enforce laws addressing restrictions on competition by enterprises within their jurisdiction.

2.2. The Parties shall refrain from granting export aids favouring certain undertakings or the production of products other than primary products. The Parties also declare their readiness, as from the third year from the date of entry into force of this Agreement, to establish for other aids which distort or threaten to distort competition in so far as they affect trade between the Community and Russia, strict disciplines, including the outright prohibition of certain aids. These categories of aids and the disciplines applicable to each shall be defined jointly within a period of three years after entry into force of this Agreement.

Upon request by one Party, the other Party shall provide information on its aid schemes or in particular individual cases of State aid.

2.3. During a transitional period expiring five years after the entry into force of the Agreement, Russia may take measures inconsistent with paragraph 2.2, second sentence, provided that these measures are introduced and applied in the circumstances referred to in Annex 9.

2.4. In the case of State monopolies of a commercial character, the Parties declare their readiness, as from the third year from the date of entry into force of this Agreement, to ensure that there is no discrimination between nationals and companies of the Parties regarding the conditions under which goods are procured or marketed.

In the case of public undertakings or undertakings to which Member States or Russia grant exclusive rights, the Parties declare their readiness, as from the third year from the date of entry into force of this Agreement, to ensure that there is neither enacted nor maintained any measure distorting trade between the Community and Russia to an extent contrary to the Parties' respective interests. This provision shall not obstruct the performance, in law or fact, of the particular tasks assigned to such undertakings.

2.5. The period defined in paragraphs 2.2 and 2.4 may be extended by agreement of the Parties.

3   Consultations may take place within the Cooperation Committee at the request of the Community or Russia on the restrictions or distortions of competition referred to in paragraphs 1 and 2 and on the enforcement of their competition rules, subject to limitations imposed by laws regarding disclosure of information, confidentiality and business secrecy. Consultations may also comprise questions on the interpretation of paragraphs 1 and 2.

4   The Party with experience in applying competition rules shall give full consideration to providing the other Party, upon request and within available resources, technical assistance for the development and implementation of competition rules.

5   The above provisions in no way affect a Party's rights to apply adequate measures, notably those referred to in Article 18, in order to address distortions of trade.

## Article 54

### Intellectual, industrial and commercial property protection

1   Pursuant to the provisions of this Article and Annex 10, the Parties confirm the importance they attach to ensure adequate and effective protection and enforcement of intellectual, industrial and commercial property rights.

2   The Parties confirm the importance they attach to the obligations arising from the following multilateral conventions:

- Paris Convention for the protection of industrial property (Stockholm Act, 1967 and amended in 1979),
- Madrid Agreement concerning the international registration of marks (Stockholm Act, 1967, and amended in 1979),
- Nice Agreement concerning the international classification of goods and services for the purposes of the registration of marks (Geneva, 1977, and amended in 1979),

- Budapest Treaty on the international recognition of the deposit of microorganisms for the purposes of patent procedure (1977, modified in 1980),
- Patent Cooperation Treaty (Washington 1970, amended and modified in 1979 and 1984),
- Protocol relating to the Madrid Agreement concerning the international registration of marks (Madrid, 1989).

3 The implementation of the provisions of this Article and Annex 10 shall be regularly reviewed by the Parties in accordance with Article 90. If problems in the area of intellectual, industrial and commercial property affecting trading conditions were to occur, urgent consultations shall be undertaken, at the request of either Party, with a view to reaching mutually satisfactory solutions.

## Article 61

### Mining and raw materials

1 The Parties shall cooperate with a view to fostering the development of the sectors of mining and raw materials. Special attention shall be paid to cooperation in the sector of non-ferrous metals.
2 The cooperation shall focus in particular on the following areas:

- exchange of information on all matters of interest to the Parties concerning the mining and raw materials sectors, including trade matters,
- the adoption and implementation of environmental legislation,
- training.

3 Such cooperation shall be regularly reviewed by the Parties in a special committee or body to be set up in accordance with the provisions of Article 93.
4 This Article is without prejudice to Articles dealing more specifically with raw materials, in particular Articles 21, 65 and 66.

## Article 105

In so far as matters covered by this Agreement are covered by the Energy Charter Treaty and Protocols thereto, such Treaty and Protocols shall upon entry into force apply to such matters but only to the extent that such application is provided for therein.

## Article 106

This Agreement is concluded for an initial period of 10 years. The Agreement shall be automatically renewed year by year provided that neither Party gives the other Party written notice of denunciation of the Agreement at least six months before it expires.

**Energy Charter Treaty 1994 (as it applied to energy trade between EU and Russia before the Russian withdrawal)[1]**

*Article 7*

1 Each Contracting Party shall take the necessary measures to facilitate the Transit of Energy Materials and Products consistent with the principle of freedom of transit and without distinction as to the origin, destination or ownership of such Energy Materials and Products or discrimination as to pricing on the basis of such distinctions, and without imposing any unreasonable delays, restrictions or charges.

2 Contracting parties shall encourage relevant entities to co-operate in:

   a   modernising Energy Transport Facilities necessary to the Transit of Energy Materials and Products

   b   the development and operation of Energy Transport Facilities serving the Areas of more than one Contracting Party

   c   measures to mitigate the effects of interruptions in the supply of Energy Materials and Product

   d   facilitating the interconnection of Energy Transport Facilities

3 Each Contracting Party undertakes that its provisions relating to transport of Energy Materials and Products and the use of Energy Transport Facilities shall treat Energy Materials and Products in Transit in no less favourable a manner than its provisions treat such materials and products originating in or destined for its own Area, unless an existing international agreement provides otherwise.

4 In the event that Transit of Energy Materials and Products cannot be achieved on commercial terms by means of Energy Transport Facilities the Contracting parties shall not place obstacles in the way of new capacity being established, except as may be otherwise provided in applicable legislation which is consistent with paragraph 1.

5 A Contracting Party through whose Area Energy Materials and Products may transit shall not be obliged to,

   a   permit the construction or modification of Energy Transport Facilities; or

   b   permit new or additional Transit through existing Energy Transport Facilities, which it demonstrates to the other Contracting parties concerned would endanger the security or efficiency of its energy systems, including the security of supply. Contracting parties shall, subject to paragraphs (6) and (7), secure established flows of Energy Materials and Products to, from or between the Areas of other Contracting parties.

1 The latest (amended) version of the ECT 1994 can be found via: <http://www.europarl.europa.eu/meetdocs/2014_2019/documents/itre/dv/energy_charter_/energy_charter_en.pdf> accessed 08 August 2017.

6 A Contracting Party through whose Area Energy Materials and Products transit shall not, in the event of a dispute over any matter arising from that Transit, interrupt or reduce, permit any entity subject to its control to interrupt or reduce, or require any entity subject to its jurisdiction to interrupt or reduce the existing flow of Energy Materials and Products prior to the conclusion of the dispute resolution procedures set out in paragraph (7), except where this is specifically provided for in a contract or other agreement governing such Transit or permitted in accordance with the conciliator's decision.

7 The following provisions shall apply to a dispute described in paragraph (6), but only following the exhaustion of all relevant contractual or other dispute resolution remedies previously agreed between the Contracting parties party to the dispute or between any entity referred to in paragraph (6) and an entity of another Contracting Party to the dispute:

a A Contracting Party to the dispute may refer it to the Secretary-General by a notification summarizing the matters in dispute. The Secretary-General shall notify all Contracting parties of any such referral.

b Within 30 days of receipt of such a notification, the Secretary-General, in consultation with the parties to the dispute and the other Contracting parties concerned, shall appoint a conciliator. Such a conciliator shall have experience in the matters subject to dispute and shall not be a national or citizen of or permanently resident in a party to the dispute or one of the other Contracting parties concerned.

c The conciliator shall seek the agreement of the parties to the dispute to a resolution thereof or upon a procedure to achieve such resolution. If within 90 days of his appointment he has failed to secure such agreement, he shall recommend a resolution to the dispute or a procedure to achieve such resolution and shall decide the interim tariffs and other terms and conditions to be observed for Transit from a date which he shall specify until the dispute is resolved.

d The Contracting parties undertake to observe and ensure that the entities under their control or jurisdiction observe any interim decision under subparagraph (c) on tariffs, terms and conditions for 12 months following the conciliator's decision or until resolution of the dispute, whichever is earlier.

e Notwithstanding subparagraph (b) the Secretary-General may elect not to appoint a conciliator if in his judgement the dispute concerns Transit that is or has been the subject of the dispute resolution procedures set out in subparagraphs (a) to (d) and those proceedings have not resulted in a resolution of the dispute.

f The Charter Conference shall adopt standard provisions concerning the conduct of conciliation and the compensation of conciliators.

8 Nothing in this Article shall derogate from a Contracting Party's rights and obligations under international law including customary international law,

existing bilateral or multilateral agreements, including rules concerning submarine cables and pipelines.

9  This Article shall not be so interpreted as to oblige any Contracting Party which does not have a certain type of Energy Transport Facilities used for Transit to take any measure under this Article with respect to that type of Energy Transport Facilities. Such a Contracting Party is, however, obliged to comply with paragraph (4).

10  For the purposes of this Article:

a  "Transit" means (i) the carriage through the Area of a Contracting Party, or to or from port facilities in its Area for loading or unloading, of Energy Materials and Products originating in the Area of another state and destined for the Area of a third state, so long as either the other state or the third state is a Contracting Party; or (ii) the carriage through the Area of a Contracting Party of Energy Materials and Products originating in the Area of another Contracting Party and destined for the Area of that other Contracting Party, unless the two Contracting parties concerned decide otherwise and record their decision by a joint entry in Annex N. The two Contracting parties may delete their listing in Annex N by delivering a joint written notification of their intentions to the Secretariat, which shall transmit that notification to all other Contracting parties. The deletion shall take effect four weeks after such former notification.

b  "Energy Transport Facilities" consist of high-pressure gas transmission pipelines, high-voltage electricity transmission grids and lines, crude oil transmission pipelines, coal slurry pipelines, oil product pipelines, and other fixed facilities specifically for handling Energy Materials and Products.

*Article 12*

**Compensation for losses**

1  Except where Article 13 applies, an Investor of any Contracting Party which suffers a loss with respect to any Investment in the Area of another Contracting Party owing to war or other armed conflict, state of national emergency, civil disturbance, or other similar event in that Area, shall be accorded by the latter Contracting Party, as regards restitution, indemnification, compensation or other settlement, treatment which is the most favourable of that which that Contracting Party accords to any other Investor, whether its own Investor, the Investor of any other Contracting Party, or the Investor of any third state.

2  Without prejudice to paragraph (1), an Investor of a Contracting Party which, in any of the situations referred to in that paragraph, suffers a loss in the Area of another Contracting Party resulting from (a) requisitioning of its Investment or part thereof by the latter's forces or authorities; or (b) destruction of

its Investment or part thereof by the latter's forces or authorities, which was not required by the necessity of the situation, shall be accorded restitution or compensation which in either case shall be prompt, adequate and effective.

## Article 19

### Environmental aspects

1 In pursuit of sustainable development and taking into account its obligations under those international agreements concerning the environment to which it is party, each Contracting Party shall strive to minimize in an economically efficient manner harmful Environmental Impacts occurring either within or outside its Area from all operations within the Energy Cycle in its Area, taking proper account of safety. In doing so each Contracting Party shall act in a Cost-Effective manner. In its policies and actions each Contracting Party shall strive to take precautionary measures to prevent or minimize environmental degradation. The Contracting parties agree that the polluter in the Areas of Contracting parties, should, in principle, bear the cost of pollution, including transboundary pollution, with due regard to the public interest and without distorting Investment in the Energy Cycle or international trade. Contracting parties shall accordingly:

   a   take account of environmental considerations throughout the formulation and implementation of their energy policies;

   b   promote market-oriented price formation and a fuller reflection of environmental costs and benefits throughout the Energy Cycle;

   c   having regard to Article 34(4), encourage co-operation in the attainment of the environmental objectives of the Charter and co-operation in the field of international environmental standards for the Energy Cycle, taking into account differences in adverse effects and abatement costs between Contracting parties;

   d   have particular regard to Improving Energy Efficiency, to developing and using renewable energy sources, to promoting the use of cleaner fuels and to employing technologies and technological means that reduce pollution;

   e   promote the collection and sharing among Contracting parties of information on environmentally sound and economically efficient energy policies and Cost-Effective practices and technologies;

   f   promote public awareness of the Environmental Impacts of energy systems, of the scope for the prevention or abatement of their adverse Environmental Impacts, and of the costs associated with various prevention or abatement measures;

   g   promote and co-operate in the research, development and application of energy efficient and environmentally sound technologies, practices and processes which will minimize harmful Environmental Impacts of all aspects of the Energy Cycle in an economically efficient manner;

h   encourage favourable conditions for the transfer and dissemination of such technologies consistent with the adequate and effective protection of Intellectual Property rights;

i   promote the transparent assessment at an early stage and prior to decision, and subsequent monitoring, of Environmental Impacts of environmentally significant energy investment projects;

j   promote international awareness and information exchange on Contracting parties' relevant environmental programmes and standards and on the implementation of those programmes and standards;

k   participate, upon request, and within their available resources, in the development and implementation of appropriate environmental programmes in the Contracting parties.

2   At the request of one or more Contracting parties, disputes concerning the application or interpretation of provisions of this Article shall, to the extent that arrangements for the consideration of such disputes do not exist in other appropriate international fora, be reviewed by the Charter Conference aiming at a solution.

3   For the purposes of this Article:

a   "Energy Cycle" means the entire energy chain, including activities related to prospecting for, exploration, production, conversion, storage, transport, distribution and consumption of the various forms of energy, and the treatment and disposal of wastes, as well as the decommissioning, cessation or closure of these activities, minimizing harmful Environmental Impacts;

b   "Environmental Impact" means any effect caused by a given activity on the environment, including human health and safety, flora, fauna, soil, air, water, climate, landscape and historical monuments or other physical structures or the interactions among these factors; it also includes effects on cultural heritage or socio-economic conditions resulting from alterations to those factors;

c   "Improving Energy Efficiency" means acting to maintain the same unit of output (of a good or service) without reducing the quality or performance of the output, while reducing the amount of energy required to produce that output;

d   "Cost-Effective" means to achieve a defined objective at the lowest cost or to achieve the greatest benefit at a given cost.

## Article 21

### Taxation

1   Except as otherwise provided in this Article, nothing in this Treaty shall create rights or impose obligations with respect to Taxation Measures of the

Contracting parties. In the event of any inconsistency between this Article and any other provision of the Treaty, this Article shall prevail to the extent of the inconsistency.

2    Article 7(3) shall apply to Taxation Measures other than those on income or on capital, except that such provision shall not apply to:

    a    an advantage accorded by a Contracting Party pursuant to the tax provisions of any convention, agreement or arrangement described in sub-paragraph (7)(a)(ii); or

    b    any Taxation Measure aimed at ensuring the effective collection of taxes, except where the measure of a Contracting Party arbitrarily discriminates against Energy Materials and Products originating in, or destined for the Area of another Contracting Party or arbitrarily restricts benefits accorded under Article 7(3).

3    Article 10(2) and (7) shall apply to Taxation Measures of the Contracting parties other than those on income or on capital, except that such provisions shall not apply to:

    a    impose most favoured nation obligations with respect to advantages accorded by a Contracting Party pursuant to the tax provisions of any convention, agreement or arrangement described in subparagraph (7)(a)(ii) or resulting from membership of any Regional Economic Integration Organization; or

    b    any Taxation Measure aimed at ensuring the effective collection of taxes, except where the measure arbitrarily discriminates against an Investor of another Contracting Party or arbitrarily restricts benefits accorded under the Investment provisions of this Treaty.

4    Article 29(2) to (6) shall apply to Taxation Measures other than those on income or on capital.

5

    a    Article 13 shall apply to taxes.

    b    Whenever an issue arises under Article 13, to the extent it pertains to whether a tax constitutes an expropriation or whether a tax alleged to constitute an expropriation is discriminatory, the following provisions shall apply: (i) The Investor or the Contracting Party alleging expropriation shall refer the issue of whether the tax is an expropriation or whether the tax is discriminatory to the relevant Competent Tax Authority. Failing such referral by the Investor or the Contracting Party, bodies called upon to settle disputes pursuant to Article 26(2)(c) or 27(2) shall make a referral to the relevant Competent Tax Authorities; (ii) The Competent Tax Authorities shall, within a period of six months of such referral, strive to resolve the issues so referred. Where non-discrimination issues are concerned, the Competent Tax Authorities shall apply the non-discrimination provisions of the relevant tax convention or, if there is no non-discrimination provision in the relevant tax convention applicable to the tax or no such tax convention is in force between the Contracting parties concerned, they shall apply the non-discrimination principles under the Model Tax Convention on Income and Capital of the Organisation for Economic Co-operation and Development; (iii) Bodies called upon to settle disputes pursuant to Article 26(2)(c) or 27(2) may take into account any conclusions arrived at by the Competent Tax Authorities regarding whether the tax is an expropriation. Such bodies shall take into account any conclusions arrived at within the six-month period prescribed in subparagraph (b)(ii) by the Competent Tax Authorities regarding whether the tax is discriminatory. Such bodies may also take into account any conclusions arrived at by the Competent Tax Authorities after the expiry of the six-month period; (iv) Under no circumstances shall involvement of the Competent Tax Authorities, beyond the end of the six-month period referred to in subparagraph (b)(ii), lead to a delay of proceedings under Articles 26 and 27.

6   For the avoidance of doubt, Article 14 shall not limit the right of a Contracting Party to impose or collect a tax by withholding or other means.

For the purposes of this Article:

a   The term "Taxation Measure" includes: (i) any provision relating to taxes of the domestic law of the Contracting Party or of a political subdivision thereof or a local authority therein; and (ii) any provision relating to taxes of any convention for the avoidance of double taxation or of any other international agreement or arrangement by which the Contracting Party is bound.

b   There shall be regarded as taxes on income or on capital all taxes imposed on total income, on total capital or on elements of income or of capital, including taxes on gains from the alienation of property, taxes on estates, inheritances and gifts, or substantially similar taxes, taxes on the total amounts of wages or salaries paid by enterprises, as well as taxes on capital appreciation.

c   A "Competent Tax Authority" means the competent authority pursuant to a double taxation agreement in force between the Contracting parties or, when no such agreement is in force, the minister or ministry responsible for taxes or their authorized representatives.

d   For the avoidance of doubt, the terms "tax provisions" and "taxes" do not include customs duties.

## Article 22

### State and privileged enterprises

1   Each Contracting Party shall ensure that any state enterprise which it maintains or establishes shall conduct its activities in relation to the sale or

provision of goods and services in its Area in a manner consistent with the Contracting Party's obligations under Part III of this Treaty.

2 No Contracting Party shall encourage or require such a state enterprise to conduct its activities in its Area in a manner inconsistent with the Contracting Party's obligations under other provisions of this Treaty.

3 Each Contracting Party shall ensure that if it establishes or maintains an entity and entrusts the entity with regulatory, administrative or other governmental authority, such entity shall exercise that authority in a manner consistent with the Contracting Party's obligations under this Treaty.

4 No Contracting Party shall encourage or require any entity to which it grants exclusive or special privileges to conduct its activities in its Area in a manner inconsistent with the Contracting Party's obligations under this Treaty.

5 For the purposes of this Article, "entity" includes any enterprise, agency or other organization or individual.

## Article 23

### Observance by sub-national authorities

1 Each Contracting Party is fully responsible under this Treaty for the observance of all provisions of the Treaty, and shall take such reasonable measures as may be available to it to ensure such observance by regional and local governments and authorities within its Area.

2 The dispute settlement provisions in Parts II, IV and V of this Treaty may be invoked in respect of measures affecting the observance of the Treaty by a Contracting Party which have been taken by regional or local governments or authorities within the Area of the Contracting Party.

## Article 26

### Settlement of disputes between an investor and a contracting party

1 Disputes between a Contracting Party and an Investor of another Contracting Party relating to an Investment of the latter in the Area of the former, which concern an alleged breach of an obligation of the former under Part III shall, if possible, be settled amicably.

2 If such disputes cannot be settled according to the provisions of paragraph (1) within a period of three months from the date on which either party to the dispute requested amicable settlement, the Investor party to the dispute may choose to submit it for resolution:

a to the courts or administrative tribunals of the Contracting Party party to the dispute;

b in accordance with any applicable, previously agreed dispute settlement procedure; or

c in accordance with the following paragraphs of this Article.

3

    a    Subject only to subparagraphs (b) and (c), each Contracting Party hereby gives its unconditional consent to the submission of a dispute to international arbitration or conciliation in accordance with the provisions of this Article.

    b    (i) The Contracting parties listed in Annex ID do not give such unconditional consent where the Investor has previously submitted the dispute under subparagraph (2)(a) or (b). (ii) For the sake of transparency, each Contracting Party that is listed in Annex ID shall provide a written statement of its policies, practices and conditions in this regard to the Secretariat no later than the date of the deposit of its instrument of ratification, acceptance or approval in accordance with Article 39 or the deposit of its instrument of accession in accordance with Article 41.

    c    A Contracting Party listed in Annex IA does not give such unconditional consent with respect to a dispute arising under the last sentence of Article 10(1).

4    In the event that an Investor chooses to submit the dispute for resolution under subparagraph (2)(c), the Investor shall further provide its consent in writing for the dispute to be submitted to:

    a    (i) The International Centre for Settlement of Investment Disputes, established pursuant to the Convention on the Settlement of Investment Disputes between States and Nationals of other States opened for signature at Washington, 18 March 1965 (hereinafter referred to as the "ICSID Convention"), if the Contracting Party of the Investor and the Contracting Party party to the dispute are both parties to the ICSID Convention; or (ii) The International Centre for Settlement of Investment Disputes, established pursuant to the Convention referred to in subparagraph (a)(i), under the rules governing the Additional Facility for the Administration of Proceedings by the Secretariat of the Centre (hereinafter referred to as the "Additional Facility Rules"), if the Contracting Party of the Investor or the Contracting Party to the dispute, but not both, is a party to the ICSID Convention;

    b    a sole arbitrator or ad hoc arbitration tribunal established under the Arbitration Rules of the United Nations Commission on International Trade Law (hereinafter referred to as "UNCITRAL"); or

    c    an arbitral proceeding under the Arbitration Institute of the Stockholm Chamber of Commerce.

5

    a    The consent given in paragraph (3) together with the written consent of the Investor given pursuant to paragraph (4) shall be considered to satisfy the requirement for: (i) written consent of the parties to a dispute for purposes of Chapter II of the ICSID Convention and for purposes of the Additional Facility Rules; (ii) an "agreement in writing" for purposes of article II of the United Nations Convention on the Recognition and Enforcement of Foreign Arbitral Awards, done at New York, 10 June 1958 (hereinafter referred to as the "New York Convention"); and (iii) "the parties to a contract [to] have agreed in writing" for the purposes of article 1 of the UNCITRAL Arbitration Rules.

b   Any arbitration under this Article shall at the request of any party to the dispute be held in a state that is a party to the New York Convention. Claims submitted to arbitration hereunder shall be considered to arise out of a commercial relationship or transaction for the purposes of article I of that Convention.

6   A tribunal established under paragraph (4) shall decide the issues in dispute in accordance with this Treaty and applicable rules and principles of international law.

7   An Investor other than a natural person which has the nationality of a Contracting Party party to the dispute on the date of the consent in writing referred to in paragraph (4) and which, before a dispute between it and that Contracting Party arises, is controlled by Investors of another Contracting Party, shall for the purpose of article 25(2)(b) of the ICSID Convention be treated as a "national of another Contracting State" and shall for the purpose of article 1(6) of the Additional Facility Rules be treated as a "national of another State".

8   The awards of arbitration, which may include an award of interest, shall be final and binding upon the parties to the dispute. An award of arbitration concerning a measure of a sub-national government or authority of the disputing Contracting Party shall provide that the Contracting Party may pay monetary damages in lieu of any other remedy granted. Each Contracting Party shall carry out without delay any such award and shall make provision for the effective enforcement in its Area of such awards.

## Article 27

### Settlement of disputes between contracting parties

1   Contracting parties shall endeavour to settle disputes concerning the application or interpretation of this Treaty through diplomatic channels.

2   If a dispute has not been settled in accordance with paragraph (1) within a reasonable period of time, either party thereto may, except as otherwise provided in this Treaty or agreed in writing by the Contracting parties, and except as concerns the application or interpretation of Article 6 or Article 19 or, for Contracting parties listed in Annex IA, the last sentence of Article 10 (1), upon written notice to the other party to the dispute submit the matter to an ad hoc tribunal under this Article.

3   Such an ad hoc arbitral tribunal shall be constituted as follows:

a   The Contracting Party instituting the proceedings shall appoint one member of the tribunal and inform the other Contracting Party to the dispute of its appointment within 30 days of receipt of the notice referred to in paragraph (2) by the other Contracting Party;

b   Within 60 days of the receipt of the written notice referred to in paragraph (2), the other Contracting Party party to the dispute shall appoint one member. If the appointment is not made within the time limit prescribed, the Contracting Party having instituted the proceedings may, within 90 days of the receipt of the written notice referred to in paragraph (2), request that the appointment be made in accordance with subparagraph (d);

c   A third member, who may not be a national or citizen of a Contracting Party party to the dispute, shall be appointed by the Contracting parties to the dispute. That member shall be the President of the tribunal. If, within 150 days of the receipt of the notice referred to in paragraph (2), the Contracting parties are unable to agree on the appointment of a third member, that appointment shall be made, in accordance with subparagraph (d), at the request of either Contracting Party submitted within 180 days of the receipt of that notice;

d   Appointments requested to be made in accordance with this paragraph shall be made by the Secretary-General of the Permanent Court of International Arbitration within 30 days of the receipt of a request to do so. If the Secretary-General is prevented from discharging this task, the appointments shall be made by the First Secretary of the Bureau. If the latter, in turn, is prevented from discharging this task, the appointments shall be made by the most senior Deputy;

e   Appointments made in accordance with subparagraphs (a) to (d) shall be made with regard to the qualifications and experience, particularly in matters covered by this Treaty, of the members to be appointed;

f   In the absence of an agreement to the contrary between the Contracting parties, the Arbitration Rules of UNCITRAL shall govern, except to the extent modified by the Contracting parties to the dispute or by the arbitrators. The tribunal shall take its decisions by a majority vote of its members;

g   The tribunal shall decide the dispute in accordance with this Treaty and applicable rules and principles of international law;

h   The arbitral award shall be final and binding upon the Contracting parties to the dispute;

i   Where, in making an award, a tribunal finds that a measure of a regional or local government or authority within the Area of a Contracting Party listed in Part I of Annex P is not in conformity with this Treaty, either party to the dispute may invoke the provisions of Part II of Annex P;

j   The expenses of the tribunal, including the remuneration of its members, shall be borne in equal shares by the Contracting parties to the dispute.

The tribunal may, however, at its discretion direct that a higher proportion of the costs be paid by one of the Contracting parties to the dispute;

k   Unless the Contracting parties to the dispute agree otherwise, the tribunal shall sit in The Hague, and use the premises and facilities of the Permanent Court of Arbitration;

l   A copy of the award shall be deposited with the Secretariat which shall make it generally available.

*Article 29*

*Interim provisions on trade-related matters*

1   The provisions of this Article shall apply to trade in Energy Materials and Products while any Contracting Party is not a party to the GATT and Related Instruments.

2

a   Trade in Energy Materials and Products between Contracting parties at least one of which is not a party to the GATT or a relevant Related Instrument shall be governed, subject to subparagraphs (b) and (c) and to the exceptions and rules provided for in Annex G, by the provisions of GATT 1947 and Related Instruments, as applied on 1 March 1994 and practised with regard to Energy Materials and Products by parties to GATT 1947 among themselves, as if all Contracting parties were parties to GATT 1947 and Related Instruments.

b   Such trade of a Contracting Party which is a state that was a constituent part of the former Union of Soviet Socialist Republics may instead be governed, subject to the provisions of Annex TFU, by an agreement between two or more such states, until 1 December 1999 or the admission of that Contracting Party to the GATT, whichever is the earlier.

c   As concerns trade between any two parties to the GATT, subparagraph (a) shall not apply if either of those parties is not a party to GATT 1947.

3   Each signatory to this Treaty, and each state or Regional Economic Integration Organization acceding to this Treaty, shall on the date of its signature or of its deposit of its instrument of accession provide to the Secretariat a list of all tariff rates and other charges levied on Energy Materials and Products at the time of importation or exportation, notifying the level of such rates and charges applied on such date of signature or deposit. Any changes to such rates or other charges shall be notified to the Secretariat, which shall inform the Contracting parties of such changes.

4   Each Contracting Party shall endeavour not to increase any tariff rate or other charge levied at the time of importation or exportation:

a   in the case of the importation of Energy Materials and Products described in Part I of the Schedule relating to the Contracting Party referred to in article II of the GATT, above the level set forth in that Schedule, if the Contracting Party is a party to the GATT;

    b    in the case of the exportation of Energy Materials and Products, and that of their importation if the Contracting Party is not a party to the GATT, above the level most recently notified to the Secretariat, except as permitted by the provisions made applicable by subparagraph (2)(a).

5    A Contracting Party may increase such tariff rate or other charge above the level referred to in paragraph (4) only if:

    a    in the case of a rate or other charge levied at the time of importation, such action is not inconsistent with the applicable provisions of the GATT other than those provisions of GATT 1947 and Related Instruments listed in Annex G and the corresponding provisions of GATT 1994 and Related Instruments; or

    b    it has, to the fullest extent practicable under its legislative procedures, notified the Secretariat of its proposal for such an increase, given other interested Contracting parties reasonable opportunity for consultation with respect to its proposal, and accorded consideration to any representations from such Contracting parties.

6    Signatories undertake to commence negotiations not later than 1 January 1995 with a view to concluding by 1 January 1998, as appropriate in the light of any developments in the world trading system, a text of an amendment to this Treaty which shall, subject to conditions to be laid down therein, commit each Contracting Party not to increase such tariffs or charges beyond the level prescribed under that amendment.

7    Annex D shall apply to disputes regarding compliance with provisions applicable to trade under this Article and, unless both Contracting parties agree otherwise, to disputes regarding compliance with Article 5 between Contracting parties at least one of which is not a party to the GATT, except that Annex D shall not apply to any dispute between Contracting parties, the substance of which arises under an agreement that:

    a    has been notified in accordance with and meets the other requirements of subparagraph (2)(b) and Annex TFU; or

    b    establishes a free-trade area or a customs union as described in article XXIV of the GATT.

## Article 45

### Provisional application

1    Each signatory agrees to apply this Treaty provisionally pending its entry into force for such signatory in accordance with Article 44, to the extent that such provisional application is not inconsistent with its constitution, laws or regulations.

2

a Notwithstanding paragraph (1) any signatory may, when signing, deliver to the Depositary a declaration that it is not able to accept provisional application. The obligation contained in paragraph (1) shall not apply to a signatory making such a declaration. Any such signatory may at any time withdraw that declaration by written notification to the Depositary.

b Neither a signatory which makes a declaration in accordance with sub-paragraph (a) nor Investors of that signatory may claim the benefits of provisional application under paragraph (1).

c Notwithstanding subparagraph (a), any signatory making a declaration referred to in subparagraph (a) shall apply Part VII provisionally pending the entry into force of the Treaty for such signatory in accordance with Article 44, to the extent that such provisional application is not inconsistent with its laws or regulations.

3

a Any signatory may terminate its provisional application of this Treaty by written notification to the Depositary of its intention not to become a Contracting Party to the Treaty. Termination of provisional application for any signatory shall take effect upon the expiration of 60 days from the date on which such signatory's written notification is received by the Depositary.

b In the event that a signatory terminates provisional application under subparagraph (a), the obligation of the signatory under paragraph (1) to apply Parts III and V with respect to any Investments made in its Area during such provisional application by Investors of other signatories shall nevertheless remain in effect with respect to those Investments for twenty years following the effective date of termination, except as otherwise provided in subparagraph (c).

c Subparagraph (b) shall not apply to any signatory listed in Annex PA. A signatory shall be removed from the list in Annex PA effective upon delivery to the Depositary of its request therefor.

4 Pending the entry into force of this Treaty the signatories shall meet periodically in the provisional Charter Conference, the first meeting of which shall be convened by the provisional Secretariat referred to in paragraph (5) not later than 180 days after the opening date for signature of the Treaty as specified in Article 38.

5 The functions of the Secretariat shall be carried out on an interim basis by a provisional Secretariat until the entry into force of this Treaty pursuant to Article 44 and the establishment of a Secretariat.

6 The signatories shall, in accordance with and subject to the provisions of paragraph (1) or subparagraph (2)(c) as appropriate, contribute to the costs of the provisional Secretariat as if the signatories were Contracting parties under Article 37(3). Any modifications made to Annex B by the signatories shall terminate upon the entry into force of this Treaty.

7 A state or Regional Economic Integration Organization which, prior to this Treaty's entry into force, accedes to the Treaty in accordance with Article 41

shall, pending the Treaty's entry into force, have the rights and assume the obligations of a signatory under this Article.

## Draft Convention on Ensuring International Energy Security

### Article II.2

### Aims

The Parties shall intend and seek:

a   to maintain an optimal sustainable balance between energy supply and demand providing progressive socio-economic development of countries in accordance with the model of development chosen by them;
b   to enhance the efficiency of production, refinement, transportation and use of Energy Materials and Products;
c   to diversify on an economically acceptable basis and with no detriment to existing contractual relations, the production, transportation, forms of trade and consumption of Energy Materials and Products to the extent that such diversification contributes to the objective of this Convention;
d   to encourage scientific and technological cooperation in the energy sector, including with the aim of increasing the share of non-conventional and renewable energy sources in the world energy balance, increasing energy efficiency and energy saving in all elements of the energy value chain;
e   to ensure non-discriminatory access to international energy markets, their openness and the development of their competitiveness;
f   to improve the transparency of the elements of the energy value chain with no detriment to the economic operators' obligations to preserve confidentiality;
g   to ensure uninterrupted energy supply to international markets, including via Transit through EMP Transport Facilities;
h   to ensure the technological reliability of the energy infrastructure;
i   to ensure the physical security of the energy infrastructure, including through resisting international terrorism threats;
j   to contribute to the resolution of energy problems of the poorest segments of the developing countries' population;
k   to create reserve capacity for the production and transportation of Energy Materials and Products necessary for ensuring international

### Article V.4

### Transit through a REIO

If the Parties to the Convention are not only REIOs but also their Member States, the definition of Transit and corresponding Transit provisions of the Convention shall apply to the REIOs as well as to each of these States.

# The Treaty Establishing Energy Community, 2005

## Title I: Principles

### Article 3

For the purposes of Article 2, the activities of the Energy Community shall include:

a   the implementation by the Contracting Parties of the acquis communautaire on energy, environment, competition and renewables, as described in Title II below, adapted to both the institutional framework of the Energy Community and the specific situation of each of the Contracting Parties (hereinafter referred to as 'the extension of the acquis communautaire'), as further described in Title II;

b   the setting up of a specific regulatory framework permitting the efficient operation of Network Energy markets across the territories of the Contracting Parties and part of the territory of the European Community, and including the creation of a single mechanism for the cross-border transmission and/or transportation of Network Energy, and the supervision of unilateral safeguard measures (hereinafter referred to as 'the mechanism for operation of Network Energy markets'), as further described in Title III;

c   the creation for the Parties of a market in Network Energy without internal frontiers, including the coordination of mutual assistance in case of serious disturbance to the energy networks or external disruptions, and which may include the achievement of a common external energy trade policy (hereinafter referred to as 'the creation of a single energy market'), as further described in Title IV.

## Title III

### Chapter VII

#### Safeguard Measures

### Article 36

In the event of a sudden crisis on the Network Energy market in the territory of an Adhering Party, the territory under the jurisdiction of the United Nations Interim Administration Mission in Kosovo, or a territory of the European Community referred to in Article 27, where the physical safety or security of persons, or Network Energy apparatus or installations or system integrity is threatened in this territory, the concerned Party may temporarily take necessary safeguard measures.

*Title VII*

*Implementation of Decisions and Dispute Resolution*

*Article 92*

1    At the request of a Party, the Secretariat or the Regulatory Board, the Ministerial Council, acting by unanimity, may determine the existence of a serious and persistent breach by a Party of its obligations under this Treaty and may suspend certain of the rights deriving from application of this Treaty to the Party concerned, including the suspension of voting rights and exclusion from meetings or mechanisms provided for in this Treaty.

2    The Ministerial Council may subsequently decide by simple majority to revoke any decisions taken under this Article.

## Procedural Act 2008/1021/MC-EnC of the Ministerial Council of the Energy Community

*Article 3*

*Tasks*

1    The Security of Supply Coordination Group shall facilitate the coordination of security of supply measures and advise the Energy Community institutions on issues relating to gas and electricity security of supply.

2    The Security of Supply Coordination Group shall regularly monitor the state of security of supply of network energy within the Energy Community, share experience on security of supply mechanisms and develop comprehensive risk analysis. The conclusions of the Group's annual meetings shall be submitted to the Ministerial Council, the Permanent High Level Group and the Regulatory Board.

3    The tasks of the Security of Supply Coordination Group are without prejudice to the obligations of the Parties to adopt and update security of supply statements in accordance with Article 29 of the Treaty. The Security of Supply Coordination Group shall support the Parties in the preparation and updating of national emergency measures.

4    In the event of an existing or imminent threat to security of supply or in the event of a supply disruption affecting a Party and involving another Party or a third country, the Security of Supply Coordination Group shall, where appropriate, coordinate measures taken at national levels. In doing so, it shall follow the principles established by Article 9 of Directive 2004167lEC in both the gas and electricity sectors.

5    In the cases mentioned in paragraph 4, the Chair of the Security of Supply Coordination Group or any Party directly affected may request an ad-hoc meeting of the Ministerial Council to take measures in response to the existing or imminent threat to security of supply.

6   The activities of the Security of Supply Coordination Group may relate to, but are not restricted to, all issues falling within the scope of Directives 200416TlEC and 2005/89/EC as well as mutual assistance within the meaning of Chapter IV in Title IV of the Treaty and the handling of unilateral safeguard measures in accordance with Article 39 of the Treaty.

## General Agreement on Trade in Services (GATS)

### Article XIV

#### General Exceptions

Subject to the requirement that such measures are not applied in a manner which would constitute a means of arbitrary or unjustifiable discrimination between countries where like conditions prevail, or a disguised restriction on trade in services, nothing in this Agreement shall be construed to prevent the adoption or enforcement by any Member of measures:

a   necessary to protect public morals or to maintain public order;
b   necessary to protect human, animal or plant life or health;
c   necessary to secure compliance with laws or regulations which are not inconsistent with the provisions of this Agreement including those relating to:

    i   the prevention of deceptive and fraudulent practices or to deal with the effects of a default on services contracts;

    ii   the protection of the privacy of individuals in relation to the processing and dissemination of personal data and the protection of confidentiality of individual records and accounts;

    iii   safety;

d   inconsistent with Article XVII, provided that the difference in treatment is aimed at ensuring the equitable or effective imposition or collection of direct taxes in respect of services or service suppliers of other Members;
e   inconsistent with Article II, provided that the difference in treatment is the result of an agreement on the avoidance of double taxation or provisions on the avoidance of double taxation in any other international agreement or arrangement by which the Member is bound.

### Article XIV

#### Security Exceptions

1   Nothing in this Agreement shall be construed:

    a   to require any Member to furnish any information, the disclosure of which it considers contrary to its essential security interests; or b to prevent any Member from taking any action which it considers necessary for the protection of its essential security interests:

   i relating to the supply of services as carried out directly or indirectly for the purpose of provisioning a military establishment;

   ii relating to fissionable and fusionable materials or the materials from which they are derived;

   iii taken in time of war or other emergency in international relations; or

c to prevent any Member from taking any action in pursuance of its obligations under the United Nations Charter for the maintenance of international peace and security.

2 The Council for Trade in Services shall be informed to the fullest extent possible of measures taken under paragraphs 1(b) and (c) and of their termination.

## General Agreement on Tariffs and Trade (GATT) 1948

### Article V

### Freedom of Transit

1 Goods (including baggage), and also vessels and other means of transport, shall be deemed to be in transit across the territory of a contracting party when the passage across such territory, with or without trans-shipment, warehousing, breaking bulk, or change in the mode of transport, is only a portion of a complete journey beginning and terminating beyond the frontier of the contracting party across whose territory the traffic passes. Traffic of this nature is termed in this article "traffic in transit". ARTICLE V 9

2 There shall be freedom of transit through the territory of each contracting party, via the routes most convenient for international transit, for traffic in transit to or from the territory of other contracting parties. No distinction shall be made which is based on the flag of vessels, the place of origin, departure, entry, exit or destination, or on any circumstances relating to the ownership of goods, of vessels or of other means of transport.

3 Any contracting party may require that traffic in transit through its territory be entered at the proper custom house, but, except in cases of failure to comply with applicable customs laws and regulations, such traffic coming from or going to the territory of other contracting parties shall not be subject to any unnecessary delays or restrictions and shall be exempt from customs duties and from all transit duties or other charges imposed in respect of transit, except charges for transportation or those commensurate with administrative expenses entailed by transit or with the cost of services rendered.

4 All charges and regulations imposed by contracting parties on traffic in transit to or from the territories of other contracting parties shall be reasonable, having regard to the conditions of the traffic.

5  With respect to all charges, regulations and formalities in connection with transit, each contracting party shall accord to traffic in transit to or from the territory of any other contracting party treatment no less favourable than the treatment accorded to traffic in transit to or from any third country.

6  Each contracting party shall accord to products which have been in transit through the territory of any other contracting party treatment no less favourable than that which would have been accorded to such products had they been transported from their place of origin to their destination without going through the territory of such other contracting party. Any contracting party shall, however, be free to maintain its requirements of direct consignment existing on the date of this Agreement, in respect of any goods in regard to which such direct consignment is a requisite condition of eligibility for entry of the goods at preferential rates of duty or has relation to the contracting party's prescribed method of valuation for duty purposes.

7  The provisions of this Article shall not apply to the operation of aircraft in transit, but shall apply to air transit of goods (including *baggage*).

## Article XI

### General Elimination of Quantitative Restrictions

1  No prohibitions or restrictions other than duties, taxes or other charges, whether made effective through quotas, import or export licences or other measures, shall be instituted or maintained by any contracting party on the importation of any product of the territory of any other contracting party or on the exportation or sale for export of any product destined for the territory of any other contracting party.

2  The provisions of paragraph 1 of this Article shall not extend to the following:

a  Export prohibitions or restrictions temporarily applied to prevent or relieve critical shortages of foodstuffs or other products essential to the exporting contracting party;

b  Import and export prohibitions or restrictions necessary to the application of standards or regulations for the classification, grading or marketing of commodities in international trade;

c  Import restrictions on any agricultural or fisheries product, imported in any form, necessary to the enforcement of governmental measures which operate:

i  to restrict the quantities of the like domestic product permitted to be marketed or produced, or, if there is no substantial domestic production of the like product, of a domestic product for which the imported product can be directly substituted; or

ii  to remove a temporary surplus of the like domestic product, or, if there is no substantial domestic production of the like product, of a domestic product for which the imported product can be directly substituted, by making the surplus available to certain groups of domestic consumers free of charge or at prices below the current market level; or

   iii  to restrict the quantities permitted to be produced of any animal product the production of which is directly dependent, wholly or mainly, on the imported commodity, if the domestic production of that commodity is relatively negligible.

3   Any contracting party applying restrictions on the importation of any product pursuant to sub-paragraph (c) of this paragraph shall give public notice of the total quantity or value of the product permitted to be imported during a specified future period and of any change in such quantity or value. Moreover, any restrictions applied under (i) above shall not be such as will reduce the total of imports relative to the total of domestic production, as compared with the proportion, which might reasonably be expected to rule between the two in the absence of restrictions. In determining this proportion, the contracting party shall pay due regard to the proportion prevailing during a previous representative period and to any special factors which may have affected or may be affecting the trade in the product concerned.

## Article XII

### Restrictions to Safeguard the Balance of Payments

1   Notwithstanding the provisions of paragraph 1 of Article XI, any contracting party, in order to safeguard its external financial position and its balance of payments, may restrict the quantity or value of merchandise permitted to be imported, subject to the provisions of the following paragraphs of this Article.

2

   a   Import restrictions instituted, maintained or intensified by a contracting party under this Article shall not exceed those necessary:

      i  to forestall the imminent threat of, or to stop, a serious decline in its monetary reserves, or

      ii  in the case of a contracting party with very low monetary reserves, to achieve a reasonable rate of increase in its reserves.

   b   Due regard shall be paid in either case to any special factors which may be affecting the reserves of such contracting party or its need for reserves, including, where special external credits or other resources are available to it, the need to provide for the appropriate use of such credits or resources.

   c   contracting parties applying restrictions under subparagraph (a) of this paragraph shall progressively relax them as such conditions improve, maintaining them only to the extent that the conditions specified in that sub-paragraph still justify their application. They shall eliminate the restrictions when conditions would no longer justify their institution or maintenance under that sub-paragraph.

3   (a) Contracting parties undertake, in carrying out their domestic policies, to pay due regard to the need for maintaining or restoring equilibrium in their balance of payments on a sound and lasting basis and to the desirability of avoiding an uneconomic employment of productive resources. They recognize that, in order to achieve these ends, it is desirable so far as possible to adopt measures which expand rather than contract international trade.

  a   Contracting parties applying restrictions under this Article may determine the incidence of the restrictions on imports of different products or classes of products in such a way as to give priority to the importation of those products which are more essential.

  b   Contracting parties applying restrictions under this Article undertake:

    i   to avoid unnecessary damage to the commercial or economic interests of any other contracting party;

    ii   not to apply restrictions so as to prevent unreasonably the importation of any description of goods in minimum commercial quantities the exclusion of which would impair regular channels of trade; and

    iii   not to apply restrictions which would prevent the importations of commercial samples or prevent compliance with patent, trade mark, copyright, or similar procedures.

  c   The contracting parties recognize that, as a result of domestic policies directed towards the achievement and maintenance of full and productive employment or towards the development of economic resources, a contracting party may experience a high level of demand for imports involving a threat to its monetary reserves of the sort referred to in paragraph 2 (a) of this Article. Accordingly, a contracting party otherwise complying with the provisions of this Article shall not be required to withdraw or modify restrictions on the ground that a change in those policies would render unnecessary restrictions which it is applying under this Article.

4

  a   Any contracting party applying new restrictions or raising the general level of its existing restrictions by a substantial intensification of the measures applied under this Article shall immediately after instituting or intensifying such restrictions (or, in circumstances in which prior consultation is practicable, before doing so) consult with the contracting parties as to the nature of its balance of payments difficulties, alternative corrective measures which may be available, and the possible effect of the restrictions on the economies of other contracting parties.

  b   On a date to be determined by them, the contracting parties shall review all restrictions still applied under this Article on that date. Beginning one year after that date, contracting parties applying import restrictions under this Article shall enter into consultations of the type provided for in sub-paragraph (a) of this paragraph with the contracting parties annually.

c

    i   If, in the course of consultations with a contracting party under sub-paragraph (a) or (b) above, the contracting parties find that the restrictions are not consistent with provisions of this Article or with those of Article XIII (subject to the provisions of Article XIV), they shall indicate the nature of the inconsistency and may advise that the restrictions be suitably modified.

    ii  If, however, as a result of the consultations, the contracting parties determine that the restrictions are being applied in a manner involving an inconsistency of a serious nature with the provisions of this Article or with those of Article XIII (subject to the provisions of Article XIV) and that damage to the trade of any contracting party is caused or threatened thereby, they shall so inform the contracting party applying the restrictions and shall make appropriate recommendations for securing conformity with such provisions within the specified period of time. If such contracting party does not comply with these recommendations within the specified period, the contracting parties may release any contracting party the trade of which is adversely affected by the restrictions from such obligations under this Agreement towards the contracting party applying the restrictions as they determine to be appropriate in the circumstances.

d   The contracting parties shall invite any contracting party which is applying restrictions under this Article to enter into consultations with them at the request of any contracting party which can establish a prima facie case that the restrictions are inconsistent with the provisions of this Article or with those of Article XIII (subject to the provisions of Article XIV) and that its trade is adversely affected thereby. However, no such invitation shall be issued unless the contracting parties have ascertained that direct discussions between the contracting parties concerned have not been successful. If, as a result of the consultations with the contracting parties, no agreement is reached and they determine that the restrictions are being applied inconsistently with such provisions, and that damage to the trade of the contracting party initiating the procedure is caused or threatened thereby, they shall recommend the withdrawal or modification of the restrictions. If the restrictions are not withdrawn or modified within such time as the contracting parties may prescribe, they may release the contracting party initiating the procedure from such obligations under this Agreement towards the contracting party applying the restrictions as they determine to be appropriate in the circumstances.

e   In proceeding under this paragraph, the contracting parties shall have due regard to any special external factors adversely affecting the export trade of the contracting party applying the restrictions.

f   Determinations under this paragraph shall be rendered expeditiously and, if possible, within sixty days of the initiation of the consultations.

5   If there is a persistent and widespread application of import restrictions under this Article, indicating the existence of a general disequilibrium which is restricting international trade, the contracting parties shall initiate discussions to consider whether other measures might be taken, either by those contracting parties the balance of payments of which are under pressure or by those the balance of payments of which are tending to be exceptionally favourable, or by any appropriate intergovernmental organization, to remove the underlying causes of the disequilibrium. On the invitation of the contracting parties, contracting parties shall participate in such discussions.

## Article XX

### General exceptions

Subject to the requirement that such measures are not applied in a manner which would constitute a means of arbitrary or unjustifiable discrimination between countries where the same conditions prevail, or a disguised restriction on international trade, nothing in this agreement shall be construed to prevent the adoption or enforcement by any contracting party of measures:

a   necessary to protect public morals;

b   necessary to protect human, animal or plant life or health;

c   relating to the importations or exportations of gold or silver;

d   necessary to secure compliance with laws or regulations which are not inconsistent with the provisions of this agreement, including those relating to customs enforcement, the enforcement of monopolies operated under paragraph 4 of Article II and Article XVII, the protection of patents, trademarks and copyrights, and the prevention of deceptive practices;

e   relating to the products of prison labour;

f   imposed for the protection of national treasures of artistic, historic or archaeological value;

g   relating to the conservation of exhaustible natural resources if such measures are made effective in conjunction with restrictions on domestic production or consumption;

h   undertaken in pursuance of obligations under any intergovernmental commodity agreement which conforms to criteria submitted to the contracting parties and not disapproved by them or which is itself so submitted and not so disapproved;

i   involving restrictions on exports of domestic materials necessary to ensure essential quantities of such materials to a domestic processing industry during periods when the domestic price of such materials is held below the world price as part of a governmental stabilization plan; provided that such restrictions shall not operate to increase the exports of or the protection afforded to such domestic industry, and shall not depart from the provisions of this agreement relating to non-discrimination;

j   essential to the acquisition or distribution of products in general or local short supply; provided that any such measures shall be consistent with the principle that all contracting parties are entitled to an equitable share of the international supply of such products, and that any such measures, which are inconsistent with the other provisions of the agreement shall be discontinued as soon as the conditions giving rise to them have ceased to exist. The Contracting Parties shall review the need for this sub-paragraph not later than 30 June 1960.

## Article XXI

### Security exceptions

Nothing in this agreement shall be construed a

to require any contracting party to furnish any information the disclosure of which it considers contrary to its essential security interests; or Articles XXI, XXII and XXIII;

b   to prevent any contracting party from taking any action which it considers necessary for the protection of its essential security interests

  i   relating to fissionable materials or the materials from which they are derived;

  ii  relating to the traffic in arms, ammunition and implements of war and to such traffic in other goods and materials as is carried on directly or indirectly for the purpose of supplying a military establishment;

  iii taken in time of war or other emergency in international relations; or

c   to prevent any contracting party from taking any action in pursuance of its obligations under the united nations charter for the maintenance of international peace and security.

## Article XXII

### Consultation

1   Each contracting party shall accord sympathetic consideration to, and shall afford adequate opportunity for consultation regarding, such representations as may be made by another contracting party with respect to any matter affecting the operation of this Agreement.

2   the contracting parties may, at the request of a contracting party, consult with any contracting party or parties in respect of any matter for which it has not been possible to find a satisfactory solution through consultation under paragraph 1.

# Memorandum on an Early Warning Mechanism in the Energy Sector within the Framework of the EU-Russia Energy Dialogue

## Section 13

### Final Provisions

This Memorandum does not constitute an interactional agreement or other legally binding document and does not establish rights and obligations governed by international law.

This Memorandum is made in two copies, both of them in Russian and English. The Memorandum is signed in Moscow on 16 November 2009.

# Russian Constitution 1993

### Article 15

1   The *Constitution* of the Russian Federation shall have the supreme juridical force, direct application and shall be used on the whole territory of the Russian Federation. Laws and other legal acts adopted in the Russian Federation shall not contradict the *Constitution* of the Russian Federation.

2   The bodies of state authority, bodies of local self-government, officials, private citizens and their associations shall be obliged to observe the *Constitution* of the Russian Federation and laws.

3   Laws shall be officially published. Unpublished laws shall not be used. Normative legal acts concerning human rights, freedoms and duties of man and citizen may not be used, if they are not officially published for general knowledge.

4   The universally-recognised norms of international law and international treaties and agreements of the Russian Federation shall be a component part of its legal system. If an international treaty or agreement of the Russian Federation establishes other rules than those envisaged by law, the rules of the international agreement shall be applied.

# Vienna Convention of the Law of Treaties 1969

### Article 25

### Provisional application

1   A treaty or a part of a treaty is applied provisionally pending its entry into force if:

a   the treaty itself so provides; or

b   the negotiating States have in some other manner so agreed.

2   Unless the treaty otherwise provides or the negotiating States have otherwise agreed, the provisional application of a treaty or a part of a treaty with respect to a State shall be terminated if that State notifies the other States between which the treaty is being applied provisionally of its intention not to become a party to the treaty.

## Draft Energy Charter Protocol on Transit 1998

### Preamble

The Contracting Parties to this Protocol,

Having regard to the European Energy Charter adopted in the Concluding Document of The Hague Conference on the European Energy Charter, signed at The Hague on 17 December 1991;

Being Contracting Parties to the Energy Charter Treaty adopted in the Final Act of the European Energy Charter Conference, signed in Lisbon on 17 December 1994 (hereinafter referred to as the "Treaty");

In pursuit of the ultimate purpose of the Treaty as stated in its Article 2;

Recalling the provisions of the Treaty, notably Article 7 establishing the principle of freedom of Transit;

Recognising the basic principles in international law establishing the freedoms of the high seas including the freedom to lay submarine cables and pipelines.

Noting Contracting Parties' rights and obligations pursuant to Articles 4 and 29 of the Treaty;

Acknowledging the importance of open energy markets, access to Energy Transport Facilities, as well as security of energy supply;

Wishing to strengthen further a clear and coherent set of international rules and principles promoting secure, efficient, uninterrupted and unimpeded Transit and International Energy Swap Agreements, as a means of promoting the economic growth and security of energy supply of all Contracting Parties;

Desiring to further liberalise the existing regimes of the Contracting Parties relating to Transit;

Wishing to develop further stable, equitable, favourable, objective, non-discriminatory and transparent market conditions for Transit;

Aiming to avoid Transit being impeded by any territorial disputes between or among Contracting Parties, which, as such, shall not be addressed by this Protocol;

Reaffirming their commitment to secure established flows and not to interrupt or reduce the existing flow of Energy Materials and Products in Transit;

Desiring to prevent unauthorised taking of Energy Materials and Products in Transit;

Acknowledging the existence of certain obstacles of a technical and non-technical nature to secure, efficient, uninterrupted and unimpeded Transit;

Recognising the need to ensure environmentally sound Transit of Energy Materials and Products in order to minimise and remedy damage to the environment;

Reaffirming the importance of protecting human, animal or plant life or health, and the maintenance of public order; and

Recalling that pursuant to Understanding 1(b) of the Treaty, the provisions of the Treaty and this Protocol do not oblige any Contracting Party to introduce mandatory third party access;

## Article 1

### Definitions

For the purposes of this Protocol, the definitions contained in the Treaty, and in particular those contained in Articles 1, 7 and 19, shall apply.

As used in this Protocol:

1   "Contracting Party" means a state or Regional Economic Integration Organisation which has consented to be bound by this Protocol and for which this Protocol is in force.

2   "Available Capacity" means the total physical operating capacity of the Energy Transport Facilities, less the physical operating capacity:

    a   necessary for the fulfilment of obligations by the owner or operator of the Energy Transport Facilities under any valid and legally binding agreements relating to the transportation of Energy Materials and Products;

    b   necessary for the fulfilment of any other binding obligations pursuant to laws and regulations to the extent those laws and regulations are intended to ensure the supply of Energy Materials and Products within the territory of a Contracting Party;

    c   regarding hydrocarbons, necessary to account for the reasonable requirements, including forecasted requirements, for the transportation of Energy Materials and Products which are owned by the owners or operators of the Energy Transport Facilities or their Affiliates1; and

    d   necessary for the efficient operation of the Energy Transport Facilities, including any operating margin necessary to ensure the security and reliability of the system.

3   "Entity" means:

    a   with respect to a Contracting Party:

       i   a natural person having the citizenship or nationality of or who is permanently residing in that Contracting Party in accordance with its applicable law;

       ii   a company or other organisation organised in accordance with the law applicable in that Contracting Party.

    b   with respect to a "third state", a natural person, company or other organisation which fulfils, mutatis mutandis, the conditions specified in sub-paragraph (a) for a Contracting Party.

4  "Internationally Accepted Accounting Standards" means the standards which are accepted by a recognised consensus of, or have substantial authoritative support from, international accounting standard bodies with respect to the recording of revenues, expenses, costs, assets and liabilities, disclosure of information and preparation of financial statements. These standards may be broad guidelines of general application as well as detailed standards, practices and procedures.

5  "Transit Agreement" means any agreement relating to Transit and which is entered into between:

   a    a Contracting Party and an Entity of another Contracting Party; or
   b    an Entity of a Contracting Party and an Entity of another Contracting Party.

6  "Transit Tariffs" means the payments required by the owner or operator of the Energy Transport Facilities for the Transit of Energy Materials and Products.

## Article 6

### Prohibition of unauthorised taking of energy materials and products in transit

1  A Contracting Party, through whose territory Energy Materials and Products transit shall not take from, or interfere with, the flow of Energy Materials and Products in any manner inconsistent with the provisions of the Treaty or this Protocol, taking into account whether such taking or interference is specifically provided for in a contract.

2  A Contracting Party through whose territory Energy Materials and Products transit shall take all necessary measures to prohibit and address the unauthorised taking of such Energy Materials and Products in Transit by any Entity subject to that Contracting Party's control or jurisdiction.

## Article 8

### Utilisation of available capacity

1  Each Contracting Party shall ensure that owners or operators of Energy Transport Facilities under its jurisdiction will negotiate in good faith with any other Contracting Parties or Entities of Contracting Parties requesting access to and use of Available Capacity for Transit. Such negotiations shall be based on transparent procedures, on commercial terms, and be non-discriminatory as to the origin, destination or ownership of the Energy Materials and Products.

2  Contracting Parties shall ensure that owners or operators shall be obliged to provide a duly substantiated explanation in case of refusing access to and use of Available Capacity for Transit.

3  Each Contracting Party has the right to deny the advantages of this Article to any Entity of Contracting Parties, if the denying Contracting Party establishes

that such Entity of a Contracting Party is owned or controlled directly or indirectly by an Entity of a third state in respect of which the denying Contracting Party:

a   does not maintain a diplomatic relationship; or

b   adopts or maintains measures that:

    i   prohibit transactions with Entities of that state; or

    ii   would be violated or circumvented if the benefits of this Article were accorded to Entities of that state.

4   Notwithstanding Article 8(1), where the duration of a Transit Agreement relating to Transit of hydrocarbons does not match the duration of a supply contract, the Contracting Party through whose Area the hydrocarbons transit shall ensure that the owners or operators of Energy Transport Facilities under its jurisdiction who are in negotiations on access to Available Capacity consider in good faith and under competitive conditions the renewal of such Transit Agreements. This means that the existing user upon the expiry of the Transit Agreement shall be treated neither better nor worse than other potential users at that time, except that the existing user shall be given the first opportunity to accept the conditions offered for any new Transit Agreement for that Available Capacity.

## Article 10

### Transit Tariffs

1   Each Contracting Party shall take all necessary measures to ensure that Transit Tariffs and other conditions are objective, reasonable, transparent and do not discriminate on the basis of origin, destination or ownership of Energy Materials and Products in Transit.

2   Each Contracting Party shall ensure that Transit Tariffs and other conditions are not affected by market distortions, in particular those resulting from abuse of a dominant position by any owner or operator of Energy Transport Facilities used for Transit.

3   Transit Tariffs shall be based on operational and investment costs, including a reasonable rate of return.

4   Subject to paragraphs 1, 2 and 3 of this Article, Transit Tariffs may be determined by appropriate means, including regulation, commercial negotiations or congestion management mechanisms.

## Article 20

### Regional economic integration organisation

1   For the purposes of this Protocol, the "Area" of a Contracting Party referred to in Article 7(10) (a) of the Treaty shall, as regards Contracting Parties which

are members of a Regional Economic Integration Organisation, mean the area to which the treaty establishing such a Regional Economic Integration Organisation applies.

2   A Regional Economic Integration Organisation undertakes to ensure that its provisions treat Energy Materials and Products originating in another Contracting Party and in free circulation in its Area no less favourably than Energy Materials and Products originating in its constituent member-states.

Furthermore, the rules of a Regional Economic Integration Organisation shall provide an overall standard at least equivalent to that resulting from the provisions of this Protocol.

## EU Commission Com (2002) 488 Final

*Article 12*

1   Not later than 1 January 2004, the Commission shall adopt the necessary measures for setting up a European observation system for oil and gas supply to assist in preparing and ensuring the proper implementation of Community legislation in the field of oil supply, to monitor its application and to assist in evaluating the effectiveness of the measures in force and their effects on the functioning of the internal market in petroleum products. The Commission shall ensure that adequate resources are made available to permit effective monitoring of the arrangements provided for in this Directive.

2   The European observation system for oil and gas supply shall be managed by the Commission, which will invite representatives of the Member States and the sectors concerned to meetings. It shall provide the Commission with the technical assistance necessary for the formulation and evaluation of measures taken pursuant to this Directive, and shall contribute to a better understanding of the development of the internal market and the international oil markets and the factors driving these markets.

3   The European observation system for oil and gas supply shall carry out the following tasks with regard to oil:

a   Monitor the functioning of the internal market and the international oil markets;

b   Contribute to the setting up of a system for the physical monitoring of the infrastructures inside and outside of the Community which contribute to the security of oil supply;

c   Monitor the security of oil supply and the procedures intended to guarantee security of oil supplies in crisis situations;

d   Study the development of effective security measures in the oil sector;

e   Monitor the level of security stocks of oil and petroleum products and the procedures for their use, and the implementation of measures to reduce consumption;

f   Create objective, reliable and comparable databases to fulfil its tasks.

# WTO Agreement on Subsidies and Countervailing Measures 1995

## Article 3

### Prohibition

3.1 Except as provided in the Agreement on Agriculture, the following subsidies, within the meaning of Article 1, shall be prohibited:

   a   subsidies contingent, in law or in fact, whether solely or as one of several other conditions, upon export performance, including those illustrated in Annex I;

   b   subsidies contingent, whether solely or as one of several other conditions, upon the use of domestic over imported goods.

3.2 A Member shall neither grant nor maintain subsidies referred to in paragraph 1.

# WTO Dispute Settlement Understanding (DSU) 1995

## Article 1

### Coverage and Application

1   The rules and procedures of this Understanding shall apply to disputes brought pursuant to the consultation and dispute settlement provisions of the agreements listed in Appendix 1 to this Understanding (referred to in this Understanding as the "covered agreements"). The rules and procedures of this Understanding shall also apply to consultations and the settlement of disputes between Members concerning their rights and obligations under the provisions of the Agreement Establishing the World Trade Organization (referred to in this Understanding as the "WTO Agreement") and of this Understanding taken in isolation or in combination with any other covered agreement.

2   The rules and procedures of this Understanding shall apply subject to such special or additional rules and procedures on dispute settlement contained in the covered agreements as are identified in Appendix 2 to this Understanding. To the extent that there is a difference between the rules and procedures of this Understanding and the special or additional rules and procedures set forth in Appendix 2, the special or additional rules and procedures in Appendix 2 shall prevail. In disputes involving rules and procedures under more than one covered agreement, if there is a conflict between special or additional rules and procedures of such agreements under review, and where the parties to the dispute cannot agree on rules and procedures within 20 days of the establishment of the panel, the Chairman of the Dispute Settlement Body provided for in paragraph 1 of Article 2 (referred to in this Understanding as the "DSB"), in consultation with the parties to the dispute, shall determine the rules and procedures to be followed within 10 days after a request by either Member. The Chairman shall be guided by the principle

that special or additional rules and procedures should be used where possible, and the rules and procedures set out in this Understanding should be used to the extent necessary to avoid conflict.

### Article 6

### Establishment of Panels

1  If the complaining party so requests, a panel shall be established at the latest at the DSB meeting following that at which the request first appears as an item on the DSB's agenda, unless at that meeting the DSB decides by consensus not to establish a panel (5).

2  The request for the establishment of a panel shall be made in writing. It shall indicate whether consultations were held, identify the specific measures at issue and provide a brief summary of the legal basis of the complaint sufficient to present the problem clearly. In case the applicant requests the establishment of a panel with other than standard terms of reference, the written request shall include the proposed text of special terms of reference.

## WTO Agreement 1994

### Article 3

### Functions of the WTO

1  The WTO shall facilitate the implementation, administration and operation, and further the objectives, of this Agreement and of the Multilateral Trade Agreements, and shall also provide the framework for the implementation, administration and operation of the Plurilateral Trade Agreements.

2  The WTO shall provide the forum for negotiations among its Members concerning their multilateral trade relations in matters dealt with under the agreements in the Annexes to this Agreement. The WTO may also provide a forum for further negotiations among its Members concerning their multilateral trade relations, and a framework for the implementation of the results of such negotiations, as may be decided by the Ministerial Conference.

3  The WTO shall administer the Understanding on Rules and Procedures Governing the Settlement of Disputes (hereinafter referred to as the "Dispute Settlement Understanding" or "DSU") in Annex 2 to this Agreement.

4  The WTO shall administer the Trade Policy Review Mechanism (hereinafter referred to as the "TPRM") provided for in Annex 3 to this Agreement.

5  With a view to achieving greater coherence in global economic policy-making, the WTO shall cooperate, as appropriate, with the International Monetary Fund and with the International Bank for Reconstruction and Development and its affiliated agencies.

# Bibliography

*Case Law*

*Court of Justice of the European Union:*

Case 26/62 *NV Algemene Transport en Expeditie Onderneming van Gend & Loos v Netherlands Inland Revenue Administration* [1963] ECR 1.

Case 6/64 *Flaminio Costa v ENEL* [1964] ECR 585.

Case C-13/68 *SPA Salgoil v Italian Ministry of Foreign Trade* [1968] ECR 453.

Case 11/70 *Internationale Handelsgesellschaft mbH v Einfuhr- und Vorratsstelle für Getreide und Futtermittel* [1970] ECR 1125.

Case 22/70 *Commission of the European Communities v Council of the European Communities* [1971] ECR 263, 274.

Case 106/77 *Amministrazione delle Finanze dello Stato v Simmenthal SpA* [1978] ECR 629.

Case 72/83 *Campus Oil Limited and others v Minister for Industry and Energy and others* [1984] ECR 2727.

Case C-222/84 *Marguerite Johnston v Chief Constable of the Royal Ulster Constabulary* [1986] ECR 1651

Joined cases 351/85 and 360/85 *Fabrique de fer de Charleroi SA and Dillinger Hüttenwerke AG v Commission of the European Communities* [1987] ECR 3639.

Case C-347/88 *Commission v Hellenic Republic* [1990] ECR I-4747.

Case C-213/89 *The Queen v Secretary of State for Transport, ex parte: Factortame Ltd and others* [1990] ECR I- 2433.

Cases C-159/91 and C-160/91 [1993] *Poucet v Assurances générales de France (AGF) et Caisse mutuelle régionale du Languedoc-Roussillon (Camulrac), Pistre v Caisse autonome nationale de compensation de l'assurance vieillesse des artisans (Cancava)* ECR 637.

Case C-268/94 *Portugal v Council* [1996] ECR I-06177.

Case C-70/95 *Sodemarev Rgione Lombardia* [1997] ECR I-3395.

Case C-56/99 *Gascogne Limousin viands SA v Office national interprofessionnel des viandes de l'élevage et de l'aviculture (Ofival)* [2000] ECR I-3079.

Cases C-466/98 *Commission v United Kingdom* [2002] ECR I-9427.

C-467/98 *Commission v Denmark* [2002] ECR I-9519.

C-468/98 *Commission v Sweden* [2002] ECR I-09575.

C-469/98 *Commission v Finland* [2002] ECR I-9627.

C-471/98 *Commission v Belgium* [2002] ECR I-9681.

C-472/98 *Commission v Luxemburg* [2002] ECR I-9741.

C-475/98 *Commission v Austria* [2002] ECR I-09797.

C-476/98 *Commission v Germany* [2002] ECR I-9855.

C-379/98 *Preussen Elektra AG v Schleswag* AG [2001] ECR I-2099.

Case C-522/04 *Commission of the European Communities v Kingdom of Belgium* [2007] ECR I-5701.

Case C-66/08 *Seyman Kozlowski* [2008] ECR I-6041.

Case C-205/06 *Commission of the European Communities v Republic of Austria* [2009] ECR I-1301.

Case C-249/06 *Commission of the European Communities v Kingdom of Sweden* [2009] ECR I-1335.

Case C-118/07 *Commission of the European Communities v Republic of Finland* [2009] ECRI-10889.

Case C-384/09 *Prunus and Polonium* [2011] ECRI-3319.

Cases C-411/10 and C-493/10[2011] ECR I-0000.

The CJEU Opinion 2/15, Opinion pursuant to Article 218(11) TFEU — Free Trade Agreement between the European Union and the Republic of Singapore, 16 May 2017.


**Arbitration awards**

*Eastern Sugar BV (Netherlands) v The Czech Republic* [2007] Partial Award, SCC Case No 088/2004.

*Hulley Enterprises Limited (Cyprus) v The Russian Federation*, Final Arbitral Award [18 July 2014] PCA Case No AA226.

*Yukos Universal Limited v Russian Federation* Arbitration (2), Final Arbitration Award [18 July 2014] PCA Case No AA227.


**United Kingdom**

*Morgan and Baker v Hinton Organics (Wessex) Ltd and CAJE* [2009] EWCA Civ 107 CA.


**Books:**

Aalto P, *The EU–Russian Energy Dialogue: Europe's Future Energy Security* (Ashgate2008).

Barton B, Redgwell C, Ronne A and Zillman D N, 'Introduction' in Barton B and others (eds), *Energy Security: Managing Risk in a Dynamic Legal and Regulatory Environment* (Oxford University Press2004).

Belyi V A, 'The EU's External Energy Policy' in Roggenkamp M, Redgwell C, Ronne A and del Guayo I (eds), *Energy Law in Europe: National, EU an International Regulation* (Oxford University Press2007).

Bockenforde E W, *What holds Europe together?* (Central European Press2006).

Borgmann-Prebil Y and Ross M, 'Promoting European Solidarity: Between Rhetoric and Reality' in Ross and Borgmann-Prebil, *Promoting Solidarity in the European Union* (Oxford University Press2010).

Bretherton C and Vogler J, *The European Union as a Global Actor* (Routledge2006).

Butler E W, *Russian Foreign Relations and Investment Law* (Oxford University Press2006).

Cameron D P, *Competition in Energy Markets: Law and Regulation in the European Union* (2$^{nd}$ edn, Oxford University Press2007). Cohen A, 'Energy Security in the Caspian Basin' in Luft G and Korin A (eds), *Energy Security Challenges in the 21st Century* (Greenwood Publishing Group2009).

Cremona M, 'External Relations and External Competence: The Emergence of an Integrated Policy' in Craig P and Búrca G (eds), *The Evolution of EU Law* (Oxford University Press1999).

Dyer H and Trombetta J M, *International Handbook on Energy Security* (Edward Elgar, 2013).

Fairhurst J, *Law of the European Union* (9th edn, Pearson Education Limited2012).

Gessner V and Nelken D, *European Ways of Law – Towards a European Sociology of Law* (Hart2007).

Giddens A, *Europe in the Global Age* (Cambridge Polity Press2007).

Granholm N, Malminen J and Persson G (eds), *A Rude Awakening – Ramification of Russian Aggression towards Ukraine* (FOIJune 2014).

Grimmel A and My Giang S (eds), *Solidarity in the European Union* (Springer2017).

Haghighi S S, *Energy Security: The External Legal Relations of The European Union with Major Oil and Gas Supplying Countries* (Hart Publishing2008).

House of Lords European Union Committee, *The EU and Russia: before and beyond the crisis in Ukraine* (HL 2014–15) (The Stationery Office2015).

Judah B, Kobzova J and Popescu N, *Dealing with a Post-Bric Russia* (European Council on Foreign Relations2011).

Kaczorowska A, *European Union Law* (Routledge-Cavendish2013).

Kochenov D and Amtenbrink F, *The European Union's Shaping of the International Legal Order* (Cambridge2014).

Leal-Arcas R, *International Trade and Investment Law: Multilateral, Regional and Bilateral Governance* (Edward-Elgar2010).

Lucas E, *The New Cold War: Putin's Russia and the Threat to the West* (Palgrave Macmillan2008).

Nappert S, 'EU-Russia Relations in the Energy Field: The Continuing Role of International Law in EU–Russia relations in the energy field' in Talus K and Fratini P (eds), *EU-Russia Energy Relations* (Rixensart, Euroconfidentiel SA2010) 103–111.

Nygren B, *The rebuilding of Greater Russia: Putin's Foreign Policy towards the Baltic CIS Countries* (Routledge2008).

Petersmann E-U, *The GATT/WTO Dispute Settlement System: International Law, International Organisations and Dispute Settlement* (Kluwer1997).

Roggenkamp M, Redgwell C, Ronne A and del Guayo I, *Energy Law in Europe: National, EU, and International Regulation* (2nd edn, Oxford University Press2007).

Ross M, 'Solidarity – A New Constitutional Paradigm for the EU' in Ross and Borgmann-Prebil (eds.) *Promoting Solidarity in the European Union* (Oxford University Press2010).

Ross M and Borgmann-Prebil Y, *Promoting Solidarity in the European Union* (Oxford University Press2010).

Saga B, 'Introduction of Competition in Gas Markets: Effects on Contract Structures and Security of Supply' in Hancher L (ed.), *The European Energy Market: Reconciling Competition and Security of Supply*, vol 13 (Bundesanzeiger1995).

Selivanova J, *Energy Dual Pricing in WTO Law* (Cameron2008).

Selivanova Y, *Regulation of Energy in International Trade Law* (Kluwer Law International2011).

Smith C K, *Russia and European Energy Security – Divide and Dominate* (The CSIS Press2008).

Smith C K, *Russia-Europe Energy Relations – Implications for U.S. Policy*, Center for Strategic & International Studies (CSIS, February 2010).

Steurmer M, *Putin and the Rise of Russia* (Pegasus Books2009).

Stjerno S, *Solidarity in Europe: The History of an Idea* (Cambridge University Press, 2009).

Strik P, *Shaping the Single European Market in the Field of Foreign Direct Investment* (Bloomsbury Publishing2014).

Talus K, *EU Energy Law and Policy – A Critical Account* (Oxford University Press2013).

Westphal K, 'Germany and the EU-Russia Energy Dialogue' in Aalto P (ed.), *The EU-Russian Energy Dialogue: Europe's Future Energy Security* (Ashgate2008).

Youngs R, *Energy Security: Europe's New Foreign Policy Challenge* (Routledge2009).

Youngs R, *The EU's Role in World Politics: A Retreat from Liberal Internationalism* (Routledge2010).


### Journal Articles:

Alhajji F A, 'What is Energy Security? (5/5)' (2008) LI (2) *Middle East Economic Survey*.

Anand A, 'Russia in the G20: "Bearly" fitting in?' (2012) 32(2) *SAIS Review of International Affairs* (Summer/Fall 2012).

Assenova M, 'Protests against Rising Energy Prices in Bulgaria: Will Sofia Follow Warsaw and Kyiv's Lead on Shale Gas?' (2013) 10(29) *Eurasia Daily Monitor*.

Bast A and Bogdandy A, 'The European Union's Vertical Order of Competences: The Current Law and Proposals for its Reform' (2002) 39*Common Market Law Review* 227.

Belyi V A and Nappert S, 'A New Charter: Myth or Reality?' (2009) 2*Oil Gas & Energy Law*.

Belyi A, Nappert S and Pogoretskyy V, 'Modernising the Energy Charter Process? The Energy Charter Conference Road Map and the Russian Draft Convention on Energy Security' (2011) 29(3) *Journal of Energy and Natural Resources Law*.

Brill A, 'A Modest Approach for Effective Multilateral Institutions' (2012) 32(2) *The SAIS Review of International Affairs*.

Chester L, 'Conceptualising energy security and making explicit its polysemic nature' (2010) 3(4) *Energy Policy* 202.

Christie H E, 'Energy Vulnerability and EU-Russia Energy Relations' (2009) 5(2) *Journal of Contemporary European Research* 274.

De Jong S, Wouters J and Sterkx S, 'The 2009 Russian-Ukrainian Gas Dispute: Lessons for European Energy Crisis Management after Lisbon' (2010) 15*European Foreign Affairs Review* 511.

Emerson M, Tassinari F and Vahl M, 'A New Agreement between the EU and Russia: Why, what and when?' (May 2006) No 103*CEPS Policy Brief*.

Espuny F T, 'EU-Russia Energy Dialogue at the Origins of the European Foreign Energy Policy' (2009) 2*Oil Gas & Energy Law*.

Flynn C, 'Russian roulette: the ECT, transit and Western European energy security' (2006) 4*Oil, Gas & Energy Law*.

Gray C B, 'Europe should tackle Gazprom Monopoly' [2009] Nos1–2 *European Affairs* 45.

Hanson P, 'The Russian Budget: Why So Much Fuss?' (21 December 2012) No 121*Russian Analytical Digest* 1–2.

Harsem Ø and Claes D H, 'The interdependence of European–Russian energy relations' (2013) 59*Energy Policy* 784–791.

Hartwig I and Nicolaides P, 'Elusive Solidarity in an Enlarged European Union' (2003) 3*Eipascope* 19.

Haukkala H, 'Towards a Pan-European energy order? Energy as an object of contention in EU-Russia relations' (2014) 12(4) *Oil, Gas & Energy Law* 1–26.

Issawi C., 'The 1973 Oil Crisis and After', (Winter, 1978–1979), Vol. 1, No. 2*Journal of Post Keynesian Economics*, pp. 3–26.

Kerr W A, 'Taming the Bear: The WTO after the Accession of Russia' (2012) 13(2) *The Estey Centre Journal of International Law and Trade Policy* 150.

Kjarstand J and Johnson F, 'Prospects of the European Gas Market' (2007) 35*Energy Policy* 874.

Konoplyanik A, 'Russia-EU summit: WTO, the Energy Charter Treaty and the Issue of Transit Energy' (2005) *International Energy Law and Taxation Review*, 2, 30–35.

Konoplyanik A, 'The Evolution of contractual structure of Russian gas supplies to Europe' (2006) 10*Perspectives in Energy* 16.

Konoplyanik A and Wälde W T, 'Energy Charter Treaty and its Role in International Energy' (2006) 4*Journal of Energy and Natural Resources Law*.

Konoplyanik A, 'A Common Russia-EU Energy Space: The New EU Russia Partnership Agreement, Acquis Communautaire and the Energy Charter' (2009) 27(2) *Journal of Energy and Natural Resources Law*.

Konoplyanik A, 'A Common Russia-EU Energy Space (The new EU-Russia Partnership Agreement, acquis communautaire, the Energy Charter and the new Russian initiative)' (2009) 2*Oil Gas and Energy Law*.

Konoplyanik A, 'Energy Charter Plus – Russia to Take the Lead Role in Modernizing ECT?' (2009) 4*Oil Gas & Energy Law*.

Konoplyanik A, 'Energy Charter and the Russian initiative – future prospects of the legal base of international cooperation' (2009) 2*Oil Gas & Energy Law*.

Konoplyanik A, 'Gas Transit in Eurasia: Transit Issues between Russia and the European Union and the European Union and the Role of the Energy Charter' (2009) 27(3) *Journal of Energy and Natural Resources Law*.

Krasner D S, 'Structural causes and regime consequences: regimes as intervening variables' (1982) 36(2) *International Organisation* 1–21.

Kratochvil P and Tichy L, 'EU and Russian discourse on energy relations' (2013) 56*Energy Policy*, 391–406.

Kuzemko C, 'Ideas, power and change: explaining EU-Russian energy relations' (2014) 21(1) *Journal of European Public Policy* 58–75.

Leal-Arcas R, 'EU Legal Personality in Foreign Policy?' (2006) 24*Boston University International Law Journal* 165, 167.

Liesen R, 'Transit Under the 1994 Energy Charter Treaty' (1999) 17*Journal of Energy and Natural Resources Law*.

Luong P J and Weinthal E, 'Prelude to the resource curse – explaining oil and gas development strategies in the Soviet successor states and beyond' (2001) 34*Comparative Political Studies* 367–399.

Maican O-H, 'Some Legal Aspects of Energy Security in the Relations Between EU and Russia' (2009) 9(4) *Romanian Journal of European Affairs* 29.

Maltby T, 'European Union energy policy integration: A case of European Commission policy entrepreneurship and increasing supranationalism' (2013) 55*Energy Policy* 435–444.

Marhold A, 'The World Trade Organization and Energy: Fuel for Debate' (2013) 2(8) *European Society of International Law – ESIL Reflections*, p. 5, http://www.esil-sedi.eu/sites/default/files/Marhold%20-%20ESIL%20Reflections.pdf.

Moorhead T, 'European Union Law as International Law' (2012) 5(1) *European Journal of Legal Studies* 126–143.

Nappert S, 'EU-Russia Relations in the Energy Field: The Continuing Role of International Law' (2009) 2*Oil Gas & Energy Law*.

Natorski M and Surrallés A, 'Securitizing Moves to Nowhere? The Framing of the European Union's Energy Policy' (2008) 4(2) *Journal of Contemporary European Research* 71.

Nies S, 'Oil and gas delivery to Europe: An Overview of Existing and Planned Infrastructure' (2008) 3*Oil, Gas & Energy Law*.

Piebalgs A, 'EU-Russia Energy Relations: Common Goals and Concerns' (2009) 2 *Oil Gas & Energy Law*.

Romanova T, 'The Russian Perspective on the Energy Dialogue' (2008) 16(2) *Journal of Contemporary European Studies* 220–221.

Roth M, 'Poland as a policy entrepreneur in European external energy policy: towards greater energy solidarity vis-à-vis Russia?' (2011) 16(3) *Geopolitics* 600–625.

Sangiovanni A, 'Solidarity in the European Union' (2013) 33(2) *Oxford Journal of Legal Studies* 213–241.

Selivanova Y, 'World Trade Organization and Energy Pricing: Russia's Case' (2004) 38(4) *Journal of World Trade* 559–602.

Selivanova J and Ratliff J, 'Major Events and Policy Issues in EC Competition Law, 2009–2010: Part 1' (2011) 22(3) *International Company and Commercial Law Review* 67–95.

Seliverstov S, 'Energy Security of Russia and the EU: Current Legal Problems' (2009) 2 *Oil Gas & Energy Law*.

Sharples J, 'Russo-Polish energy security relations: a case of threatening dependency, supply guarantee, or regional energy security dynamics?' (2012) 6(1) *Political Perspectives* 35.

Shtilkind I T, 'Energy Charter Treaty: A critical Russian Perspective' (2005) 3(1) *Oil Gas & Energy Law*.

Stegen S K, 'Deconstructing the "energy weapon": Russia's threat to Europe as case study' (2011) 39(10) *Energy Policy* 6505–6513.

Stelzenmuller C, 'Germany's Russia Question – A new Ostpolitik for Europe' (April/ March 2009) 89 *Foreign Affairs*.

Stern J, 'Natural Gas Security Problems in Europe: The Russian – Ukrainian Crisis of 2006' (2006) 13(1) *Asia-Pacific Review* 32–59.

Turksen U, 'Current Problems and Future Prospects for EU Solidarity in Energy Trade' (2014) 12(4) *Oil, Gas and Energy Law*.

Turksen U, 'Investment Disputes in the Russian Federation' (2016) 14(4) *Oil, Gas and Energy Law*.

Turksen U and Antto V, 'The Geoeconomics of the South Stream Pipeline Project' *Columbia Journal of International Affairs*, (Special Issue on Energy Security) January, 2016.

Vazquez M C, 'The Four Doctrines of Self-Executing Treaties' (1995) 89 *American Journal of International Law* 695.

Vihma A and Turksen U, 'The Geoeconomics of the South Stream Pipeline Project' (2015) 69(1) *Columbia Journal of International Affairs*.

Wagner S F, 'Energy Infrastructure Priorities for 2020 and Beyond (2011/2034 (INI))' *Committee on Industry, Research and Energy*, 14 June 2011.

Wagnsson C, 'Divided power Europe: normative agencies among the EU "big three"' (2010) 17(8) *Journal of European Public Policy* 1089–1105.

Yakovlev A, 'In Search for a New Social Base or Why the Russian Authorities Are Changing Their Relations with Business' (21 December 2012) 121 *Russian Analytical Digest* 10.


*Online publications:*

Abbasova N, 'Kazakhstan eager to join huge oil transportation systems via Azerbaijan', *AzerNews*, 6 October 2016, https://www.azernews.az/oil_and_gas/103321.html

Adomaitis N, 'Russia's Gazprom agrees to adopt EU market rules in Lithuania – PM' *Reuters Oil Report* (7 February 2014) <http://uk.reuters.com/article/2014/02/07/lithuania-gazprom-idUKL5N0LC2HU20140207>.

Assenova M, 'Russian Energy Review in 2012: Consolidating State Control in an Uncertain Market' (2013) 10(10) *Eurasia Daily Monitor* <www.jamestown.org/single/?no_ca che=1&tx_ttnews[tt_news]=40333>.

Azaria D, 'Community Interest in International Energy Law: A European Perspective', Lauterpacht Centre for International Law – University of Cambridge, 14 March 2016, <https://sms.cam.ac.uk/media/2201583>.

Balcer A, 'Corruption is not just endemic to the Russian system, it is the system: It is in the EU's interest to increase its engagement with Russian society' (LSE European Politics and Policy (EUROPP) Blog, 7 June 2012) <http://eprints.lse.ac.uk/46228/>.

Baltag C (Associate ed.), 'What's New with the Energy Charter Treaty?' (Kluwer Arbitration Blog, 13 June 2015) <http://kluwerarbitrationblog.com/2015/06/13/wha ts-new-with-the-energy-charter-treaty/>.

Belyi V A, 'A Russian Perspective on the Energy Charter Treaty' (Real Institute Elcano, ARI 98/2009, 16 June 2009) <www.realinstitutoelcano.org/wps/portal/web/rielcano_en/contenido?WCM_GLOBAL_CONTEXT=/elcano/Elcano_in/Zonas_in/ARI98-2009>.

Berg L A and Desai D, 'Overview on the Rule of Law and Sustainable Development for the Global Dialogue on Rule of Law and the Post-2015 Development Agenda', United Nations Development Programme, 2013, <http://www.undp.org/content/dam/undp/library/Democratic%20Governance/Access%20to%20Justice%20and%20Rule%20of%20La w/Global%20Dialogue%20Background%20Paper%20-%20Rule%20of%20Law%20and%20Sustainable%20Developme....pdf>

Bierman S, Arkhipov I and Mazneva E, 'Putin scraps South Stream Pipeline after EU pressure' (Bloomberg, 1 December 2014) <www.bloomberg.com/news/articles/2014-12-01/putin-halts-south-stream-gas-pipeline-after-pressure-from-eu>.

Blank S, 'Russia's Energy Weapon and European Security' (Strategic Studies Institute, September 2009) <www.acus.org/files/Stephen Blank-RussiaEnergy.pdf>.

Braun J F, 'EU Energy Policy under the Treaty of Lisbon Rules: Between a New Policy and Business as Usual' (CEPS/EPIN Working Paper 3 2011) <www.ceps.eu/system/files/book/2011/02/EPIN%20WP31%20Braun%20on%20EU%20Energy%20Policy%20under%20Lisbon.pdf>.

Brill A and Glassman K J, 'Who Should the Twenty Be? A New Membership System to Boost the Legitimacy of the G20 at a Critical Time for the Global Economy' (National Taxpayers Union, 14 June 2012) <https://papers.ssrn.com/sol3/papers.cfm?abstract_id=2235636>.

Britannia, 'King Arthur in Legend, The Holy Grail' <http://www.britannia.com/history/a rthur/grail.html>.

Buntenbach A and others, 'Solidarity in the Economic Crisis, Challenges and Expectations for European Trade Unions' (Friedrich Ebert Stiftung International Policy Analysis, May 2011) <http://library.fes.de/pdf-files/id/ipa/08073.pdf >.

Cadier D, 'Russia 2030: Potential Impact on French Policies, European Council on Foreign Relations', 15 July 2016, <http://www.ecfr.eu/article/commentary_russia_2030_potential_impact_of_french_policies>.

Castle S, 'Medvedev makes nice with the EU' *The New York Times* (Europe, June 27 2008) <www.nytimes.com/2008/06/27/world/europe/27iht-union.4.14050408.html>.

Chow C E, 'Russian Gas Stream or Dream' (Center for Strategic & International Studies Commentary, February 2015) <www.csis.org/analysis/russian-gas-stream-or-dream>.

Cohen A, 'Europe's Strategic Dependence on Russian Energy' (Backgrounder 2083 on Europe, Russia and Eurasia, 5 November 2007) <www.heritage.org/Research/Europe/bg2083.cfm>.

Comecon International Organization, 'Comecon' *Encyclopaedia Britannica* (Last updated: 4–17–2003) <www.britannica.com/topic/Comecon>.

Cottier T and others, 'Energy in WTO law and policy' (WTO Publications, 7 May 2010) <www.wto.org/english/res_e/publications_e/wtr10_forum_e/wtr10_7may10_e.pdf>.

Council of the European Union, 'Joint Statement of the EU-Russia Summit on the Launch of Negotiations for a New EU-Russia Agreement' (11214/08 Presse192, 27 June 2008) <www.consilium.europa.eu/ueDocs/cms_Data/docs/pressData/en/er/101524.pdf>.

Council of the European Union, 'Joint Statement on the Partnership for Modernisation EU-Russia Summit, 31 May-1 June 2010', 1 June 2010, <https://www.google.com.tr/url?sa=t&rct=j&q=&esrc=s&source=web&cd=1&cad=rja&uact=8&ved=0ahUKEwiNzN2ezdbVAhUBbFAKHUIEAzoQFgglMAA&url=http%3A%2F%2Feuropa.eu%2Frapid%2Fpress-release_PRES-10-154_en.pdf&usg=AFQjCNGLqwin245tXgH_RyVh69dUjqdx0w>.

Council of Europe, 'European Court of Human Rights' <www.echr.coe.int/ECHR/EN/Header/Case-Law/Decisions+and+judgments/HUDOC+database/>.

Council, Conclusions, 4 February 2011 [8 March 2011] EUCO 2/1/11 Rev 1 < http://register.consilium.europa.eu/doc/srv?l=EN&f=ST%202%202011%20REV%201>.

Council of the European Union, 'Joint EU-Russia statement on combatting terrorism' (5816/14 (OR en) PRESSE 40, 28 January 2014) <http://static.kremlin.ru/media/events/eng/files/41d4b9fc4bb11a050563.pdf>.

Delegation of the European Union to Russia, 'Investments' (Russia and EU, 13 July 2016) <http://eeas.europa.eu/delegations/russia/eu_russia/trade_relation/investments/index_en.htm>.

Desierto D, 'Namur Declaration of 05 December 2016: An EU-Values Driven Path to Negotiating and Concluding Economic and Trade Agreements', 7 December 2016, https://www.ejiltalk.org/namur-declaration-of-5-december-2016-an-eu-values-driven-path-to-negotiating-and-concluding-economic-and-trade-agreements/.

'Draft Convention on Ensuring International Energy Security' (CEIES) http://ua-energy.org/upload/files/Convention-engl1.pdf

Energy Charter Secretariat, 'The Final Act of the Energy Charter Conference with Respect to the Energy Charter Protocol on Transit (draft)' (31 October 2003) <www.energycharter.org/fileadmin/DocumentsMedia/CC_251_ENG.pdf>.

Energy Charter Secretariat, 'The Energy Charter Treaty: The Reader's Guide'<www.energycharter.org/fileadmin/DocumentsMedia/Legal/ECT_Guide_en.pdf>.

Energy Charter Treaty, 'What is Russia's status with the Energy Charter?' www.encharter.org/index.php?id=18>

Energy Community <www.energy-community.org>.

Energy Information Administration OIAF, 'International Energy Outlook 2004' (doe/eia-0484, April 2004) <www.energieverbraucher.de/files_db/dl_mg_1084170436.pdf> accessed 25 November 2016.

Energy Information AdministrationOIAF, 'International Energy Outlook 2005' (doe/eia-0482, July 2005) <www.eia.doe.gov/oiaf/ieo/pdf/0484(2005).pdf>.

EUNews Room, 'Highlights' (December 2016) <http://europa.eu/newsroom/highlights/specialcoverage/eu_sanctions/index_en.htm>.

Eur-lex, 'Agriculture' (Access to European Union Law) <http://europa.eu/legislation_summaries/agriculture/general_framework/index_en.htm>.

EurActiv, 'EU-Russia welcome "new page" in relationship' (EU news and policy debates across languages, 30 June 2008) <www.euractiv.com/section/global-europe/news/eu-russia-welcome-new-page-in-relationship/>.

EurActiv, 'Gazprom links gas price to South Stream participation' (EU news and policy debates across languages, 12 August 2012) <www.euractiv.com/energy/gazprom -links-gas-price-south-st-news-514481 >.

EurActiv, 'EU contemplates "common market" with Russia' (EU news and policy debates across languages, 22 October 2008) <www.euractiv.com/section/global-europe/news/ eu-contemplates-common-market-with-russia/>.

EurActiv, 'Europe's Southern Gas Corridor: The Great Pipeline Race' (EU News and Policy Debates across Languages, 11 October 2010) <www.euractiv.com/section/m ed-south/linksdossier/europe-s-southern-gas-corridor-the-great-pipeline-race/>.

EurActiv, 'Russia-EU energy politics' (EU news and policy debates across languages, 16 November 2011) www.euractiv.com/energy/russia-eu-energy-politics-analysis-508992

EurActiv, 'Russian-Bulgarian energy relations near melting point' (EU news and policy debates across languages, 13 November 2012) <www.euractiv.com/energy/russia n-bulgarian-energy-relatio-news-515999>.

Eurogas, 'Statistical Report' (The European Union of the Natural Gas Industry, 2012) <www.eurogas.org/uploads/media/Statistics_2011_09.12.11.pdf>.

European Coal and Steel Community, *ECSC Treaty* [*1951*] <http://europa.eu/legisla tion_summaries/institutional_affairs/treaties/treaties_ecsc_en.htm>.

European Commission, Brexit Negotiations, <https://ec.europa.eu/commission/brex it-negotiations_en>.

European Commission, 'Towards a European Strategy for the Security of Energy Supply' (Green Paper) COM (2000) 769 Final, <http://eur-lex.europa.eu/legal-content/EN/ TXT/?uri=celex:52000DC0769>.

European Commission, Communication from the Commission to the European Parliament and the Council – Codification of the Acquis communautaire (Communication) COM (2001) 645 final <http://eur-lex.europa.eu/legal-content/EN/TXT/?qid=148036024 8874&uri=CELEX:52001DC0645>

European Commission, 'A European strategy for sustainable, competitive and secure energy' (Green Paper) COM (2006)105 Final. <http://europa.eu/documents/comm/ green_papers/pdf/com2006_105_en.pdf>

European Commission, 'EU Energy Policy Data' (Commission staff working document) SEC (2007) 12. <http://iet.jrc.ec.europa.eu/remea/commission-staff-working-docum ent-eu-energy-policy-data>

European Commission, 'Second Strategic Energy Review: An EU Energy Security and Solidarity Action Plan' (Communication from the Commission to the European Parlia ment, the Council, the European Economic and Social Committee and the Committee of the Regions) COM (2008)781 final, SEC (2008) 2870–2872. <http://eur-lex. europa.eu/legal-content/en/TXT/?uri=celex%3A52008DC0781>

European Commission, Communication on security of energy supply and international cooperation – 'The EU Energy Policy: Engaging with Partners beyond Our Borders' [2011] COM (2011) 539 final, SEC (2011) 1022–1023 final. <http://ec.europa.eu/ transparency/regdoc/rep/1/2011/EN/1-2011-539-EN-F1-1.Pdf>

European Commission, 'Report from the Commission to the European Parliament and the Council under Article 7 of Decision 2006/500/EC' (Energy Community Treaty) COM (2011) 105 Final. <http://eur-lex.europa.eu/legal-content/EN/TXT/?uri=CELEX% 3A52011DC0105>

European Commission and Russia, 'Common Understanding on the Preparation of the Roadmap of the EU-Russia Energy Cooperation until 2050' (24 February 2011).

<http://ec.europa.eu/energy/international/russia/doc/20110224_understanding_roa dmap_2050.pdf>

European Council, '4 February 2011 Conclusions on Energy' [8 March 2011] EUCO 2/ 1/11 Rev 1. <https://www.consilium.europa.eu/uedocs/cms_data/docs/pressdata/ en/ec/119175.pdf>

European Union Commission, 'Communication from the Commission to the European Parliament, the Council, the European Economic and Social Committee and the Committee of the Regions: Making the internal energy market work' COM (2012) 663 final. <https:// ec.europa.eu/energy/sites/ener/files/documents/20121115_iem_0663_en.pdf>

European UnionCommission, 'European Civil Protection and Humanitarian Aid Operations, Ukraine', <http://ec.europa.eu/echo/where/europe-and-central-asia/ukraine_en>.

European Commission, 'Russia' (Europa Energy) http://ec.europa.eu/energy/en/topics/ international-cooperation/russia>.

European UnionCommission, 'European Solidarity in Action' (Humanitarian Aid and Civil Protection) <http://ec.europa.eu/echo/files/core_achievements/solidarity_in_action/ index_en.htm>.

European Union Commission, 'Single Market Act II: Twelve priority actions for new growth' (*Press Release Database IP/12/1054*, 3 October 2012) <http://europa.eu/rap id/press-release_IP-12-1054_en.htm>

European UnionCommission, 'The EU and Russia reinforce the Early Warning Mechanism to improve prevention and management in case of an energy crisis' (Press Release Database Doc IP/09/1718, 16 November 2009) <http://europa.eu/rapid/press-relea se_IP-09-1718_en.htm>.

European UnionCommission, 'The EU-Russia Partnership – basic facts and figures' (Press Release Database MEMO/11/104, 22 February 2011) <http://europa.eu/rapid/press-release_MEMO-11-104_en.htm?locale=en>.

European UnionCommission, 'Questions and Answers on the third legislative package for an internal EU gas and electricity market' (Press Release Database MEMO/11/125, 2 March 2011) <http://europa.eu/rapid/press-release_MEMO-11-125_en.htm?locale= en>.

European UnionCommission, 'EU gas market: Commission refers Bulgaria and Romania to court to ensure European law is properly implemented' (Press Release Database, 24 November 2011) <http://europa.eu/rapid/press-release_IP-11-1437_en.htm>.

European UnionCommission, 'EU starts negotiations on Caspian pipeline to bring gas to Europe' (Press Release Database, IP/11/1023, 12 September 2011) <http://europa. eu/rapid/press-release_IP-11-1023_en.htm?locale=en>.

European UnionCommission, 'Market Observatory for Energy' (Key Figures, June 2011) <http://ec.europa.eu/energy/observatory/eu_27_info/doc/key_figures.pdf>.

European UnionCommission, 'Energy Roadmap 2050' (European Union, 2012) <https://ec. europa.eu/energy/sites/ener/files/documents/2012_energy_roadmap_2050_en_0.pdf>.

European UnionCommission, 'EU welcomes Russia's WTO accession after 18 years of negotiations' (Press Release Database, 22 August 2012) <http://europa.eu/rapid/press-release_IP-12-906_en.htm?locale=en>.

European UnionCommission, 'Internal energy market: Commission refers Bulgaria, Estonia and the United Kingdom to Court for failing to fully transpose EU rules' (Press Release Database, 24 January 2013) <http://europa.eu/rapid/press-release_IP-13-42_ en.htm>.

European UnionCommission, 'Antitrust: Commission sends Statement of Objections to Gazprom for alleged abuse of dominance on Central and Eastern European gas supply markets' (Press Release Database, 22 April 2015) <http://europa.eu/rapid/press-relea se_IP-15-4828_en.htm>.

European Commission, 'Glossary: Acquis communautaire' (Agriculture and Rural Development) <http://ec.europa.eu/agriculture/glossary/acquis-communautaire_en>.

European UnionCommission, 'Towards Energy Union: Sustainable energy security package' (Press Release Database, 16 February 2016) <http://europa.eu/rapid/press-relea se_IP-16-307_en.htm>.

European Commission, 'Environment and Energy' <http://ec.europa.eu/environment/ integration/energy/unconventional_en.htm>.

European UnionCommission, Press Release, 'Antitrust: Commission invites comments on Gazprom commitments concerning Central and Eastern European gas markets', 13 March 2017, <http://europa.eu/rapid/press-release_IP-17-555_en.htm>.

European UnionParliament, 'Rule of law in Russia' – European Parliament Resolution of 13 June 2013 on the rule of law in Russia (2013/2667(RSP)) <http://www.europarl.europa. eu/document/activities/cont/201306/20130620ATT68114/20130620ATT68114EN. pdf>.

European Unionand Russia, 'Roadmap – EU Russia Energy Cooperation until 2050' (March 2013) <https://ec.europa.eu/energy/sites/ener/files/documents/2013_03_ eu_russia_roadmap_2050_signed.pdf>.

Europe's Energy Portal, 'Energy Prices Report' (Energy Prices from past to present) <www.energy.eu/#dependence>.

EUROSTAT, 'EU imports of energy products – recent developments', April 2017, <http://ec.europa.eu/eurostat/statistics-explained/index.php/EU_imports_of_ener gy_products_-_recent_developments>.

Farnesina, 'Italian Ministry of Foreign Affairs, New Italian/Russian Relations' (Macro Areas) <www.esteri.it/MAE/EN/Politica_Estera/Aree_Geografiche/Europa/I_nuovi_ rapporti.htm>.

Feifer G, 'Too Special a Friendship: Is Germany Questioning Russia's Embrace?' European Dialogue, 25 July 2011, <http://www.eurodialogue.eu/too-special-friendship-germa ny-questioning-russias-embrace>.

Feifer G, 'Too special a friendship: Is Germany questioning Russia's embrace?' (The Big Read, 24 January 2013) <www.rferl.org/content/germany_and_russia_too_special_a_ relationship/24262486.html>.

Fernandes S and Rubio E, 'Solidarity within the Eurozone: how much, what for, for how long?' (2012) 51 Notre Europe, Policy Paper <www.institutdelors.eu/media/solida rityemu_s.fernandes-e.rubio_ne_feb2012.pdf?pdf=ok>.

Forecastchart, 'Historical Oil Prices Chart' <www.forecast-chart.com/chart-crude-oil. html>.

France Diplomatie, 'France and Russia, Economic Relations', http://www.diplomatie. gouv.fr/en/country-files/russia/france-and-russia/

Friedrich-Elbert Stiftung, 'Partnership with Russia in Europe: Economic and Regional Topics for a Strategic Partnership' (Fifth Roundtable Discussion Potsdam, March 2007) <http://library.fes.de/pdf-files/id/04688.pdf>.

Galouchko K, 'Ruble slides most in emerging markets on sanctions, Brent' (Bloomberg, 13 November 2014) <www.bloomberg.com/news/2014-11-13/ruble-slides-most-in-em erging-markets-on-sanctions-brent.html>.

Gotev G, 'Orbán says EU's Energy Union is a threat to Hungary' (EurActive, 20 February 2015) <www.euractiv.com/sections/eu-priorities-2020/orban-says-eus-energy-union- threat-hungary-312290>.

Gotev G, 'Russia says it will shift gas transit from Ukraine to Turkey' (EurActiv, 15 January 2015) <www.euractiv.com/section/energy/news/russia-says-it-will-shift-gas-transit-from-ukraine-to-turkey/>.

Gregory R P, 'Putin's Gas Problem' (Project Syndicate, 26 February 2015) <www.project-syndicate.org/commentary/russia-ukraine-gas-pipeline-by-paul-r–gregory-2015-02#YJZP0vsfOeFMCa3v.99>.

Gurbanov I, 'In Search of New Partners: Putin's Turkish Stream for Turkey' (Energy Corridors Review, 25 December 2014) <https://www.naturalgasworld.com/new-partners-putin-turkish-stream-turkey>.

Guzeloglu A and Guzeloglu F E, 'TurkStream Gas Pipeline Project is approved by the Council of Ministers of the Republic of Turkey', 25 December 2016, <http://www.lexology.com/library/detail.aspx?g=0200a112-b285-4838-a5c2-98d3b6e0c924&utm_source=Lexology+Daily+Newsfeed&utm_medium=HTML+email+-+Body+-+General+section&utm_campaign=Lexology+subscriber+daily+feed&utm_content=Lexology+Daily+Newsfeed+2016-12-30&utm_term>

Helm D, 'Russia, Germany and the European Energy Policy' (Open Democracy, 14 December 2006) <www.opendemocracy.net/globalization-institutions_government/energy_policy_4186.jsp>.

Hille K and Weaver C, 'Rouble suffers worst fall since 1998 crisis' *Financial Times* (4 December 2014) <https://www.ft.com/content/4bb50fcc-7937-11e4-9567-00144feabdc0>.

Honorata N, 'Poland's energy security strategy' [2011] March 2011 *Journal of Energy Security Issue* <www.ensec.org/index.php?option=com_content&view=article&id=279:assessing-polands-energy-security-strategy&catid=114:content0211&Itemid=374>.

Hughes J, 'EU Relations with Russia: Partnership or Asymmetric Interdependency?' [2006] LSE Research online <http://eprints.lse.ac.uk/651/1/Hughes.EU-Russia.2006.pdf>.

Index Mundi, Italy Natural Gas Production, <http://www.indexmundi.com/italy/natural_gas_production.html>

International Energy Agency (IEA), 'Energy Policies of IEA Countries: European Union, 2014 Review'<www.iea.org/Textbase/npsum/EU2014SUM.pdf>.

International Energy Charter (IEC), 'List of all Investment Dispute Settlement Cases' <www.energycharter.org/what-we-do/dispute-settlement/all-investment-dispute-settlement-cases/>.

International Energy Charter (IEC), 'Latest News' <www.encharter.org/>.

International Energy Charter (IEC), 'Transit Protocol' <www.energycharter.org/what-we-do/trade-and-transit/transit-protocol/>.

International Energy Charter (IEC), 'The energy charter treaty' <www.energycharter.org/process/energy-charter-treaty-1994/energy-charter-treaty/>.

International Energy Charter(IEC), 'Overview', 2015, http://www.energycharter.org/process/international-energy-charter-2015/overview/.

Judah B, Kobzova J and Popescu N, 'Dealing with a Post-Bric Russia' (European Council on Foreign Relations, November 2011) 49–53 <www.ecfr.eu/page/-/ECFR44_RUSSIA_REPORT_AW.pdf>.

Juncker J C, 'State of the Union 2015: Time for Honesty, Unity and Solidarity' (European Commission Press Release Database, 9 September 2015) <http://europa.eu/rapid/press-release_SPEECH-15-5614_en.htm>.

Konoplyanik A, 'Russia-EU, G-8, ECT and Transit Protocol' (2006) 3 *Russian/CIS Energy & Mining Law Journal* <http://www.konoplyanik.ru/ru/publications/articles/415_RussiaEU_G8_CT_and_Transit_Protocol.pdf>.

Konstadinides T, 'Civil protection in Europe and the Lisbon "solidarity clause": A genuine legal concept or an article exercise' (2011) *Uppsala Faculty of Law Working Article 3*, <www2.statsvet.uu.se/LinkClick.aspx?fileticket=ywEQQ722UuI%3D&tabid=3159&language=sv-SE>.

Kovacevic A, 'The Impact of the Russia-Ukraine Gas Crisis in South Eastern Europe' (Oxford Institute for Energy Studies, March 2009) <www.oxfordenergy.org/wpcms/wp-content/uploads/2010/11/NG29-TheImpactoftheRussiaUkrainianCrisisinSouthEasternEurope-AleksandarKovacevic-2009.pdf>.

Kremlin, 'Conceptual Approach to the New Legal Framework for Energy Cooperation (Goals and Principles)' (21 April 2009) <http://en.kremlin.ru/supplement/258>.

Lamy P, 'Doha Round will benefit energy trade' (20th World Energy Congress, Rome, 16 November 2007) <www.wto.org/english/news_e/sppl_e/sppl80_e.htm>.

Labelle M, 'The day Hungary cleaved from Europe: The true cost of Russian gas' (The Energy SCEE Commentary, 23 February 2015) <http://energyscee.com/2015/02/23/the-day-hungary-cleaved-from-europe-the-true-cost-of-russian-gas/>.

Leonard M and Popescu N, 'A Power Audit of EU-Russia Relations' (Policy Paper, European Council on Foreign Relations, 2 November 2007) 50 <http://fride.org/uploads/file/A_power_audit_of_relations_eu-russia.pdf>.

Levada Center2014, <http://www.levada.ru/en/2014/11/05/levada-center-and-kiis-about-crisis-in-ukraine/>

Maltby T, 'The development of EU foreign policy: Enlargement and the case of external energy security policy towards Russia, 2000–2010' [2010] Political Studies Association, <www.psa.ac.uk/journals/pdf/5/2010/1630_1484.pdf>.

Ministry of Energy of the Russian Federation, 'The Energy Strategy of Russia for the Period up to 2030' (Russian Government 2010) <www.energystrategy.ru/projects/docs/ES-2030(Eng).pdf>.

Mironova I, 'Russia and the Energy Charter Treaty' (IEC, 7 August 2014) <www.energycharter.org/what-we-do/knowledge-centre/occasional-papers/russia-and-the-energy-charter-treaty/>.

Nowak Z, Godzimirski J and Ćwiek-Karpowicz J, 'Russia's Grand Gas Strategy – the power to dominate Europe?' (Energy Post, 25 May 2015) <http://energypost.eu/russias-grand-gas-strategy-power-dominate-europe/>.

Osterath B, 'What ever happened with Europe's fracking boom?', DW, Environment <http://www.dw.com/en/what-ever-happened-with-europes-fracking-boom/a-18589660>.

Paltsev S, 'Russian Natural Gas Export Potential Up to 2050' (July 2011) MIT Center for Energy and Environmental Policy Research <http://citeseerx.ist.psu.edu/viewdoc/download?doi=10.1.1.208.194&rep=rep1&type=pdf>.

Pawlak P, 'Cybersecurity and cyberdefence: EU Solidarity and Mutual Defence Clauses' (June 2015) *European Parliament Briefing* <www.europarl.europa.eu/RegData/etudes/BRIE/2015/559488/EPRS_BRI(2015)559488_EN.pdf>.

Permanent Mission of the Russian Federation to theEuropean Union, 'EU-Russia Summits' <https://russiaeu.ru/en/russia-eu-summits>.

Picardo E, 'How US & European Union Sanctions Impact Russia' (Investopedia, 15 January 2015) <www.investopedia.com/articles/investing/011515/how-us-european-union-sanctions-impact-russia.asp>.

Piebalgs A and Shmatko I S, 'Memorandum on an Early Warning Mechanism in the Energy Sector within the Framework of the EU-Russia Energy Dialogue' (24 February

2016) <https://ec.europa.eu/energy/sites/ener/files/documents/2009_11_16_ewm_signed_en.pdf>.

Pirani S, Stern J and Yafimava K, 'The Russo-Ukrainian gas dispute of January 2009: a comprehensive assessment' (Oxford Institute for Energy Studies, February 2009) <www.oxfordenergy.org/wpcms/wp-content/uploads/2010/11/NG27TheRussoUkrainianGasDisputeofJanuary2009AComprehensiveAssessmentJonathanSternSimonPiraniKatjaYafimava-2009.pdf>.

Putin V V and Aznar J M, 'Joint Statement on energy dialogue in Russia-European Union Summit, annex 2' (Moscow, Presse 171, 29 May 2002) <www.consilium.europa.eu/uedocs/cms_data/docs/pressdata/en/er/70903.pdf>.

Ratner M, Belkin B, Nichol J and Woehrel S, 'Europe's Energy Security: Options and Challenges to Natural Gas Supply Diversification' (US Congressional Research Service No 7–5700, 20 August 2013) <www.fas.org/sgp/crs/row/R42405.pdf>.

Rettman A, 'Polish FM in Wikileaks: Germany is Russia's Trojan horse' (EU Observer, 16 September 2011) (as cited in Judah B, Kobzova J and Popescu N, 'Dealing with a Post-Bric Russia' (European Council on Foreign Relations, November 2011)) <www.ecfr.eu/page/-/ECFR44_RUSSIA_REPORT_AW.pdf>.

Richards T and Herman L, 'Relationship between International Trade and Energy' (WTO – Research and Analysis, World Trade Report, 2010) <www.wto.org/english/res_e/publications_e/wtr10_richards_herman_e.htm>.

Riley A, 'Commission v Gazprom: Time to do a deal? The Russian energy giant has strong incentives to do a deal' (Natural Gas World, 3 August 2015) <www.naturalgaseurope.com/european-commission-vs-gazprom-time-to-do-a-deal-24881 >.

Roche P, Abraham S and Petit S, 'Russia's withdrawal from the Energy Charter Treaty' (Norton Rose Fulbright, August 2009) <www.nortonrosefulbright.com/knowledge/publications/22691/russias-withdrawal-from-the-energy-charter-treaty>.

Russian National Security Council (SCRF), 'The Russian Federation National Security Strategy 2009 until 2020' (Approved decree of the President of Russian Federation of May 12 2009 No 537) <www.scrf.gov.ru/documents/99.html>.

Schneider F, Buehn A and Montenegro E C, 'Shadow Economies All over the World: New Estimates for 162 Countries from 1999 to 2007' (The World Bank, July 2010) <http://documents.worldbank.org/curated/en/311991468037132740/pdf/WPS5356.pdf>.

Smeenk T, 'Russian Gas for Europe: Creating Access and Choice', Clingendael International Energy Programme, 2010, <http://www.rug.nl/research/portal/files/13025746/16_thesis.pdf>

Smith C K, 'Russian Energy Pressure Fails to Unite Europe' (24 January 2007) 13(1) *CSIS Euro-Focus* <https://csis-prod.s3.amazonaws.com/s3fs-public/legacy_files/files/media/csis/pubs/eurofocus_v13n01.pdf>.

Sputnik News, 'Putin's Performance Hits Record 89% Approval Rating – Independent Poll', 24 June 2016, <https://sputniknews.com/russia/201506241023791005/>.

Stern J, 'The Russian-Ukrainian gas crisis of January 2006' (Oxford Institute for Energy Studies, 16 January 2006) <www.oxfordenergy.org/wpcms/wp-content/uploads/2011/01/Jan2006-RussiaUkraineGasCrisis-JonathanStern.pdf>. Tagliapietra S, 'The EU antitrust case: no big deal for Gazprom', Bruegel, 15 March 2017, <http://bruegel.org/2017/03/the-eu-antitrust-case-no-big-deal-for-gazprom/>.

Technology Centre, <www.technologycentre.org>.

Woehrel S, 'Russian Energy Policy Toward Neighbouring Countries' (Congressional Research Service, 2 September 2009) <www.fas.org/sgp/crs/row/RL34261.pdf>.

World Bank, 'Russian Economic Report 28: Reinvigorating the Economy' (Press Release, 8 October 2012) <www.worldbank.org/en/news/press-release/2012/10/08/russian-economic-report-28>.

WTO, 'Agreement on Subsidies and Countervailing Measures (SCM Agreement)' <www.wto.org/english/docs_e/legal_e/24-scm.pdf>.

WTO, 'Dispute Settlement System Training Module (Chapter 4): Legal basis for a Dispute' <www.wto.org/english/tratop_e/dispu_e/disp_settlement_cbt_e/c4s1p1_e.htm>.

WTO, 'Dispute Settlement Understanding', <https://www.wto.org/english/tratop_e/dispu_e/dsu_e.htm>

WTO, 'Energy Services' (9 September 1998) Background Note by the Secretariat, S/C/W/52, para 36.

WTO, 'Member Information: Russian Federation and the WTO' (Russian Federation) <www.wto.org/english/thewto_e/countries_e/russia_e.htm>.

WTO, 'Understanding the WTO – Principles of the Trading System' <www.wto.org/english/thewto_e/whatis_e/tif_e/fact2_e.htm>.

WTO, 'Understanding the WTO, the organisation, members and observers' < www.wto.org/english/thewto_e/whatis_e/tif_e/org6_e.htm >

WTO, 'Working Party Seals Deal on Russia's Membership Negotiations' (WTO News Items, 10 November 2011) <www.wto.org/english/news_e/news11_e/acc_rus_10nov11_e.htm>.

XE, 'Currency Charts: RUB to USD' <www.xe.com/currencycharts/?from=RUB&to=USD>.

Yafimava K, 'The EU Third Package for Gas and the Gas Target Model: major contentious issues inside and outside the EU' (April 2013) *NG 75 Oxford Institute for Energy Studies* <www.oxfordenergy.org/wpcms/wp-content/uploads/2013/04/NG-75.pdf>.

### *Media:*

BBC, 'Russia "forced" into oil shutdown', BBC News (9 January 2007) <http://news.bbc.co.uk/1/hi/6243573.stm>.

BBC, 'Russia tells Ukraine to pay gas debt or supplies may halt', BBC News (12 May 2014) <www.bbc.co.uk/news/business-27374070>.

BBC, 'Russia's trade ties with Europe', BBC News (Europe, 4 March 2014) <www.bbc.co.uk/news/world-europe-26436291>.

BBC, 'Russia signs 30-year gas deal with China', BBC News (21 May 2014) <www.bbc.co.uk/news/business-27503017>.

BBC, 'Ukraine Crisis: Russia halts gas supplies to Kiev', BBC News, (16 June 2014) <www.bbc.co.uk/news/world-europe-27862849>.

BBC, 'Bulgaria halts work on gas pipeline after US talks', BBC News (8 June 2014) <www.bbc.co.uk/news/business-27755032>.

BBC, 'Russia opposition politician Boris Nemtsov shot dead' BBC News (Europe, 28 February 2015) <www.bbc.co.uk/news/world-europe-31669061>.

BBC, 'Sir John Sawers, ex-MI6 chief, warns of Russia "danger"' BBC News (UK, 28 February 2015) <www.bbc.co.uk/news/uk-31669195>.

Caroll J, (quoting from Pope Francis), 'Pope Francis Proposes a Cure for Populism', *The New Yorker*, 28 March 2017, <http://www.newyorker.com/news/news-desk/pope-francis-proposes-a-cure-for-populism>.

Chaffin J, 'Europe cools on Russia's WTO Accession', *Financial Times* (5 December 2012) <www.ft.com/cms/s/0/ff524424-3eff-11e2-9214-00144feabdc0.html>.

Der Spiegel, 'SPIEGEL Interview with Ex-Chancellor Gerhard Schröder' 23 October 2006, <http://www.spiegel.de/international/spiegel/spiegel-interview-with-ex-chancellor-gerhard-schroeder-i-m-anything-but-an-opponent-of-america-a-444069.html>.

Elder M, 'Russia exerts its power', *Financial Times* News (31 October 2008) <www.ft.com/content/07d25ee2-a6e1-11dd-95be-000077b07658>.

Farchy J, Hille K and Mitchell T, 'Russia – Putin courts China as west turns away: gas deal centerpiece of Russian President's Beijing visit', *Financial Times* (19 May 2014) <https://www.ft.com/content/0344dc50-df44-11e3-86a4-00144feabdc0>.

Gaillard E, 'Russia cannot walk away from its legal obligations', *Financial Times* Letters (18 August 2009). <http://www.shearman.com/~/media/Files/Old-Site-Files/IA081809FINANCIALTIMESRussiacannotwalkawayfromlegalobligations.pdf>.

Galpin R, 'Russia loses ground in central Asian energy battle', BBC News (Moscow, 2 June 2010) <www.bbc.co.uk/news/10131641>.

Milner M, 'Eon Drops out of Endesa Fight', *The Guardian*, 3 April 2007, <https://www.theguardian.com/business/2007/apr/03/spain>.

Rankin J, 'Russia ordered to pay $50bn in damages to Yukos shareholders', *The Guardian*, 24 July 2014, <https://www.theguardian.com/business/2014/jul/28/russia-order-pay-50bn-yukos-shareholders-khodorkovsky-court>.

Roberts J, 'Will Central Asia's Oil and Gas go East or West?' BBC News (Asia-Pacific, 1 June 2010) <www.bbc.co.uk/news/10185429>.

Roberts J, 'Turkmenistan key to EU energy needs?' BBC News (Asia, 20 November 2014) <www.bbc.co.uk/news/world-asia-30125544>.

RT, 'Bulgaria halts Russia's South Stream gas pipeline project' RT Business (8 June 2014) <http://rt.com/business/164588-brussels-bulgaria-halts-south-stream/ >.

Sikorski R and Westerwelle G, 'A New Vision of Europe', *The New York Times*, 17 September 2012, <http://www.nytimes.com/2012/09/18/opinion/a-new-vision-of-europe.html>.

Soldatkin V, 'Russia tightens squeeze on Ukraine with gas price rise', Reuters' Bonds news (1 April 2014) <www.reuters.com/article/2014/04/01/ukraine-crisis-gas-idUSL5N0MT14Z20140401>.

Than K, 'Inside Hungary's $10.8 billion nuclear deal with Russia' (Reuters Special Report, 30 March 2015) <www.reuters.com/article/2015/03/30/us-russia-europe-hungary-specialreport-idUSKBN0MQ0MP20150330>.

Thompson D, 'Panama Papers: Putin associates linked to "money laundering"', BBC News, 3 April 2016, <http://www.bbc.com/news/world-europe-35918845>.

Thorpe N, 'Hungary challenged on nuclear choice with Russia', BBC News (12 June 2015) < www.bbc.co.uk/news/world-europe-33078832 >.

Williamson H, 'Germany blocks ex-Soviets' NATO entry', *Financial Times*, 1 April 2008, <https://www.ft.com/content/ab8eb6a6-ff44-11dc-b556-000077b07658>

The Economist, 'Economics – the Rule of Law, Order in the Jungle', 13 March 2008, <http://www.economist.com/node/10849115>

# Index

Note: Italic page numbers indicate figure; bold page numbers indicate table